W9-CUI-718

KING MOB

KING MOB

*The Story of Lord George Gordon
and the Riots of*

1780

CHRISTOPHER HIBBERT

DORSET PRESS
New York

This edition published by Dorset Press,
a division of Marboro Books Corporation,
by arrangement with Christopher Hibbert
1989 Dorset Press

ISBN 0-88029-399-3

Printed in the United States of America
M 9 8 7 6 5 4 3 2 1

For
My Mother and Father

'Such a time of terror
you have been fortunate
in not seeing'

Dr. Johnson to Mrs. Thrale.

NOTE

FOR almost a week during the early June of 1780 London was in the hands of a reckless, drunken and desperate mob. This is the story of those few days and of the remarkable man by whose name they are remembered.

It is based entirely upon contemporary pamphlets, newspapers, documents and trial reports in the British Museum, the Inner Temple Library, the Bodleian Library and the Public Record Office; and upon the diaries, memoirs and letters, published and unpublished, of eye-witnesses. Some of the greatest diarists and letter writers of the eighteenth century were in London at the time and gave vivid descriptions of the scenes of havoc. Henry Angelo, Edmund Burke, the Burney family, George Crabbe, Lady Anne Erskine, Edward Gibbon, Doctor Johnson, Frederick Reynolds, Samuel Romilly, Horace Walpole and Nathaniel Wraxall were among the many observant witnesses who have given the bare facts of the story their colour and life.

I am also most grateful to Mr. J. M. Bullock, Mr. J. Paul de Castro, Mr. Percy Colson and Dr. John Williams for drawing my attention to various sources of information which I would not otherwise have consulted.

I am also grateful to my wife for her careful reading of numerous eighteenth-century newspapers and official documents in the British Museum and the Public Record Office and for extracting from them many curious and illuminating facts which have not before been published.

CONTENTS

		Page
NOTE		vii
1	THE MAD SCOTCHMAN	1
2	THE ANVIL OF ROME	15
3	A MEAN SET OF PEOPLE	25
4	THE SURGING OF THE SEA	33
5	DENS OF POPERY	53
6	SO MANY INFERNALS	66
7	THE SKY LIKE BLOOD	74
8	UNDER MARTIAL LAW	88
9	A BLACK NIGHT	97
10	AMERICAN TREACHERY AND ENGLISH TREASON . . .	113
11	LOOK UPON THE PRISONER	128
12	GORDON AND LIBERTY	152
	BIBLIOGRAPHY	173
	INDEX	181

ILLUSTRATIONS

facing page

Lord George Gordon, President of the Protestant Association . 20

Two Scandalous Political Satires issued in 1780 . . . 21

Brackley Kennet, Lord Mayor of London 36

The Petitioners marching to the Houses of Parliament on the
afternoon of 2nd June, 1780 36

Alderman Frederick Bull 37

The Burning of Newgate on the night of 6th June, 1780 . . 84

The Riot in Broad Street
from an engraving after the painting by FrancisWheatley, R.A. 85

The Riots in Moorfields 100

At Langdale's Distillery
from illustrations by Hablot K. Browne in *Barnaby Rudge* . 100

Israel Bar Abraham Gordon 101

The illustrations with the exception of those facing page 100 are
reproduced from engravings in the Department of Prints and Drawings,
British Museum.

KING MOB

I

THE MAD SCOTCHMAN

'THEY were, and are, all mad', Walpole said of them, dismissing in a spasm of irritation all the members of the Gordon family past and present.

The exasperated judgment was not entirely groundless. The Gordons had for generations shown occasional signs of something more than eccentricity and at the time of Walpole's verdict several members of the family were said to be extremely odd.

The young and beautiful Duchess of Gordon herself was already indeed tirelessly driving her unconventional way through the fashionable drawing-rooms of London and Edinburgh where her callous wit, her rudeness, her ruthless opportunism and outrageous vulgarity were among the most refreshing delights that an admiring if frequently shocked society had to offer. Her determined efforts to introduce Robert Burns into Edinburgh society enhanced her reputation for extravagant irresponsibility.

She had begun her wild life early. In the Edinburgh of her childhood she was on occasions to be seen with her sister galloping madly down High Street on the back of a capering pig; and she was constantly expected, so a rival once said of her, to do the same down the staircase of Gloucester House. She married off three of her daughters to Dukes, and a fourth to a future Marquess after having light-heartedly assured his parents that there was 'not a drop of Gordon blood in Louisa's body'.

Her mother-in-law, the widow of the third Duke, described as a woman who looked like 'a raw-boned Scotch metaphysician that has got a red face by drinking water' was quite as strange. She was a Gordon by birth as well as by marriage and doubts had been openly expressed at the time of her engagement as to the wisdom of the Duke marrying a member of his own family and thus increasing the Gordon strain in their children. But Lady Catherine was as determined and

passionate as she was odd and she had her way and married the Duke
and gave him six children before he died, still a young man, at Amiens.

Never much caring for social life and spending most of her time in
Scotland, her eccentricities were not generally known or gossiped
about in society, until a few years after the Duke's death when she
conceived a passion for Stanislaus Poniatowski, the young and handsome King of Poland. His great grandmother had been a Gordon and
the Duchess felt that this family link between them would be sufficient
excuse for her asking the King to tea, although she had never met him
and had so far only had an opportunity of admiring his good looks from
a distance. Before he arrived, so the story went, she sent for her two
youngest children and dressing them up, or rather undressing them,
as cupids, she gave them each a bow and a quiver of little silver arrows.
The King on being shown into the drawing-room was surprised to be
greeted not only by the Duchess reclining in theatrical wistfulness upon
a sofa but also by a shower of silver darts, one of which hit him on the
head narrowly missing his eye.[1]

And so it was as an excited and half-naked little boy shooting arrows
at a King over the lovesick body of a whimsical Duchess that Lord
George Gordon gave his first display of capricious behaviour and was
brought for the first time to public attention.

His birth in Upper Grosvenor Street about three years earlier, on
Boxing Day 1751, had almost coincided with the death of his young
father and for that reason, and because he was the sixth child, had been
little noticed outside the family. He was a healthy baby and his mother
felt able, soon after his birth, to take him and his three sisters and two
brothers back to Scotland, where she thought they would grow up
more happily than in London and where she herself felt more at home.

The family estates in Scotland were vast, stretching for miles across

[1] The elder of these two cupids, Lord William Gordon, was later to maintain the
family reputation for eccentricity. He publicly repented of his brief elopement with
Lady Sarah Bunbury, with whom King George III had been so much in love, by
making a flamboyant pilgrimage to Rome. In Naples he was introduced by Lady
Hamilton to Nelson at a picnic and remained his devoted admirer. He wrote long
verses commemorating naval victories which he sent on to the Admiral in bulky
envelopes of red satin. As a rather cruel wit his company was enjoyed by George
Selwyn with whom he frequently dined and at a dinner party at which they were
both present he gave an example of this quick malicious humour which has happily been preserved by Walpole. It was at the Duke of Queensberry's. The Duke's
mistress Madame de Gard was sitting in the hearth with her back to a raging fire
although it was a hot August evening. 'I see', Lord William said, 'the Duke likes
his meat well done.'

a lovely open countryside and here Lord George with his brothers and sisters spent a happy, contented childhood, like a prince in a kingdom which he can enjoy but does not have to understand. One day their mother introduced the children to a twenty-one year old American from New York, Staates Long Morris, a subaltern in the British Army, and she told them that she had decided to marry him. They heard later that he was an adventurer who wanted to marry their mother, who was seventeen years older than he was, because she was rich and could help him to get on in the army; and that because she was lonely and he was so young she had accepted him. But the children liked him, unable, of course, to comprehend the objections of their aunts and uncles. Their only regret was that their mother after her marriage seemed to have less and less time for them.

Lord George as the youngest suffered most deeply this neglect. As soon as he was eleven he was sent off to Eton, where he was at first bullied and unhappy but, according to Doctor Robert Watson, who was in later years to know him well, soon settled down and 'gave many proofs of a rising genius'. The only surviving evidence that this rather extravagant claim might be justified is a charming letter written to his old nurse in London. It is certainly a remarkably literate letter for a schoolboy—even though an eighteenth-century Etonian—not yet twelve years old:

To Mrs. Lewis in Castle Street, near the White Hart, Seven Dials, London.

Dear Nurse,
I hope you will excuse my negligence in writing, as it has been a very hard time with me. I think very long to see you and Richard. Your cake was very acceptable to me; only I wish you had not put yourself in such trouble.

Our holydays begin Monday week and last four weeks. My mother, I fancy, spends the winter in Scotland; but I shall come to town whenever she comes up, at which time I shall not fail to come and see you.

I have not had the least ailment since I saw you than a cold or two which nobody escapes.
I am, Dear Nurse,
Your affectionate and humble servant
G. Gordon
Eton December the 9th, 1763.

His mother had already by this time bought a commission for him in the army and he had, in fact, been promoted lieutenant in the year before, not long after his tenth birthday. His brother William was also, however, an army officer and the Duchess feeling that her influence at the Horse Guards could not effectively be used for George while she had the interests both of her elder son and her husband to consider, now got him appointed a midshipman in the Navy.

Although the decision that George should adopt a naval career was taken by the Duchess without his consent, and in fact without his knowledge, he accepted the decision, when he heard of it, with pleasure. Within a year of his leaving Eton he was at sea.

The hardships and dangers of a midshipman's life in the eighteenth century are well known,[1] and there is no reason to suppose that the young midshipman Gordon had an easier time of it than any other specimen of that 'lowest form of animal life in the British Navy'. Indeed it is likely that he had a harder time than most at the hands of his superior officers, for within a few days of his joining his ship he made a nuisance of himself in a way which was typical of the man he was later to become. While waiting in Portsmouth harbour for the order to sail a tender delivered to his ship a quantity of biscuits which were riddled with weevils and which the men spent most of the morning sorting out and eventually throwing overboard. Midshipman Gordon was horrified. As soon as the captain came aboard he went up to him to complain on behalf of the men, of the incompetence, and probable dishonesty of the purser and the naval suppliers. The captain and the entire crew were astounded by the new midshipman's extraordinary impudence. It earned him the rather contemptuous dislike of his officers and the amused admiration of his men. It was the first of several incidents in his naval career which made his sailors revere him as a sort of seaman's lawyer, odd, talkative, erratic and somehow lovable who would argue their case for them whether they wanted him to or not, and which made his captain and the Admiralty Board consider him a 'damned nuisance wholly unsuitable for promotion'. So unsuitable, in fact, did they consider the emotional and meddlesome young officer that they saw to it he never got promotion. He remained, in spite of his connections, a lieutenant for more than ten years.

[1] 'No man will be a sailor', said Johnson, 'who has contrivance enough to get himself into jail; for being in a ship is being in a jail, with the chance of getting drowned. The man in jail has more room, better food and commonly better company.' In the Seven Years War, of 135,220 sailors lost only 1,512 were killed in battle, most of the remainder dying of scurvy and other diseases.

With the arrival of his ship in Jamaican waters the remarkable midshipman further alienated his officers by using the influence of his young, American stepfather, who was serving in America and who was already with the Duchess's help a general, to obtain long shore leaves in the West Indies and in the colonies on the mainland. To the amazement of his fellow-midshipmen he did not spend these leaves in enjoying himself as a midshipman should, but in studying the way of life of the Americans and the social conditions of the negroes. He was deeply moved by what he saw.

In the West Indies his impressionable, emotional nature was appalled by the 'bloody treatment of the negroes'. Even his sailors were not treated like these poor defenceless slaves, these pitiable examples of man's inhumanity to man. What sort of world was it, he was later vehemently to complain, that allowed such inequality and such injustice, that viewed without concern the sugar planters growing rich at the expense of the whipped, hungry, bleeding bodies of their slaves? The anger was real and heartfelt.

But in America it simmered down and cooled away. Here was a new and quite different society and one which he could and did respect and admire. There was no inequality here. The Americans were a kind and simple people, generous, sincere, honest and free, already aware of their great destiny. His admiration was whole-hearted and uncritical. He took the entire people and their country to his heart. It was an immediate and affectionate esteem which was to colour his thought for years to come and to provide at least one motive for the actions of the future.

One day, a few years after this significant visit to America, when he was on leave in Scotland, a friend suggested to him that he should enter Parliament. He was by now dismayed by the repeated frustrations of his naval career and was easily persuaded to try his hand at a political one.

His entry into politics was marked by that ebullient, erratic enthusiasm which had characterized his life in the navy. The electors of Inverness-shire, whose member he sought to be, were astonished by his tireless determination to succeed and the methods he used in his efforts to do so. He had already, during a summer leave spent among the people of the Hebrides, learned Gaelic and he made much use of his ability to talk to the people of Inverness in their native tongue. This was only one of the many flattering accomplishments which endeared him to the electors. For he not only talked like a Highlander but he dressed like one too and behaved like one. He played the bagpipes to perfection and danced the Highland reels with fervour and grace. He spoke with interest and knowledge about fish to the fishermen, about sheep to the shepherds, about wool to the wool brokers and about barley to the distillers, not caring who had a vote and who had not, delighting the enfranchised and the unenfranchised alike with the apparent breadth of his sympathies and the charm of his enthusiasm. Towards the close of his campaign he strained his limited financial resources by giving a splendid ball to which everyone of importance in the constituency was invited, and to ensure its success he brought over by yacht from the Isle of Skye fifteen beautiful and lively girls of the clan Macleod.

This, his opponent General Fraser decided, was going too far. The young naval officer whom he had at first treated with a rather patronizing indulgence seemed to be well on the way to running away with all his votes. He consulted his father Lord Lovat who in turn spoke to the Duke of Gordon, Lord George's elder brother. It was decided that as Lord George had set his heart on getting into Parliament the only solution was to buy him a different seat, as this would be cheaper and more reliable than bribing all the voters in Inverness-shire. So General Fraser bought by arrangement with George Selwyn its owner and Lord Melbourne, one of its two representatives, the pocket borough of Luggershall in Wiltshire for his tiresome opponent who, reluctantly, for he was enjoying the contest in Scotland, and under pressure from his family, accepted it. As all the votes in Luggershall were, of course, included in General Fraser's purchase, Lord George did not even trouble to visit the constituency but merely waited for the result of his election to be announced.

He was dining with his brother in London when he heard the expected news. He took his seat in the House a few days later. He was twenty-two. The year was 1774.

For the first year or so he was little noticed. He attended the House infrequently and remained surprisingly quiet when he did so. His vote was generally cast for the Opposition but this seemed more out of respect and admiration for Edmund Burke, under whose powerful influence he had fallen, than through any definite convictions of his own. But as the military operations against the American colonies developed into a costly, unpopular and futile war, his voice was heard more and more often raised in violent opposition. He was a fluent if somewhat incoherent speaker and the more frequently he spoke the more he enjoyed it. He began to relish his political life and his lank, long-haired impressive, Puritan-looking figure, clothed usually in sombre black but occasionally made even more striking by startling plaid trousers, became a familiar sight in Westminster.

Once he had established himself as a Parliamentary speaker he devoted his earnest attention to matters other than the 'mad, cruel and accursed American war'. He became a regular speaker in debates and one of the Tory Ministry's most aggressive critics. But the better known he became, the less the Opposition members could rely upon him for his unquestioning support. While he would attack Lord North and the King's friends with satisfying vehemence one day, the next he would turn upon the Opposition. He was, they discovered, too exasperatingly independent in his views to be reliable. So erratic, in fact, did he now become in his allegiances, so unpredictable in his opinions, that a pleasant *bon mot* went around the coffee houses to the effect that there were now 'three parties in Parliament—the Ministry, the Opposition and Lord George Gordon'.

He himself put it a different way when he said that he belonged to none of the factions in the House but to the 'party of the people'. And this protestation of political allegiance went to the heart of the matter. In his opinion, always implied and often voiced, neither party, nor any of the overlapping factions in an increasingly confused political world, could be trusted to safeguard the interests of the people and it was they whom he at least intended to support. 'Justice for the people', he frequently complained, 'is not to be expected from either party.' 'The Ministers have lost the confidence of the people', was another accusation, 'and the Opposition have not found it.' Obviously Lord North and the King could not be trusted but even Fox and Burke were suspect. They 'used in those days', he later grumbled, 'to make a great deal of noise in favour of petitions for the redress of grievances. I always doubted their sincerity in those windy harangues. I thought they were no real friends to the people.'

It was in his own opinion a damning reproof. For the will of the people was 'sacred'; the voice of the people was 'the voice of God'. Members on both sides of the House listened to expressions such as these with a vaguely apprehensive contempt. They had enough of that sort of tomfoolery, one of them said voicing the opinion of most, from that 'damned fellow Wilkes'.[1] One revolutionary in the House was bad enough without having to listen to a new one and a dull one at that.

For his speeches, fluent as they were and outrageous as they later became, were at this time undoubtedly dull. Even his friends had to admit that. They were long, involved, disorderly and generally inconclusive. In delivering them his normally pleasant speaking voice would drawl in monotonous complaint and then grow harsh and too loud in this impatient sincerity and rising anger. During a debate on free trade with Ireland he produced an enormously long pamphlet, and, in a speech of exceptional boredom, quoted voluminous extracts from it. 'Two hundred members', *The Gentleman's Magazine* reported, 'thinned to fifty before he was half-way through.' In desperation a Member appealed to the Speaker, who declined to decide whether a pamphlet might thus be introduced into the debate, although he admitted that he could not see that it was in the least relevant to the motion. 'But still Lord George continued to read on, till he so tired the House that most of the Members left their seats.' In spite of this reception the next day, quite unabashed, he began to read the pamphlet again. 'It is really so excellent', he said, 'it ought to be read every day in the week.' At this, it is not surprising to learn, 'a general murmur took place'.

In spite of the long practice in which he indulged himself, he never became a distinguished or even an adequate Parliamentary orator, but in the course of time his speeches did lose all trace of their former plaintive drabness and became enlivened by occasional flashes of wit and artful turns of phrase. Sometimes indeed their grotesque sarcasm, their unashamed rudeness or their splendid splenetic fury, seemed to raise them at moments to a sort of grandeur.

It seemed unfortunate, Shelburne once said, that with all that fine fury and good intention and with all those words he should ultimately have nothing to say. It was an understandable verdict. His emotional exaggerated anger and the welter of words with which he chose to

[1] John Wilkes, the demagogue, the most 'wicked and agreeable fellow' that William Pitt had ever met had also voiced his respect for the opinion of the people in similar terms. 'I firmly and sincerely believe', he once declared, 'the voice of the people to be the voice of God. I wish always to hear it loud and distinct. When I do I will obey it as a divine call'. His sincerity, however, unlike Lord George's, was questionable. One day in the House of Commons he whispered to the Speaker that he had to present a petition from 'a set of the greatest scoundrels on earth'. A few minutes later he was on his feet. 'Sir', he declared, 'I hold in my hand a petition from a most intelligent, independent and enlightened body of men.'

express it, lost him the support and the attention of many who shared his sympathies; while the supreme importance he so often attached to matters of little concern gave to his views an aspect of absurdity, which they did not always deserve. His views seemed absurd to his contemporaries because few men of influence, certainly no aristocrat, had propounded them before. Lord George believed passionately in the rights of the people, not as a politician should do, but as a humanitarian is obliged to do. He had all the humanitarian's emotional weakness, all the Romantic's enthusiasm, without the politician's hard-headed sense. His actions, contradictory as they sometimes seemed, and foolhardy as they often were, were the result of this unreasoning, overwhelming pity for the poor and the oppressed which forced him into positions and attitudes that were as ridiculous as they were useless.

His vanity, and self-confidence made this impossible for him to understand, while his irritating impatience with criticism and advice finally induced many of his friends to let him 'go to the devil in his own way'. They gave him up because his fragmented, neurotic personality was quite beyond their comprehension. And yet they recognized that unpredictable and misguided as the man undoubtedly was, there lay within him a sincere and essential passion for the rights of the people, a determination to help the wronged and underprivileged to which all his other characteristics, contradictory as they were, were subject.

Such fundamental beliefs as these, however, did not cut much ice in the House of Commons. And Lord George was quite unable to voice them adequately.

His behaviour during the debate on Burke's plan for the alteration of the Crown's revenues was typical of many episodes in which he irritated the House and gave good reason for the contempt in which most members held him.

Burke's speech when explaining his Bill lasted for nearly three and a half hours and was, Walpole thought, 'temperate, moderate, sprinkled with wit and humour, and had such a universal effect on the whole House, that it was thought he could that day have carried any point he had proposed'. Even Lord North complimented him and agreed to the Bill being brought in. And then Lord George stood up and to the annoyance of every Member present in a very full House, attacked the Bill because it did not go far enough, particularly regarding sinecures and places of profit. It was a 'mean dirty bill', he said, 'a mere tub to the whale, a greasy bait to draw off the attention of poor duped John Bull from the foul nest of the real grievous abominations of the evil things of this reign'. He insisted upon a division, but he found himself quite alone when the House divided. Not one Member on either side followed him. He was in a minority of one.

George Selwyn, the witty Member for Gloucester and a friend of George's brother William, who had sat fast asleep during most of the debate as was his usual habit, gave Lord George a lift to White's in his coach when it was over. Selwyn had some time previously been rewarded by the Government for regularly casting his vote in their favour, by an extremely profitable appointment in the Board of Works and when he entered White's he announced to the customers drinking there: 'I have brought the whole opposition in my coach.' And added that he hoped one coach would always hold them 'if they mean to take away the Board of Works'.[1]

It was a good remark and it was, of course, repeated in the drawing-rooms and coffee houses. It emphasized the reputation for overweening folly which the young Member for Luggershall, 'the Duke of Gordon's half-cracked brother', was earning for himself.

But however stupid, irritating, rude, reckless and ambitious Lord George might seem in the House of Commons, outside it he was as likeable as he was charming, as gracious as he was kind.

The happy voyage he went on in William Cane's yacht during a long summer recess at this time has been pleasantly recorded by William Hickey, one of his fellow guests. It shows the fiery young man in a quite different and revealing light.

William Cane, Lord George's host during this voyage, was a happy, generous, charming and extravagant man, an epicure noted for the excellence of his table and the perfection of his cellar. Although he was not as rich as his way of living led most of his friends to suppose, he enjoyed an income of about two thousand a year which enabled him to keep a town house in Berners Street with six indoor menservants as well as his elegant country house at Erith in Kent. And it was at Erith

[1] This was not the only occasion upon which Selwyn made a caustic remark at Lord George's expense. Once, so it was said, when the two men were discussing Lord George's constituency, Selwyn doubted whether Gordon would be chosen, again to represent Luggershall. 'Oh yes', replied Lord George, 'if you would recommend me, they would choose me if I came from the coast of Africa.' 'That', said Selwyn 'is according to what part of the coast you came from; they would certainly [rattling the coins in his pocket] if you came from the Guinea coast.'

during the warm June of 1776 that Lord George had been asked to meet his fellow guests.

Cane had chosen these guests carefully and well. They were all, so it seemed to William Hickey, 'men of superior talents'. As well as Hickey himself, who had been an intimate friend of his ever since they had been schoolboys together at Westminster, and Lord George Gordon, Cane had invited George Dempster, a young but already well-known Member of Parliament and the recently created secretary of the Order of the Thistle, the badge of which he proudly wore on a ribbon round his neck; Sir Charles Bingham, afterwards created Earl of Lucan; and John Stephenson, a brilliant businessman who had just returned from India with an immense fortune made while serving in the office of the East India Company at Bombay.

They were all young, energetic, intelligent and high-spirited; they all liked to eat well and to drink well; and they all shared the same political views, and this, one of the party thought, with the controversial and argumentative Lord George Gordon among them, might be important. But Cane knew that, tiresome and intractable as Lord George was in public life, in private conversation he was witty, gracious and polite. William Hickey, writing some years later, described him as being at this time 'a gay, volatile and elegant young man of the most affable and engaging manners', and so he appeared to them all.

The mood of the party was set when the guests had been in the house only a few hours. After dinner, as soon as his wife and mother-in-law had retired to the drawing-room, Cane stood up and asked each guest to fill a bumper of champagne and drink a toast to the American patriots. The toast was well received and his guests drank it with enthusiasm, not only that first evening at Erith but every day while they were at sea.

After a leisurely and enjoyable crossing, the *Henrietta* anchored off Boulogne and as the tide was out the passengers had to get into a yawl to be rowed to shore. When still some way from the shore, the yawl grounded and while the oarsmen were trying to dislodge it, a group of Amazonian fish-women, their petticoats rolled up to their waists, exposing massive thighs, came up to them and regardless of their protestations lifted them out in their vast, fish-smelling arms and carried them onto the beach.

They walked up the beach together, laughing and joking, and strolled across the harbour towards the shop of Messrs. Meriton and Smith, the English wine merchants, both of whom Cane knew. They spent most of the morning in the shop, sampling the wine, until they were all a little drunk. Gordon, cheerful and excited, suggested a 'dash off to Paris for a couple of days' and to this the others readily agreed; so Cane asked the hospitable wine merchants if they would arrange for three carriages to be at their door at daybreak.

In Paris the party stayed at a 'handsome hotel' in the Rue St. Sauveur. On the day after their arrival Lord George met an attractive young girl at the Comédie and excused himself from a dinner party early the following evening in order to 'pay his respects to her'. For the idea of a holiday in Paris without some sort of amatory adventure was, to him, unthinkable. He was, like most young men of energy and compassion, extremely sensual. He drank in comparative moderation, he derived no pleasure from the cruel sports indulged in by his contemporaries and he never gambled, but his appetite for women was boundless. It was also indiscriminate. For in his sexual life as in his public life his enthusiasm was not tempered with discernment nor his energy with judgment. There was in his choice of bed companion, an undeniable lack of taste, a conscious rejection of fastidiousness, a deep and passionate *nostalgie de la boue*. Some years after this trip to Paris when he had quarrelled with the Church and called the Archbishop of Canterbury a whore, Mrs. Montagu said, with more than a little truth behind the malice, that if Lord George had called the Archbishop the Whore of Babylon 'then it was very uncivil as it is the only whore his Lordship dislikes'. He was known to make visits of punctilious regularity to a famous prostitute who had a house in Tottenham Court Road and he had, it was said, even asked her to marry him but she 'preferring the species to the individual' had declined the generous offer.

Happy after his night with the 'certain young woman' from the Comédie, Lord George returned to his friends at the hotel in the Rue St. Sauveur and together they rode back to Boulogne and to the *Henrietta* waiting for them in the harbour.

At supper that evening, celebrating the escape from customs duty of enormous quantities of champagne supplied by Meriton and Smith, the passengers were in even higher spirits than usual. And when the conversation turned, as it nearly always did on the American war, Lord George suggested that 'in compliment to the worthy patriots of our injured colonies' the cutter should be renamed *The Congress*. The others agreed to this with the habitual enthusiasm which any reference to American patriotism aroused. Bumper after bumper was drunk to 'the success of *The Congress* 'and a bowl of punch was ordered for the crew.

The following day as the cutter sailed towards Spithead its new name was the cause of an amusing incident. A lieutenant on board a warship lying at anchor, watched the cutter approach and asked Johnson its master whose it was. 'Squire Cane's, sir,' Johnson called, adding with a hint of defiance as the cutter shot ahead and the lieutenant saw the name *Henrietta* written on her stern, 'Name of *The Congress*, sir!'

'Damn your blood, you impudent scoundrel!' shouted the lieutenant, 'I wish I had you here and I'd "congress" you.'

The party spent only a few hours in Portsmouth wandering around the docks and then moved on to Weymouth where they passed ten pleasant days in 'as good a tavern as any in England', enjoying the sea air, the company at the Rooms and the theatre. On the 16th they returned to Portsmouth on their way home and in the evening taking a last stroll together along the sea front, they met Admiral Gambier who asked them to dine with him.

In the company of the admiral, Gordon spoke of the bitterness of his own frustrated naval career. 'There is', he complained, 'no encouragement in the Navy nowadays to induce any man to enter it; it is all job and trick. This I know too well by woeful experience having already been nine years a lieutenant without hope of promotion.'

Hickey listened to his friend's complaint with a doubtful sympathy. He did not find it strange, he commented later, that the Administration should do what they could to obstruct the advancement of a man so uncompromisingly hostile to it. Making, as he did, such 'violent speeches against all its measures', Hickey wrote, 'he could not reasonably expect that the Administration should think themselves bound to give him rank in his profession.'

That the Ministry used what means they could to prevent his promotion cannot be doubted, and soon after this conversation with Admiral Gambier, Gordon himself accepted the impossibility of his obtaining it. He made one last request for a command which was, as he had expected, refused, and he went to see the dissipated Lord Sandwich to tell him what he thought of him. He took his letter of resignation and his commission with him, and when Lord Sandwich said that it was just a little difficult to give him a command at the moment, but that there were many ships being built, and perhaps his Lordship might get one of those, Lord George cut him short and took the letter and commission out of his pocket. He would not have accepted a command anyway, he said, as he would not 'imbrue his hands in the blood of men struggling for freedom', and so handed in his resignation.

His naval career now behind him, Lord George threw himself with even greater zeal and energy into his political activities.

2

THE ANVIL OF ROME

WHEN Lord George returned to Westminster, the country was simmering with discontent. Lord North, charming and amiable, was still surprisingly in office, mumbling his seemingly muddled, inconsequential way through one crisis and into another. His resignation, expected for many months, was now, according to Nathaniel Wraxall 'anxiously anticipated and seemed to be inevitable'.

At the head of a despised and hated government, he was lampooned, insulted and attacked in a way and with a regularity which his easygoing, good natured temperament found distressing. He longed to retire to a quiet life but the King, whose obedient servant he was and whose features so strongly resembled his own that it was sometimes suggested he was a royal changeling, would not hear of it. Unwillingly, he carried on.

And yet despite his troubles and his political allegiances, he retained much of his personal popularity. His mind, behind that fat, loose 'booby-looking' face with its prominent, rolling eyes and inflated cheeks which, as Walpole unkindly said, gave him 'the air of a blind trumpeter', was unexpectedly shrewd and perspicacious. And when all was said and done, to the ordinary men, he seemed 'a proper Englishman', with an Englishman's appetites and interests, with most of his virtues and practically all of his failings. He was a sympathetic character which the King, of course, was not.

The King indeed, in spite of an impressive parade of private virtues, was quite as disliked as the most unpopular of his Ministers. Like most of the members of his tasteless, vain and self-important family he was as dull as he was hard-working, as stubborn as ungracious; as well-intentioned as uncompromising; sharing with them all a belief in the far-reaching importance of the details of court procedure and protocol and a Germanic passion for uniforms.

It was he, it was believed, who, even more than his Tory ministers, was pressing for further and more extensive efforts to crush the American rebellion. The efforts that had so far been made, had proved both unsuccessful and humiliating and had induced the French to take advantage of the difficulties of their traditional enemy and to declare war in support of the Americans.

The subsequent 'disgraceful naval campaigns' had resulted in the French fleet becoming 'Masters of the Channel' and might, it was feared at one time, have ended in the capture of Plymouth. The morale of the Royal Navy had rarely, if ever, been lower. After the recall of Howe, Admiral Byron, the poet's grandfather, had given painful proof that 'Foul Weather Jack' was a well merited epithet. The appointment of the elegant and sensual Rodney to succeed Byron as supreme naval commander in American waters did not improve the position. One after the other the islands of the West Indies fell with ignominious ease into the hands of the enemy. The operations on the mainland fared no better.

It was a shameful and depressing time. It seemed indeed to one who lived through it that England had never been overspread by a 'deeper gloom'.

Prices were rising while wages, despite a recent increase in some trades, still bore no particular relevance to the cost of living. The streets of London seemed full, a German tourist thought, of sullen dispirited and bitter people who looked as if they were waiting for an opportunity to start a fight. It was a prophetic observation.

Back in Parliament Lord George fell with renewed vigour upon Lord North and the King's friends. He had now found a new weapon with which to attack them, and having found it effective he wielded it with haphazard violence. The weapon was the national and traditional fear of Roman Catholicism.

The English Catholics had until recently been subject to severe and unmerited restrictions not only as members of a proscribed religion but also as citizens. So severe, in fact, were many of these restrictions and so outdated, that the laws in which they were contained had been, by tacit agreement, largely ignored. And as this was so, relief for Catholics was not contemplated even by the more enlightened Members of a Protestant Parliament, and neither expected nor requested by the Catholics themselves.

There was, however, one part of the anti-Catholic law which the

Government itself found irksome and this was a clause in a statute of William III which enforced upon anyone joining the army the necessity of taking the attestation oath, and thereby swearing that he was a Protestant. There were, of course, Catholics in the army but they were enlisted as Protestants and treated as such, and although when a government badly needed soldiers it was customary for certain parts of the attestation oath to be omitted in an attempt to encourage Catholics to join up, recruiting among Catholics was never very successful.

At the beginning of 1778 when the military operations in America were going badly and it had seemed likely that Spain and France would come into the war on the American side, the Government had decided that an attempt must be made to persuade Catholics to enlist.

A profitable area for recruitment was the Highlands of Scotland where the men were desperately poor and therefore more easily persuaded, and brave and hardy too.

It was, therefore, agreed that a confidential agent should be sent to Scotland with instructions to ask a leading Catholic Bishop what hopes there were of Catholics joining the army if it were made easier for their consciences to allow them to do so, and what social favours they would ask in return for their military services.

The agent chosen was Sir John Dalrymple, a Baron of the Scottish Exchequer, who obtained an interview with Bishop Hay in Edinburgh and learned from him the terms which would be considered acceptable to the Scottish Catholics. Dalrymple reported these terms to the Government in London, and as England was now at war with France they were immediately pronounced satisfactory.

Dalrymple was then asked by Lord North to find out whether English Catholics would enlist if favours similar to those suggested by Bishop Hay were offered to them. He thereupon called on Bishop Challoner, the leading Catholic in London. But Challoner was an old man of eighty-seven, timid and anxious to be left in peace. He raised, Dalrymple complained, 'twenty difficulties', and said, with the premonitory intuition of an old man close to death, that measures such as those proposed would anger the Protestants more than the Government expected and in particular the dissenting sects, now mercifully quiet.

Dalrymple had no more success with other English Catholics than he had had with Bishop Challoner. They were all afraid apparently of the persecution which might follow any steps to improve their social and legal position, and some of them even suspected that Dalrymple was a secret agent of America or France trying to trick them into an admission of disloyalty and persuade them to agree to some traitorous enterprise.

At last, almost despairing of success, Dalrymple called on William Sheldon, a young, ambitious, energetic lawyer who saw in the Government's dilemma the first real opportunity the Catholics had had for more than seventy-five years, and at the same time a chance for the profitable exercise of his own talents. Sheldon went to see the heads of all the leading Catholic families beginning with the Duke of Norfolk, the Earl of Shrewsbury and Lord Petre. 'They generally concurred, some demurred but said they would follow the opinion of the majority.' He also called on the Opposition leaders to discover what dissent there was likely to be in Parliament to the Catholic Relief Bill which was already taking shape in his mind.

Reassured that the opposition would be negligible and ineffective, as every good Whig could not but agree to uphold the traditional belief of his party in religious toleration, he began to prepare his Bill.

Burke was asked to write the preamble but the draft he submitted was considered unsuitable and John Dunning, one of the most skilful lawyers of the day, was asked to try his more practised hand and afterwards to introduce the Bill into Parliament.

Dunning was a natural choice for this duty not only because of his gifts as a speaker but also because of his great popularity on both sides of the House.[1] He was almost grotesquely ugly, his ungainly figure and lumbering walk being distinguishable a 'mile off in a hailstorm' and his voice was harsh and guttural; but he had a quick, sharp wit and an irresistible manner which made his physical presence quite acceptable. Like Wilkes it did not take him long 'to talk his face away'.

It was, however, eventually decided that the Bill should be introduced by Sir George Savile, a likeable and uncontroversial Member, who had so far had nothing to do with Catholic relief and was in fact known not greatly to care for most of those Catholics whom he knew; and that Dunning should second it.

Both Savile and Dunning were completely independent in their views and it was therefore possible to present the Bill quite uncontentiously. Indeed many Members supposed that Savile's interest in it was

---

[1] It was he who two years later was to introduce the famous motion that it was 'the opinion of this committee that the influence of the Crown has increased, is increasing and ought to be diminished'.

roused only by reason of his owning large estates in Ireland, where American agents were offering passages across the Atlantic to his Catholic tenants, and promising them more freedom over there than they could hope to have at home.

And so accepted as a non-party measure the Bill passed into law with remarkable rapidity. On Friday, 15 May, 1778, it was introduced into a poorly attended and not particularly interested House and little more than a fortnight later it had passed its three readings in both Houses without a division. On 3 June it received the royal assent.

In spite of the anger and fear it was afterwards to raise and the disaster it was to cause, it was neither generous nor far-reaching. The Catholics were still, in most essential respects, outcasts, and they remained so until the Emancipation Act of 1829.

The 1778 Bill, by repealing the Act of William III, granted to Catholics only a few limited reliefs. They were now able, openly and without restrictions, to purchase and inherit land, which had previously not been possible except by legal trickery and conspiracy; their bishops, priests and schoolmasters were no longer liable to be imprisoned for life and the offer of a reward of £100 to an informer who obtained the conviction of a priest was withdrawn. An important condition of the Bill, later often forgotten and sometimes concealed by its enemies, was that it should apply only to those Catholics who took the Oath of Allegiance. All the other disabilities imposed upon Catholics and their complete exclusion from political life and places of trust remained as before.

It was believed that so limited and conditional a Bill could not possibly cause offence even to those for whom Roman Catholicism was England's most fearsome moral, social and political menace. And for a time it seemed indeed that it would be quietly accepted.

But as the international situation grew worse and the most powerful and hated Catholic countries in Europe were once more England's enemies it became easy again, as it had been in the past, to earn a cheap popularity by speaking out against the English Papists as untrustworthy representatives of a dangerous international conspiracy and members of a foreign and traitorous religion.

Wild and unlikely stories began to circulate and to be believed. It was spread about by zealous trouble-makers in the slums and poorer districts, that twenty thousand Jesuits were hidden in a network of underground tunnels in the Surrey bank of the Thames and were waiting for the order from Rome to blow up the bed and banks of the river and so flood London. It was not difficult in eighteenth-century London to get people to believe an absurd tale such as this. In Southwark a rumour went about, started it was thought by a mad Methodist preacher, that a gang of Benedictine monks, disguised as Irish chairmen, had poisoned all the flour in the Borough, and for days many of the inhabitants would not touch any bread until it had been tested by a dog. It was generally thought by the populace, Samuel Romilly said, 'that the King was a Papist. Some were sure of it: they pretended to know that he heard Mass privately, and that his confessor had the direction of all political concerns.'

For generations now the Pope, for many families, had been an unseen, ghost-like enemy, lurking behind clouds of wicked incense in a Satanic southern city called Rome. He was never for them quite real; a sort of ecclesiastical witch who exercised an evil power on the minds of otherwise apparently normal Englishmen; a bogey man with whom mothers and nurses frightened their children into good behaviour. He was blamed for many parochial, and practically all national, disasters. France and Spain, the traditional enemies, were the tools by which he sought to conquer England and gain control of the poor Englishmen's minds and bodies. His great hope and ultimate aim was to bring back to England the rack and the Inquisition.

The Methodist and other Dissenting ministers, played on this fear and ignorance and superstition to their own advantage. They appealed in their proselytizing not so much to men's minds as to their passions and prejudices. Even John Wesley, the greatest, and least suspect, among them, punctuated his fine emotional sermons with exhortations to remember Bloody Queen Mary and the 'raging fires of Smithfield'. He warned his congregation as they listened, rapt and silent, overwhelmed by the power of his oratory, of the 'chains forging at the anvil of Rome for the rising generation' and the 'purple power of Rome advancing by hasty strides to overspread this once happy nation'. In a pamphlet published at about this time he went so far as to 'insist upon it, that no government, not Roman Catholic, ought to tolerate men of the Roman Catholic persuasion'.

Such uncompromising, intolerant views as these were held by John Wesley and by men like him with undoubted sincerity. They honestly believed that Roman Catholicism was both evil and dangerous and

Lord George Gordon,
President of the Protestant Association

EVERY MAN IN HIS HUMOUR

" *A certain Knight, brimful of hope,*
 Knight of the Shire also,
 To gain the Papists pleas'd the Pope,
 And humbly kissed his toe.
 ' *Poh,' cried his colleague in a pother*
 ' *The toe's but a simple farce.'*
 And that he may outdo his brother
 He's gone to kiss his a—e."

A gentleman, perhaps Sir George Savile, is seen kissing the Pope's foot, while another kisses his buttock.

A PRIEST AT HIS DEVOTIONS

The tonsured King is shown praying in his private chapel. Behind the altar are portraits of Lords North and Bute. Lying on the floor of the adjoining privy are crumpled Protestant petitions.

Two Scandalous Political Satires issued in 1780

that it was their duty to fight against it with all their strength, in their never-ending mission to save the souls of their fellow men.

This growing fear of 'the progress of that soul-deceiving and all-enslaving superstition' led to the formation of various associations both in England and Scotland for the defence of the Protestant faith. Those who joined these associations were not all Methodists and Dissenters. There were amongst them many members of the Church of England and even men who belonged to no Church at all but who believed, with the others, that Roman Catholicism was a danger to the constitution, to the Protestant succession—as much a political as a religious ideal—and to the liberty of the individual.

The Protestant Associations kept the fear and hate of Popery burning with the distribution of pamphlets as ill-written as they were grotesque. 'Let us call to remembrance', one such pamphlet enjoined its readers,

> the massacre at Paris; there Popery appeared in its true colours with the blood of the saints and with the blood of the martyrs of Jesus. Whilst Popery has existence upon earth, let it be remembered though to the disgrace of humanity, let it be remembered with horror that on Saint Bartholomew's Day thousands and ten of thousands of Protestants were murdered in France in cold blood. Smithfield, Oxford, Cambridge and many other places have a voice crying aloud 'Beware of Popery, O Britons'. Let not the blood of the martyrs be forgotten, or their sufferings effaced from our memories, or from those of our children to the latest posterity. . . . To tolerate Popery is to be instrumental to the perdition of immortal souls now existing, and of millions of spirits that at present have no existence but in the prescience of God, and is the direct way to provoke the vengeance of an holy and jealous God, to bring down destruction on our fleets and armies.

Strong as feelings were in certain sects and among certain classes in England, they were even stronger in Scotland, and when it was suggested that the Catholic Relief Bill should be extended to apply to that country also, violent riots broke out in Edinburgh and Glasgow. Chapels and mass-houses were burned down[1] and the houses of Catholics attacked by the mob. Bishop Hay returning from a visit to London stepped from his carriage to see a crowd outside his house, and his

---

[1] Handbills were passed round in the streets of Edinburgh urging the passers-by to violence. One such handbill read: 'Men and Brethren—whoever shall find this letter will take it as a warning to meet at Leith Wynd on Wednesday next in the evening to pull down that pillar of Popery lately erected there. Edinburgh Jan. 29, 1779. A Protestant. Please to read this carefully keep it clean and drop it somewhere else. For King and Country. UNITY.'

chapel close by in flames. He asked a woman who was watching the fire what was happening. 'Oh, sir', she told him politely, 'we are burning the Popish chapel and we only wish we had the bishop to throw into the fire.'

Other Catholics in Scotland, frightened by the violence and the threats of violence, had already in Bishop Hay's absence written to Lord North to beg him not to grant them the relief which the Government seemed inclined to bestow. And the Government, alarmed by the news from Edinburgh, acceded to their request and announced that it was not intended to apply the provisions of the offending Bill to Scotland. The rioters had triumphed.

It was in Scotland that Lord George first came to the public notice as a champion of Protestantism. His speeches in Parliament, favourably reported and tactfully edited, had been for some time appearing in the Scottish Press. In many of these he had angrily referred to the Government's refusal to allow the Scotch, 'naked and defenceless as they are', to arm themselves for their own protection, in what seems now the unlikely event of the invasion of Scotland by the enemy. 'Earl Percy', he complained on one occasion, 'armed cap-à-pie marches at the head of all the cheesemongers and grocers from Temple Bar to Brentford; and the great Earl Douglas is not to be trusted with arms. The people of Scotland', he added, flying off at a typically explosive and outrageous tangent, 'think the King is a Papist'. He would have said more but the Speaker thought it 'time to put a stop to his proceeding'.

Such outbursts as these were naturally well received by the spiritual descendants of Knox and did much to enhance his popularity in Scotland, where indeed he was already a respected figure, admired alike for his fluency in Gaelic, his mastery of the most difficult of Highland reels, his enjoyment of Highland songs and ballads and of the esoteric sound made by bagpipes, which no Sassenach could hope fully to appreciate. He was known to wear trews of the Gordon tartan as far south of the Tweed as London and, to give hospitality at his house in Welbeck Street to any Scotsman who happened to call. He was a Scotsman born and bred and even if his forebears had been Catholics and Jacobites he himself had been brought up to respect the good sound Calvinistic doctrines more suited to the Scottish temperament.

It seemed to the Scottish Presbyterians that there was no one at Westminster more likely to help them, and at the first hint of danger

they wrote to him for his advice. He gave it with pleasure and volumi-
nously, and was subsequently invited to Edinburgh by the Scottish
Protestant Associations. He was greeted on his arrival as a heroic leader
and was delighted by a reception so flattering to his vanity. A good
deal of the credit for the ultimate anti-Catholic victory in Scotland was
naturally given to the newly found champion of the Protestant ideal.
And Lord George returned to England with a reputation for determined single-minded leadership which his outspoken, uncompromising
behaviour in Parliament did much to foster.

Soon after his return, and as a tribute to this apparent flair for leadership, he was invited by James Fisher the secretary of the London Protestant Association to become its President. He accepted the offer in a
gracious and extremely long letter.

> I have not the vanity, [he wrote] to imagine myself sufficiently qualified to
> support the dignity of so exalted a station as President; but you may assure
> the gentlemen of the Association that they may command my utmost
> exertions for the Protestant Interest till a more able and deserving President is
> pointed out. The Popish Act being introduced in a thin House, at the end of a
> session, and passed without a public debate, the people of England had
> certainly no fair opportunity given them to discover its dangerous tendency.

He went on to describe at length what he considered to be the underhand machinations of Dalrymple and the Government, emphasizing
the Catholic admittance that the relief afforded by the Act was, so far
as the Catholics themselves were concerned, 'an unlooked-for event'.
He ended on a note of caution and restraint, trusting

> that the coolness and temper in the proceedings of the Association will soon
> demonstrate to the Roman Catholics that we are far from being possessed
> of a persecuting disposition; and I hope the attention of Parliament to the
> petitions of Englishmen will be so very respectful and prudent as not to
> raise the apprehensions of the lower classes of the people . . . The Roman
> Catholics must know as well as we do, that Popery when encouraged by
> Government has always been dangerous to the liberties of the people.

The letter made evident the reasons for his own opposition to the
Catholic Relief Act. Unlike most of his fellow-members in the Protestant Association he had no personal grudge against Catholics, no
unhealthy desire to persecute them as members of a hated religion. He
did not like or trust them, it is true, but he was, in spite of the accusations which were later to be spat out against him, no bitter fanatic

burning with a frenzy of spite and intolerance. His anger rose from sources quite different. He saw in the way the Act had come about a new and most contemptible example of the 'hypocritical, underhand dealings of a despicable' Government who, behind a pretence of generosity and tolerance, were tricking men into fighting a shameful war against a noble people.

It was not only, of course, his anger with the Government and his regard for the Americans which prompted him to assume the offered championship of the Protestant cause. Nor was it entirely his belief that Popery was 'synonymous with arbitrary power' and therefore an enemy to the interests of the poeple. There were other reasons more complex and less admirable. He was at last, after years of disappointment and neglect, within sight of influence and power. He began to see himself not only as a champion of Protestantism but as a champion of that mythical entity 'the people'. In speaking with the voice of Protestantism he would be speaking with the voice of the people, and was not the voice of the people the voice of God? It was a vision which sparkled with the glittering dust of megalomania. His passion for the limelight was being inflamed by this new glimpse of power. And when he had gained that power, so much desired and so long denied him, his supporters with their delicious, intoxicating flattery urged him on from excess to excess; while he, sharing their reckless enthusiasm, did not notice where it was leading him until it was too late to turn back. It is a familiar pattern of disaster.

3

A MEAN SET OF PEOPLE

ONE afternoon early in 1780 Lord Petre, as a spokesman for the Roman Catholics, called at Lord George's house. He found the front door open and a crowd of people in the hall waiting to sign a petition for the repeal of the Catholic Relief Act. For some time now notices had been appearing regularly in the Press advertising that this petition lay waiting for signatures at Lord George Gordon's open house in Welbeck Street near Cavendish Square.

Lord Petre was shown upstairs by MacQueen, the butler, to the study on the first floor where he found Lord George in conversation with Mr. Banfield, a member of the committee of the Protestant Association, who was just expressing his concern at the recent report of a Catholic's unlikely hope that he would shortly be 'walking up to his knees in Protestant blood'.

Lord Petre was not unnaturally rather embarrassed to interrupt such a conversation and Lord George, anxious to put him at his ease, greeted him with extreme courtesy as Mr. Banfield hurriedly left.

How, Lord George asked, was Lady Petre? Would his Lordship take a glass of wine? The visitor, wanting to get his unpleasant task over quickly, refused any refreshment and came immediately to his business.

It was with pain, he told him, that he and his friends heard of his Lordship's continued support for the Protestant Association, the members of which were, they thought, 'a mean set of people', who would dwindle away were it not for their having so distinguished a supporter. They felt that it was a great tragedy that someone for whom they entertained so high a regard should devote his 'great abilities and industry' to such an unfortunate cause. Would it not be reasonable to agree to let the Relief Act remain unquestioned for say five years, to see if during that time the Catholics abuse their newly found privileges?

Lord George replied that, although 'his Lordship had been misinformed as to my abilities', it was better that he should remain in charge of the Protestant Association, as if he withdrew now, 'heated as men's minds were on the subject, there would probably spring up some Wat Tyler or Massonello who would not have patience with Government and might very possibly chuse from motives of ambition to embroil the country in a civil war'. Warming to his theme he went on to say that if the 'Papist Bill stood and any one Papist should use half the honest pains to restore the ancient and hereditary family of Stuart to the throne that I take to promote the glory of the God of Israel and the property of the people, the present illustrious sovereign and all the rest of the House of Hanover might find themselves in danger or exile in a fifth of the time your Lordship requires'.

But, protested Lord Petre, the new oath the Catholics had to take to the Government secured their allegiance to the House of Hanover. And although there was at first some doubt as to whether the new oath of allegiance was altogether acceptable to the Catholic conscience it had now been decided, at a late consultation in Paris, that they were safe in taking it.

Lord George afterwards confessed that his 'countenance, which is a great deal too flexible for political conferences', may well have shewn great 'alarm on hearing the head of the English Roman Catholics speak of a Foreign Council at Paris', the capital of an enemy power. Certainly as soon as this admission 'popt out', Lord Petre abruptly 'put up his papers into his pocket'.

But as it was late and his visitor looked tired and was possibly cold now that the fire had gone out, leaving the room very chilly, there may perhaps have been other reasons (Lord George consoled himself) apart from his too expressive face, for Lord Petre's sudden decision to leave.

It was an unfortunate and abortive interview, and during that spring Lord George was to have several more which left him equally unhappy, dissatisfied and puzzled. He had neither the patience nor the tact to carry off such a conversation with success, and his forthright interviews with the King, the first of which took place a few weeks after this meeting with Lord Petre, gave further proof of the irritating, graceless sanctimonious style in which he conducted these discussions, so unlike his usual pleasant manner in conversation with his friends.[1]

---

[1] It was about this time that Burke's friendly relations with Lord George came to an end. After his interview with Lord Petre, Lord George wrote that Burke 'never once shewed the smallest sign of that acquaintance or familiarity which had formerly subsisted between us for some years'.

As the son of a duke he was entitled to an audience with the King, and when Lord North categorically refused to present the petition of the Protestant Association or in any way to support it, he decided to call at St. James's himself to exercise his birthright.

His first audience was in the last week of January. According to his own account of what took place, the King, in spite of Lord George's unusual and impertinent request that 'some or all of his confidential counsellors', including Bute and Mansfield, should be called into the cabinet as witnesses of what passed between them, received him kindly enough. The express purpose of this interview was to deliver into the King's 'own hand the English appeal against the Popery Bill drawn up by the committee of the Protestant Association' which Lord North had refused to submit himself. Lord George asked if he might report to his committee that the King had received the appeal 'very graciously' and the King 'approved of the expression "very graciously"'.

Walpole's story is very different. He had seen a malicious report of the interview in *The Morning Post*, an often unreliable paper, and his account of the meeting is based upon this. He wrote to the Countess of Upper Ossory taking pleasure in making the most of a story which put in an unfavourable light a person for whom he felt a strong personal dislike.

> Lord George Gordon [he wrote] asked an audience, was admitted, and incontinently began reading his Irish pamphlet, and the King had patience to hear him do so for above an hour, till it was so dark that the lecturer could not see. His Majesty then desired to be excused, and said he would finish the piece himself. 'Well!' said the lunatic apostle, 'But you must give me your honour that you will read it out.' The King promised but was forced to pledge his honour. . . . It is to be hoped this man is so mad that it will soon come to perfection unless my plan is adopted of shutting up in Bedlam the few persons in this country that remain in their senses. It would be easier and much cheaper than to confine all the delirious.

The next time Lord George called upon the King this account of their earlier interview was discussed. As Lord George bowed his way out the King came up to him and said:

'Did you see the account that was given of your last audience in the papers? It's surprising what things they say! It hurt me exceedingly.'

Lord George said that he had heard of the report but as he only took the *Public Advertiser* he had not read it.

Although the scene as related by Walpole did not, it seems, take place it is undoubtedly in character, and Lord George might well have behaved in so exasperating a way at one of his later interviews with the King when there was no longer even the pretence of friendship and respect between them.

At his last interview on being shewn into the royal presence his first action was not merely, as on previous occasions, to close the inner door of the room as the Lord-in-Waiting closed the outer door, but to lock and bolt it behind him as well. He then advanced towards the King and immediately 'in solemn tones reminded him that the House of Stuart had been banished from the throne for encouraging Popery and arbitrary power; and requested him that he should order his Ministers to support the Protestant Religion', quoting extracts from a pamphlet by John Wesley.

Startled by the direct and unceremonious approach the King replied evasively that he had 'taken no part with the late Bill. Parliament did it.'

'Please recollect', said Lord George sternly. 'You *have* taken a part, and a very capital part too, by giving your royal assent to it.'

As the King made no immediate reply to this, and taking advantage of his silence to continue in this aggressive tone, Lord George brought the King's attention to his favourite and constant complaint. Was the King aware, he asked indignantly, that the 'diabolical purpose of the Bill was to arm the Roman Catholics for the American war and not from enlightenment?'

Still apparently the King did not reply and Lord George went on to rail once more at the secret underhand talks which Sir John Dalrymple, one of His Majesty's own judges in Scotland, had had with Bishop Hay.

At last the King spoke. 'I have not', he said with perhaps the expected hint of annoyance, 'been privy to any secret transaction of that nature.'

'The Judges', Lord George said ignoring the denial and delivering himself of a memorable and famous aphorism, 'are the mirrors by which the King's image is reflected.'

The King, understandably feeling that the undignified conversation had gone far enough, assured Lord George that he was a Protestant, although in favour of toleration, and changing the subject asked after his family in Scotland.

The tiresome visitor briefly thanked His Majesty for the kind inquiry and hoped he would excuse him if he returned to the subject in hand.

'Will your Majesty, or will you not, direct your confidential servants to support the Petition?'

'I am in no way pledged in the business.'

'Does that mean you will not speak to Lord North?'

The King refused to answer this last question and was obliged to bow low 'his assent several times' before Lord George accepted his dismissal and left the besieged King in peace.

Although the son of a duke might be excused for certain eccentricities of behaviour, and even for taking advantage of the King's commendable restraint, Lord George during this last interview so far overstepped the narrow limits within which court etiquette was confined, that the next time the importunate young man called at St. James's he was refused admittance.

Convinced at last that no help could be expected from the 'illeducated elector of Hanover', as he called him, or from any of his Ministers, Lord George threw his energies more determinedly than ever into the now alarming activities of the Protestant Association.

The Association had met several times since Lord Petre's reference to it at Welbeck Street as 'a mean set of people', and each time a larger hall had to be hired for the growing crowds which attended the meetings, every one of which was more rowdy and more threatening than the one before it. At one meeting it was announced to deafening cheers that there were now over one hundred thousand signatures to the monster petition at the President's house and that people were still calling to sign every day.

The committee were, however, in disagreement as to how and when this petition should be delivered. At a meeting held at The Old Crown and Rolls Tavern in Chancery Lane a suggestion put to the vote by James Fisher that it should not be delivered until the end of June was carried against the advice of Lord George Gordon and the Reverend Erasmus Middleton, a leading member of the committee. A few days later, however, Fisher called at Welbeck Street. Lord George disliked Fisher as 'a very fluent orator, specious and crouching and submissive with a plentiful command of crying and whining about religion in his speeches; and no lack of buffoonery and low jesting'. He was a lawyer with a mainly criminal practice in Whitechapel and had joined the Association, it was afterwards alleged, for reasons by no means disinterested. He had called, he told Lord George, to inform him that the committee had now come round to the President's way of thinking and agreed that the petition should be presented without delay. Before leaving Fisher asked Lord George not to mention at the next general meeting that there had been this difference in the committee. Lord George agreed but had to admit that 'from that moment neither Mr. Middleton nor I reposed any confidence at all in Mr. James Fisher'. The quarrel was, however, for the moment patched up. Lord George and Middleton had had their way and took the rest of the Association with them.

There was no doubt that the Association as a whole was behind Lord George and anxious for immediate action, and a Government spy reported that at a meeting during April the mood of the members seemed dangerous. A week later Lord North himself visited Lord George in Welbeck Street and promised him a 'large sum of money and a leading situation in Parliament provided he would desert the Association'. It was not the first bribe which the Government had offered him. Some months previously he had, on the same conditions, been offered a command at sea which formerly he had so much desired. And before that Lord North had approached the Duke of Gordon with a view to his accepting a sinecure worth £1,000 a year if he could get his brother to resign his seat in Parliament. Earlier on in his career when Lord North was anxious to get the Irish orator Henry Flood into the House as a defence against Charles James Fox, he had been offered the profitable appointment of Vice-Admiral of Scotland if he would give up his seat.

But Lord George would not be bought off. The more tempting the bribe which was offered him, the more convinced he became of his importance. Each difficulty, each repulse, increased his determination. By the early summer he had persuaded himself that he was a man with a divine mission. It is a dangerous illusion and he was obsessed by it.

Both in Parliament and at the meetings of the Protestant Association he spoke of this mission to save his country from its enemies, both spiritual and physical, with a passion which on occasions verged on hysteria. One day as a fellow Member presented a petition in Parliament and unfolded it on the floor of the House to show how long it was and how many signatures it contained. Lord George jumped up and called out in derisive indignation: 'Pooh! What is all this? With a great deal of pulling, this petition seems to extend from your chair Mr. Speaker to the door of the House. In a few days, Sir, I shall present you the Petition of the Protestant Association. It will extend, Sir, from your chair to a window at Whitehall that Kings should often think of.'

He was in the same excited, reckless mood at Coachmakers' Hall on the Tuesday of the following week when he addressed an enormous meeting of the Protestant Association on the method to be adopted for presenting the great petition which was now complete.

'The only way to go', he said admonishing by implication the more cautious members, 'is in a bold manner and shew we are to defend Protestantism with our lives. If you mean to spend your time in idle debate you had better at once choose another leader. I am ready for all, but I am not a man to do things by halves.' He wished so well to the cause himself, he told them with extravagant enthusiasm, he would go to the gallows for it. If they were lukewarm, he was certainly not. His long reddish hair, an observer noticed, 'jumped on his shoulders' and his extraordinarily deep blue eyes flashed as he stared about him. He would not present the petition at all if he were not backed up by, at least twenty thousand men.

This mention of so vast an attendance alarmed even more those fellow members on the committee, who had already advocated a more conciliatory approach; but others, as excited and reckless as himself, encouraged him to persist in his demand for an immense personal representation.   And when, after reading extracts from the 'Popish catechism just published', he moved 'that the whole body of the Protestant Association do attend in St. George's Fields on Friday 2nd June at ten o'clock in the morning to accompany him to the House of Commons in the delivery of the Protestant Petition', the motion was carried unanimously with 'bursts of applause'.

The following day this advertisement appeared in several newspapers.

PROTESTANT ASSOCIATION

Whereas no Hall in London can contain forty thousand men;

Resolved, That this Association do meet on Friday next June 2 in *St. George's Fields*, at 10 o'clock in the morning, to consider of the most prudent and respectful manner of attending their Petition, which will be presented the same day, to the House of Commons.

Resolved. For the sake of good order and regularity, that this Association, on coming to the ground, do separate themselves into 4 distinct divisions, viz. the London division, the Westminster division, the Southwark division, and the Scotch division.

Resolved, That the London division do take place upon the right of the ground towards Southwark, the Westminster division second, the Southwark division third, and the Scotch division upon the left; all wearing blue cockades in their hats to distinguish them from the Papists, and those who approve of the late act in favour of Popery.

Resolved, That the Magistrates of London, Westminster and Southwark, are requested to attend, that their presence may overawe and controul any riotous or evil minded persons, who may wish to disturb the legal and peaceable deportment of His Majesty's Protestant Subjects.

By order of the Association,

G. Gordon, President.

London. May 1780.

There was no turning back now. On Friday in St. George's Fields the crowds would assemble and march to the House of Commons 'to demand', as Walpole disdainfully put it, 'that the defender of the faith should be forced to part with his Whore of Babylon'.

During that waiting week, a journalist remembered long afterwards, there was a strange tension in the air, a feeling of excitement and vague expectant fear. The weather was hot and sultry. On Wednesday a baby was born in Spitalfields with a single eye in the middle of its head and cylindrical teeth like the teeth of a mylodon, an innocent portent of disaster. And on Thursday afternoon the weather for a short time violently broke and there were fierce storms in various parts of the country; a fire-ball, shattering through the window of a house in Oxford, pierced a mahogany chest on the landing, knocked a maid-servant down the stairs and, splintering a looking-glass, embedded it-self in the wall behind it; at Longleat a fierce hailstorm broke all the glass in Lord Weymouth's melon house and cucumber frames, and killed all the geese and ducks and poultry exposed to its fury; in Bethnal Green a weaver was struck by lightning and killed as he came running out of a brothel; and in the little village of Paddington a drunken blacksmith blinded by the sudden driving rain fell head first and drowned himself in a water butt. Each event clothed in a sort of grotesque humour was later taken as being an unheeded, ominous warning. But that was not until later. On Friday morning the skies cleared, the sun came out and the inhabitants awoke to a warm and cheerful day.

4

THE SURGING OF THE SEA

B Y ten o'clock it was already hot. The men strolling into St.
George's Fields had their collar buttons undone, their stocks
loosely tied at their throats. A few of them had stopped on their
way to quench their thirst in cool dark taverns, away from the glare of
the sun and the dryness of the dust. And it seemed to more than one
reporter that these shouting, laughing, sweating groups did not look
like men who felt deeply on questions of religion or to whom the principles of the Protestant Association would greatly appeal.

Most of the groups, however, were composed of those quiet, intent
and sober-looking men, 'the better sort of tradespeople' and 'honest
Mechanicks' who had, in weeks past, been attending the crowded,
excited meetings in Greenwood's Rooms, St. Margaret's Hall, Southwark and Coachmakers' Hall. They came with hymn-books in their
pockets and a look of martyrdom, determined, noble and self-right-
eous, in their eyes. This was the impatiently awaited day when they
would at last be able to demonstrate their steadfastness, their influence
and their strength.

St. George's Fields was a big open space south of the river where
Waterloo Station now is, and which was then bounded on its northern
side by an oak-lined street known as Melancholy Walk and on its eastern side by the appropriately called Dirty Lane. By night it was a dangerous place and only the most foolhardy citizens took a short cut
across it unarmed. In daylight gangs of streetboys chased each other
around the wooden shacks of beggars and the bushes near stagnant
ponds, while apprentices from the workshops at Newington Butts and
from the maze of streets between Bandy Leg Walk and Angel Street,
came out to play football or to make love in the long grass. For many
years it had been a favourite place for open air meetings, demonstrations
and religious services; and the crowds who came to these meetings

brought almost as much business to the busy 'Dog and Duck' at the end of Lambeth Road as did the circus opposite it. There was also a mineral spring nearby, patronized by Dr. Johnson and Mrs. Thrale. It was in this well-known part of the Fields, close to St. George's Spa, as the spring was called, and just north of the 'Dog and Duck' that the Protestant Association and its supporters were to meet.

When Lord George arrived just before eleven o'clock the crowd was loudly singing a good Protestant hymn and at the sight of the leader in his coach, cheer upon cheer could be heard above the din of the singing. Warned that a number of mischief-makers, including Roman Catholics, intended to turn the great march of protest into a fiasco and to provoke the petitioners to violence, Lord George was anxious to impress upon them all the need for restraint and 'peaceable Deportment and Behaviour'. Walking into the middle of the crowd he passed a bundle of handbills, 'inculcating the same pacifick Temper', to a member of the Committee and then stepped up on to a box to make a short speech of warning and encouragement. As soon as he began to speak the singing died away and the conversation faded to a murmur. For a few minutes only they listened. It was too hot for a speech and they were too impatient and too excited to attend to one for a moment longer than politeness and respect for their leader required. Each time he paused for breath in the blazing heat, the more impatient among the crowd surged forward to cheer his last remark or to shake him by the hand or to slap him on the back, hoping that he would thus be persuaded to take for granted their obedience and their loyalty. He was almost suffocated by them and was obliged to get down from his box long before he had finished his intended speech and to push his way through the mass of people to the coach of a friend, which with difficulty moved off down Lambeth Road towards the House of Commons, where he had arranged to accept the petition from the hands of the marching demonstrators who were to follow him there later. Some of his eager supporters stopped the coach and asked if they might accompany him. 'Pray let us attend you to the House', they said. 'By no means', Lord George replied. 'I shall be greatly obliged to you gentlemen if you will all go back.' And so they left him to go on alone.

Meanwhile in another part of the Fields a tailor was busy sewing together the several pieces of parchment on which the signatures of the petitioners were inscribed. When he had finished and the parchment was rolled up like a carpet, it was found that the strongest man there could scarcely lift the enormous bundle, which was so heavy that it had to be passed from shoulder to shoulder in the long march that followed. To practise the arrangements for this march, the crowd was divided up by the organizers into the four divisions which the advertisements published in the Press had specified; and as soon as the four divisions were sorted out, the Scottish division, led by a Highlander with kilt and drawn sword, marched off to the skirl of bagpipes round the field, followed by the divisions from the cities of London and Westminster, with the division from the Borough of Southwark bringing up the rear. Three or four times they made a circuit of the Fields practising the discipline of marching; keeping in line and in step with remarkable success for civilians unused to such military exercise. Before moving off along their route those petitioners who had not come already equipped with a blue cockade in their hats were issued with one by courtesy of the Protestant Association.[1] And for those who cared to make a contribution to the Association's fighting fund there were special cockades ornamented with gold and silver, some of which had white labels bearing the legend 'No Popery!' worked artistically in blue silk stitching. When everyone was equipped the bagpipes started up again and the great march began.

The largest body of petitioners, estimated the following day as numbering more than fifty thousand, marched off eight abreast, following their banners on which was written, the correspondent of *Adam's Weekly Courant* noticed, 'the words "No Popery" and other labels, expressive of the Business of the Day'.

Having crossed the river they marched up Fish Street Hill and Grace Church Street and then turned left down Cornhill and Cheapside. They marched in accordance with Lord George's instructions 'very quietly', not singing now, talking softly amongst themselves; impressive and peaceable. But as they passed across the narrow streets between the river and Bishopsgate, many others with motives quite different from theirs, joined them and walked along after them down Fleet Street and the Strand towards Charing Cross. Unaware of this unfortunate addition to their numbers, the leaders went on, welcoming those who more obtrusively joined them on horseback and in coaches,

---

[1] Doctor Burney said that the Association had paid £2,000 for blue ribbon and cockades. Although this figure seems excessive the Committee were certainly not short of funds. For weeks past agents had been busy in London and the surrounding towns and villages collecting subscriptions.

marching stolidly behind their banners and showing emotion or enthusiasm only when they passed a church, which they would greet with
three loud cheers. This cheering of churches—and the house of John
Wilkes in Great George Street which a party filed off to salute, and an
extra loud cheer for the Admiralty as they passed it—was the only
demonstration of enthusiasm which they allowed themselves. But the
rhythmic stamping of their feet, the mass of steady unsmiling faces, the
murmur of thousands of quiet voices within the ranks, described as
being like the surging of the waves of the sea, were sights and
sounds which were afterwards remembered, with the pang of
fear.

As the vast procession reached the bottom of Whitehall and tramped
down into Parliament Street, they met their fellow petitioners who had
taken the shorter route across Westminster Bridge and who now filled
New Palace Yard and commanded all the approaches to the Houses of
Parliament. The two groups met with an unexpected, deafening roar of
greeting which seemed to give to each a new and wilder enthusiasm, a
more unhealthy motive. The petitioners who had crossed the river by
Westminster Bridge had also been joined by ruffians and street boys,
pickpockets and prostitutes, who had come along to see if they could
turn the demonstration to their own advantage or pleasure. Seeing
these drunken trouble-makers amongst the crowd one observer said of
the petitioners that they all had 'the true aspect of abandoned vaga-
bonds'. The young Frederic Reynolds, however, has painted a more
likely picture. Reynolds, then a fifteen-year-old schoolboy of Westminster, whose father was John Wilkes's affluent solicitor and whose
first words lisped in imitation of his nurse were 'Wilkes and Liberty',
had a natural understanding of popular enthusiasms and a cynical, reactive contempt for enthusiasts.

He had come out after his midday meal with other Westminster
boys, including his friend the Duke of Bedford, 'eager for the fray' and
to witness these 'most novel and extraordinary proceedings'. He found
the crowd

occupying every avenue to the Houses of Parliament, the whole of Westminster Bridge and extending to the northern end of Parliament Street. The
greater part of it, however, was composed of persons decently dressed, who
appeared to be incited to extravagance, by a species of fanatical phrenzy.
They talked of dying in the good cause, and manifested all the violence of the
disposition imbibed under the banner of Presbyterianism. They had long lank

Brackley Kennet, Lord Mayor of London

The Petitioners marching to the Houses of Parliament on the
afternoon of 2 June, 1780

Alderman Frederick Bull

heads of hair, meagre countenances, fiery eyes, and they uttered deep ejaculations; in short, displaying all the outward and visible signs of hypocrisy and starvation.

Lord Shelburne said that they shouted out 'No Popery! We shall be burnt! Let us have the Protestant religion!' and that their fear seemed real. They shouted that they would 'rather perish in the streets than endure a Popish government'.

There was no doubt now that the former quiet steadfastness, the firm, unwavering but pacific protest, had given way to more violent emotions. The more impetuous of the petitioners, encouraged by roughs and bullies, began to make threats of force and to encourage the others to fight if they could not get their way by demonstration and negotiation. Orders were issued—no one knew where they originated—that all unpopular Members of the Lords should be stopped on their way to the House, forced to put blue cockades in their hats and to shout 'No Popery!' twice. If there was doubt as to who should be molested as being unpopular and who allowed to pass, instructions would be signalled from surrounding roof-tops by men with blue flags.

Soon after two o'clock the first coaches carrying Members of Parliament began to arrive in the streets approaching the House.

Lord Bathurst, the aged former Lord Chancellor and by now Lord President of the Council, was the first peer to receive the attention of the petitioners, who so far exceeded their instructions as to pull the old man out of his carriage, hit him across the face and pelt him with mud, jeering at him that he was 'the Pope and a silly old woman'. Excited by the sight and sense of violence, the demonstrators with the fury of suppressed emotion suddenly and thrillingly released, fell upon every carriage containing a peer whether he were a Catholic sympathizer or not. Lord Stormont's carriage was completely demolished and Lord Stormont himself was subjected to what *The Morning Chronicle* referred to next morning as 'the most impudent liberties', escaping only after having suffered half an hour's kicking and pelting. The Duke of Northumberland, whose pale secretary was dressed in sombre black, was mistaken for a Jesuit and was pulled out from his coach by his legs and beaten about the head and shoulders. He discovered on his bedraggled arrival in the House some minutes later that a pickpocket had snatched his watch in the scuffle. Lord Mansfield, the Lord Chief Justice, had all the windows of his carriage smashed in and his wig torn from his head and when at last he escaped and got to the House he was, according to

Walpole, 'quivering like an aspen'.[1] The Bishops of Lincoln and Lich-field were both attacked, their gowns were torn off, they were plastered with mud and excrement, and when the Bishop of Lincoln 'too hastily resented this treatment' he was seized by the throat with such force that the blood gurgled from his mouth. His superior, the Archbishop of York, although an adept boxer in his youth and still able to protect himself with a somewhat fragile agility, was at length obliged to say 'No Popery!', which he did in 'a pitiable and enfeebled voice'. Lords Willoughby de Broke, Ashburnham, St. John, Hillsborough, Trentham and Dudley were insulted, pelted and beaten with particular animosity. Lord Ashburnham indeed had to be dragged into the House over the heads of the crowd, badly hurt and scarcely conscious.

The Members of the House of Commons escaped more lightly, most of them merely having their names and 'No Popery!' scrawled in chalk on their carriage doors. Charles Turner, who had helped one of the bishops to escape and who had criticized Lord George in the House on several occasions, and Sir George Savile, had their coaches demolished, and Burke was abused with scandalous and obscene invective; but only Mr. Welbore Ellis and Mr. Strahan were physically attacked. Hit across the face with a whip and with blood pouring from his mouth Welbore Ellis ran away, chased by thirty or forty men, into Westminster Guildhall where the doors were locked behind him. As he stood inside the Guildhall panting for breath the door was forced by the mob outside and the windows smashed and he was forced to escape across the roof 'at the utmost hazard'.

Soon after Welbore Ellis's escape, Lord North's coach rattled at furious speed towards the Horse Guards. The people standing in the way jumped clear of the galloping horses but as the coach approached Palace Yard where the crowds were denser it was obliged to slow down and a man was able to open the door, spring inside and snatch Lord North's hat from his head. He ran away with it and later on in the day he cut it up and sold the pieces off at a shilling each.[2]

By now many of the petitioners, dismayed by the vulgarity of the demonstrations and horrified by their violence had returned home. Some, indeed, on their way had been to the offices of the Protestant

[1] Lord Mansfield was particularly suspect as a friend of the Duchess of Norfolk and because he had recently acquitted a priest indicted for saying Mass.

[2] Henry Angelo, the young son of the great fencing master, bought a piece which fifty years later still stood, faded but authentic, on the chimney-piece in his London house.

Association to withdraw their names in protest from its list of members. The petitioners who were left in Palace Yard and Parliament Street were the most ignorant and least respectable of the original number, the most bigoted and, what was more important, the most easily encouraged to violence. And there were many there to encourage them. For as the more reasonable of the petitioners went home, their places were taken by others whose only interest in religion was in the fury and injustice which so often attended it, and by professional criminals who simulated the looks and behaviour of fanatical Methodists so as to entice to further outrage those who sincerely held the frenzied beliefs which the others so outlandishly affected.

These were the men whom Samuel Romilly saw on his way to hear the Duke of Richmond speak in the House of Lords on his proposal for more representative Parliaments. Samuel Romilly then a young man of twenty-three, suffering from a severe stomach disorder which the waters at Bath had aggravated and now recovering after a prolonged course of the more gentle waters at Islington, was horrified to find his way blocked by a throng of people wearing blue cockades. 'They seemed', he wrote in one of his long, informative letters to the Reverend John Roget, his brother-in-law who was dying of tuberculosis in Switzerland, 'to consist in a great measure of the lowest rabble; men who, without doubt, not only had never heard any of the arguments for or against toleration, but who were utterly ignorant of the very purpose of the petition. To give you one instance: a miserable fanatic who accosted me, not indeed with any friendly design, but to question me where my cockade was, which I very civilly informed him I had dropped out of my hat in the crowd, told me that the reign of the Romans had lasted too long!' Moving on to a group of people 'assembled round a female preacher who by her gestures and actions seemed to be well persuaded, or desirous of persuading others that she was animated by some supernatural spirit', Romilly found that his lack of a blue cockade was a dangerous omission and that he did not long remain unquestioned as to his religious principles. 'My joining, however, in the cry of "No Popery!" ' he told Roget, 'soon pacified my inquisitors or rather indeed gained me their favour; for a very devout butcher insisted upon shaking hands with me as a token of his friendship.'

When Romilly eventually managed to force his way into the House of Lords the scene he found there was extraordinary. There were few peers present as many had followed Lord Sandwich's example in giving their coachmen orders to turn round when they saw the danger to which they would expose themselves by a too rigid attendance to their duty. The peers who had pushed their way through, stood talking excitedly in small groups, arguing with the anger which comes from indignation and fear, their faces cut, their clothes torn, some wigless with their short hair dishevelled, others holding bandages to their heads, all sweating, angry and apprehensive. The scene resembled, the correspondent of *The London Evening Post* told his readers, 'the pit at a Garrick play'.

But in spite of the ragged, agitated appearance of the Members present and the 'frequent interruptions from the thundering of the mob at the doors of the House' the liberal but pompous Duke of Richmond stood up to speak on his proposal for a 'more equal representation of the People in Parliament'. He spoke, breaking off only when it was quite impossible to make himself heard, for upwards of an hour. And then suddenly the door was burst open and a breathless Lord Mountford shouted that the mob were assembled in still greater numbers before their Lordships' doors and the life of his friend Lord Boston who was trying to get to the House was 'in the greatest danger'. The Duke of Richmond, not hearing very well what Lord Mountford had said, commented in his most gravely consequential manner that it was 'very extraordinary that the noble Lord should interrupt' him in this way. If he had said anything that was improper or disorderly, or anything which required explanation, he was willing 'to sit down till the noble Lord assigned his reason for interrupting'. Lord Mountford more frantic than ever explained again Lord Boston's predicament and at last the Duke sat down with a gesture of frustration. Immediately several peers shouted offers of assistance to Lord Mountford in his proposed rescue of Lord Boston. The Duke of Richmond, however, inveterate talker that he was and unwilling to lose the initiative, felt that the Upper House should preserve its sense of proportion even in such circumstances as these. He stood up again and said:

> It is well known that I am a friend to the people and have often stood up in defence of their rights,[1] but I am exceedingly sorry to see them so improperly assembled and acting in so unwarrantable a manner. I the more lament it on the mistaken account upon which they have been induced to

[1] He, in fact, was one of the very few Members who had been treated with respect by the demonstrators that afternoon.

behave so indefensibly, for the Act which they have been misled about, and taught to believe so encouraging to Popery, was merely an Act for giving liberty of conscience and allowing men of different religious sentiments from themselves to enjoy those sentiments at their ease. The Act, therefore, was founded in an idea of securing the general liberties of every description of subjects. *My own Bill* goes to the same point in some degree.

Having got the debate back on to more constructive lines, he was about to continue when it was brought to his notice that Lord Boston was still in the hands of the mob beneath the Committee Room windows. Whereupon Lord Radnor stood up to propose that several of their Lordships should immediately go down and 'try by their presence to extricate Lord Boston from his disagreeable situation'. Lord Townshend, whose strong nerve had enabled him to rescue the Earl of Hillsborough, immediately agreed, while several other peers stood up to remark that 'if something were not done in the business it might be too late.' But the Duke of Richmond, with a nice sense of parliamentary procedure and protocol, reminded them in the course of a long and apparently uninterrupted speech, that if they went as a House, the Mace ought to be carried before the 'learned Lord on the Woolsack who should go at their head'. Lord Mansfield timidly but creditably said that if they really thought that such a mode of conduct was proper in the circumstances, he was willing to do as they wished. The Duke of Gloucester, however, opposed this method as being dangerous and instead suggested that as he understood Mr. Wright, one of the Justices of the Peace in Bow Street, was 'about the House, he thought it much more proper that Mr. Wright should be called to the bar and receive instructions to collect the civil power and disperse the mob'. Lord Denbigh agreed and went further, observing that the mob was extremely numerous and dangerous and that although he never approved of employing the military, except in cases of extreme necessity, he believed the present case came within that description. He proposed, therefore, that as the civil magistrates would be of very little service, the military should be called out to assist them. The suggestion that troops should be used deeply shocked the Duke of Richmond, who got to his feet again to say that this was 'the way to create a riot not to suppress one. Our Government will be no better than a Military Government if troops are to be called out upon every occasion to suppress riots. I am filled with horror of the consequences which might ensue if the army are called upon.'

While this discussion about the correct approach to the problem continued, Lord Boston himself had cleverly succeeded in involving two of his fiercest tormentors, one of whom had threatened to carve the sign of the Cross on his scalp, in a heated argument as to whether the Pope were Anti-Christ or not. As the argument promised to develop into a fight Lord Boston 'his hair all dishevelled and his cloaths almost covered with powder', was able surreptitiously to slip away and at last arrived at the House, where the plans for his rescue were still being debated.

After the expressions of relief at his arrival had subsided Lord Shelburne, who thought that 'the present tumult . . . lay much deeper than the Bill relative to Roman Catholics', rose to complain 'with great warmth and energy' that he had been waiting patiently for a Minister to get up and give an account of what steps the Government had taken to guard against the tumult which, in view of the advertisements appearing in the Press, they must have expected. Had they or had they not ordered the civil power to be prepared and the Justices to be out?

In replying for the Government, Lord Hillsborough said that orders were sent through Lord North to the magistrates of Westminster 'warning them of the mob of this day and directing them to be in the way to quell any tumults that might take place'. Whereupon Lord Shelburne suggested that the absent-minded Lord North had doubtless received the order but had put it in his pocket and thought no more about it. It was a good guess for in fact Lord North had only remembered the order at two o'clock that afternoon on his way to the House.

At length after more argument, 'tumultuous altercation' and a heated exchange between Lord Denbigh and Lord Shelburne upon the advisibility of calling out the army, it was agreed that any Magistrates in or near the House should be sent for.

But only Mr. Sampson Wright and one other Justice could be found and in reply to Lord Shelburne's question, 'Have you received any orders for attending here from any Member of the Administration' Justice Wright had to admit that he had not. The interrogation continued before an increasingly indignant House:

Shelburne: 'Have you received any kind of direction from anybody to come down here?'
Wright: 'No.'
Shelburne: 'What brought you down to the House?'

Wright: 'A mere motive of curiosity in the first instance, and an idea in the second, that it was possible the interposition of a magistrate might be wanted.'

Shelburne: 'Have you made any such interposition?'

Wright: 'Yes—but to no purpose—the multitude being much too large to be manageable by a single magistrate or by any force which we could at this time collect.'

The force which he had been able to collect numbered only six constables and till more could be found, he explained, his efforts to disperse the mob would be useless.

Nevertheless Lord Mansfield, instructed by the House, ordered him and his fellow Justice, Mr. Reed, to 'try to disperse the mob and to come back and report to the House what effect their endeavours should have.'

On their return Justice Wright admitted, as everyone expected he would, that the mob was now much too large for him to disperse 'with the help of any constables I should be able to collect together'. And even as he spoke the demonstrators, later estimated as numbering fourteen thousand, were beating at the doors in an endeavour to break into the House.

In the House of Commons the atmosphere was even more alarming, as Members shouted at each other above the din made by a crowd of ruffianly, stinking and half-drunk demonstrators who had forced their way into the lobby.

The proceedings of the day had begun in relative calm as Members considered amendments to the Hair Powder Bill and the duty on starch; but immediately Lord George Gordon had stood up, a murmur of apprehension and annoyance could be heard in the House above the rumble of the steadily increasing noise outside. Lord George had before him, he had said, a Petition signed by nearly one hundred and twenty thousand of His Majesty's Subjects, 'praying for a repeal of the Act passed the last session in favour of Roman Catholics', an Act which horrified a 'populace determined to stand up for their rights against . . . the pernicious effects of a religion, subversive of all liberty, inimical to all purity of morals, begotten by fraud and superstition and teeming with absurdity, persecution and the most diabolical cruelty'. He moved to have the Petition brought up and, Mr. Alderman Bull seconding him, leave was accordingly granted, and the enormous roll of parchment was brought into the debating chamber and dumped on the floor.[1]

Lord George then moved that the Petition should be taken into immediate consideration and was again seconded by Alderman Bull. The House, however, hearing the intimidating clamour outside greeted this suggestion with scorn, and many members on both sides rose to oppose it. During the heated speeches which followed, Lord George on several occasions went out on to the gallery overlooking the lobby to keep the demonstrators informed about what was being said inside. 'Lord North calls you a mob', he shouted at them once and later 'The Member for Bristol[2] is now speaking. He is no friend to your petition.' He was seen to be extravagantly agitated, scarcely coherent, with a look in his darkly flashing eyes of an excitement which seemed hysterical. He appeared in his wild enthusiasm to be quite beyond the reach of any appeal for restraint, to be so intoxicated by the sound of the hundreds of voices shouting his name, that he was unaware that most of the reasonable petitioners had gone home, leaving behind them a mischief-making and violence-hungry rabble. And yet on occasions he seemed to realize, despite his hysteria, that the shouting, jostling people outside were not the sincere supporters that they pretended to be, that he had started something dangerous which was now beyond his power to stop.

The Chaplain to the House who saw him when he came into the dining-room after one of his excursions into the lobby, said that he 'seemed overcome with heat and fatigue', that he looked frantic with worry. As he entered the room everyone else there except the Chaplain got up and left immediately. He slumped down into a chair near the Chaplain and shut his eyes. The Chaplain told him that a man in the crowd had said that if Lord Gordon told them to go away they would go, and he tried to persuade him to use his influence with the demonstrators before it was too late. But Lord George made no reply to the Chaplain and soon after, with a sigh, got up from his chair and left the room to return to the lobby.

'Do you desire us to go away?' a petitioner, apprehensive of the company in which he found himself, called up to him.

[1] According to Father O'Leary the vast size of the petition could be attributed to the fact that parchments had been exposed in all Nonconformist 'meeting houses and vestries begging the signature of every peasant and mendicant'. Certainly, it contained many Xs marked by men and women who could not write.
[2] Edmund Burke.

'You are the best judges of what you ought to do', Lord George told him. 'But I will tell you how the matter stands: the House are going to divide upon the question, whether your petition shall be taken into consideration now or upon Tuesday. There are for taking it into consideration now, myself and six or seven others. If it is not taken into consideration now your petition may be lost. Tomorrow the House does not meet; Monday is the King's birthday; upon Tuesday the Parliament may be dissolved.'

This short speech was greeted with cheers, shouts of 'Repeal! Repeal!' and renewed chanting of Lord George's name. This chanting, later referred to as a 'constant chime', he found, in spite of his evident concern as to its sincerity, quite irresistible. Each time it reached a crescendo he would go out on to the gallery again, to be greeted by exhilarating cheers from below, and would remind the people of the success the Scots had had when they opposed the Government's wishes and would tell them to keep themselves 'steady and cool'. When he turned back into the House he was received with coldness and hostility and sometimes with threats.

Colonel Holroyd went up to him and said: 'My Lord, at first I thought you were only mad; and was going to move that you might be sent to Bedlam; now I see there is much more malice than madness in this business. If you go once more to the mob I assure you upon the faith of Parliament I will instantly move that you be committed to the Tower.'

General Conway was more ferocious; grabbing him by the collar he said in 'a very loud voice', 'I am a military man and I shall protect the freedom of debate with my sword. Do not imagine that we will be intimidated by a rabble. The entry into the House is a narrow one. Reflect that men of honour may defend this pass.'

Other Members were even more explicit. One of two gentlemen who followed him about the House with their hands on their swords threatened to plunge his blade into Lord George's body if a single one of his 'rascally adherents' came into the House.

But neither threats nor imprecations nor pleas nor warnings had any effect on the wild and feverish young man now. Like the popular general of a drunken, reckless army who is infected by the insane enthusiasm of his soldiers, he cared nothing for the consequences of his action, but only for the delirious excitement of the moment and for the dream of victory.

One moment sitting sprawled and exhausted on a chair, and the next dashing excitedly across the House, now coming forward in the gallery to present the unwilling Reverend Thomas Bowen to the people in the lobby, now being pulled back with 'a gentle violence' by General Grant, alternately arguing with a political opponent and talking to his supporters in the lobby, he seemed everywhere at once, as ubiquitous in presence as in spirit.

For six hours the hubbub continued and then at about eight o'clock the House at last divided on Lord George's motion for the immediate consideration of the Petition. Of the one hundred and ninety-eight Members who had managed to get to Parliament that day only six voted with Lord George and Alderman Bull.[1] When the news of this overwhelming defeat reached the demonstrators outside they saw in it a reason and an excuse for further violent and malicious behaviour. So menacing in fact did they now appear that at supper later on that evening Lord Frederick Cavendish told Walpole that he had thought the Members would have to throw open the doors of the House and fight their way out sword in hand. Before this unprecedented necessity was forced upon them, however, the decision to send for the Guards was eventually taken and at a little after nine o'clock a party of Foot and Horse Guards arrived under the orders of Justices Addington and Wright.

The evening was still hot and the clamour seemed more thunderous than ever as Captain Topham drew up his troop on the eastern side of Palace Yard. The crowds nervously and almost respectfully had opened up for them as they rode through 'flourishing their swords in a menacing attitude' but now as they stood still in Palace Yard, waiting for orders and apparently unwilling to use their swords otherwise than threateningly, they were surrounded by a hissing, shouting, insolent mob who pelted them with stones and 'pieces of faggot which they had taken from a neighbouring baker's'.

As the demonstrators appeared incited rather than intimidated by the cavalry, and were so little impressed by the helpless and restrained Foot Guards in Union Street and St. Margaret's Street, as to jeer and laugh at them, knocking their hats off and poking sticks at their bottoms, Justice Addington gave Captain Topham the order to charge. The crowds, however, Frederic Reynolds observed were 'wedged into

[1] These members were Sir Philip Jennings Clerke, Sir Michael Le Fleming, Sir James Lowther, Sir Joseph Mawley, Mr. Polhill and Mr. Tollemache.

such firm and compact masses that the cavalry were actually compelled to recede and return in a full gallop, in order to give their career sufficient force to penetrate them. The consequence was that after the cavalry had passed through them, the mob lay in the most ludicrous manner one over another like a pack of cards; and the only accident of which I heard was the fracture of a leg.'

This treatment while enraging many of the demonstrators made others laugh so much that they could not get up from the ground, where they lay rolling about in paroxysms of infectious laughter.

Justice Addington immediately perceived his opportunity and made use of it. Standing up in his stirrups he affected a high good humour as he told the demonstrators that if they would give their word of honour to disperse he would order the troops to march away. A few of the more respectable petitioners who had already begun to wish that they had gone home earlier on in the afternoon, shouted their agreement. Before anyone could voice his dissent Addington gave Topham orders to march his troops away and as the last trooper turned his horse round a man called for three cheers for 'grand old Addington', which 'at least six hundred of the petitioners' accorded him before retiring 'very quietly'.

Other petitioners soon after went away too and at ten o'clock when the Members began to leave the House to go home there were only a few straggling groups of demonstrators left in Palace Yard and the roads leading towards it.

Lord George was one of the last to leave. His coach had gone back to Welbeck Street and in order to get a lift home he went up to Sir James Lowther who had been one of the few men to vote with him earlier on in the evening. Sir James sat on a bench between Sir Philip Jennings Clerke another of his supporters and Sir George Savile the friendly and gregarious proposer of the offending Bill. They were all three talking to Lord John Cavendish who, as Gordon approached them, was complaining of an insult he had just received from a soldier which put him 'in mind of the time of Oliver Cromwell'.

'Have you a carriage?' Lord George asked Lowther.

'Yes, I have.'

'Are you engaged?'

'I would carry Sir Philip here.'

'If you have room please give me leave to go along with you.'

Lord George looked pale and exhausted and sad, and as Sir Philip afterwards commented, a somehow 'pitiable figure'. The crushing defeat which he had suffered had drained the energy and frenzy out of him and left him in silent despair. Sir James told him he would be glad of his company and wishing Savile and Cavendish a good night, the three others went downstairs together and got into the coach which was awaiting them in the street outside. 'Very little conversation passed in the coach', Sir James remembered, 'I carried Sir Philip Clerke to the top of St. James's Street and asked Lord George Gordon where he desired to be set down? He said, "At my own house." I said, "You seem very tired." He said, "Very much so." I believe he was rather sleepy during the whole time he was there.'

Sir James got out as the coach drew up at his own house and he sent it on with Lord George who arrived home at about a quarter to eleven. Mrs. Yond, his old housekeeper, who was waiting up for him, let him in and he went straight to bed.

For an hour as Lord George slept, the town was silent and curiously still as if exhausted by the sweltering heat of the day and the excitement of its events.

And then a little before midnight, a group of 'resolute, half-drunk, venomous-looking' men were seen marching down Great Queen Street towards Lincoln's Inn Field, bearing the banners which had been seen earlier on that day proclaiming the evils of popery. They marched along in surprising and alarming quiet and order, with blue cockades in their hats or stuck into the lapels of their coats. But these men, in spite of their badges and occasional perfunctorily shouted Protestant catchwords, were not the 'lank Puritanical' figures whom Reynolds had noticed that afternoon in Palace Yard. In their hands they carried lighted torches and over their shoulders spades and pickaxes, blacksmiths' hammers, staves and crowbars. It was equipment which was later to be painfully familiar, as naturally associated with the symbols of the Protestant Association as now it seemed incongruous.

By the time the formidable-looking gang had reached Lincoln's Inn Fields it had collected behind it crowds of followers, hangers-on and spectators, so that when a young girl looked out of her bedroom window the whole square appeared a bobbing sea of heads and hats and faces, which the few torches lit up in little patches of flickering light.

Soon the crowds converged upon the west side of the square as the gang of marching men crossed over into Duke Street and stopped outside the chapel of the Sardinian Ambassador.

They waited for a moment or two in the street outside the chapel as scores of street urchins ran up to support them, shouting at the top of their voices and jumping up and down with excitement. Then the leader of the gang went forward and with careful and heavily humorous deliberation, pushed his crowbar through one of the windows splintering the stained glass. The signal for destruction had been given. The crowd surged forward, broke open the doors of the chapel in an instant and rushed inside. Many innocent spectators standing near the doors were forced into the chapel by the people behind pushing forward to get a good view of the demolition and were obliged to remain there quite unable to get out again. They saw hundreds of street boys and prostitutes, drunks, pickpockets and rowdies rush into the chapel and smash everything in it in a matter of minutes. A woman so alarmed by the sight and the din of smashing glass and the screams and shouts of the mob fell down in a fit and died. The pregnant wife of the Ambassador frightened 'out of her wits' by the din in the chapel next to her house, fainted and was rescued by Walpole's cousin who came along and carried her away.

All the vestments and altar ornaments, the smashed-up altar and pews and anything else which would burn were passed out over the heads of the mob into the street and there piled up and burned. Hearing of the riot while spending the evening at a friend's house in Long Acre, Henry Angelo anxious not to miss anything dashed over to Lincoln's Inn Fields to see this enormous bonfire in the street and on his way he passed many other bonfires. In Great Queen Street he 'counted ten fires blazing to burn those whom the mob called papishes'. Some of these fires had crosses soaked in tar burning in them, like the symbolic warnings of the Ku Klux Klan. When he arrived in Lincoln's Inn Fields, Angelo saw 'the rabble, the greater part boys not above the age of fifteen, throwing hassocks, dead cats and other missiles at each other'.

There were no Justices there to quell the riot or, if there were, they were anxious not to make their presence felt. Only one man, Sampson Rainforth, the King's tallow chandler made any real effort to fulfil his duties as a citizen. Helped by a Mr. Maberley, he forced his way into the chapel and grabbed a man he took to be one of the ring-leaders by the collar and tried to drag him out. But some of the other rioters recognized him and as he later deposed in court, said of him ' "Damn him! That is the late High Constable. Knock him on the head!" Then they rescued the man.' And Rainforth and Maberley themselves were lucky to escape.

As there were still, Rainforth estimated, between two and three hundred men in the chapel and no sign yet of the riot abating, he told Maberley to 'get some of Sir John Fielding's people' while he himself ran away to Somerset House Barracks for the Guards. He returned with about a hundred foot guards with fixed bayonets and immediately made what he called a 'prison in the street by a ring of soldiers three deep' and ordered every person in the chapel to be taken into custody.

This was not as difficult a task as it would have been when Rainforth had left for Somerset House, for now the rioters had pushed the bonfire against the doors of the chapel which was itself beginning to burn, and out of which most of the wreckers had consequently fled. The soldiers under Rainforth's direction were, however, able to arrest thirteen men and march them off to the Savoy. But as Justice Wright complained the next day none of them were ring-leaders and many indeed were merely spectators.[1] Even those who had actually joined in the destruction of the chapel had done so only in the drunken high spirits of the moment 'little knowing what they had been about'. All thirteen men arrested were gainfully employed, not one was a professional criminal. 'Several' indeed, according to *The Gazetteer and New Daily Advertiser* 'confessed themselves to be of the Roman Catholick religion'. There were two carpenters, three painters, a glazier, a sadler, a printer, a waiter, a tailor, a footman, a coachman and, inexplicably, an officer in the Russian Army. By Tuesday afternoon, after three examinations, all but two of them had been released.

As these thirteen unfortunate scapegoats were taken off to the Savoy the chapel was blazing fiercely. Fearing for their own homes, the owners of adjoining houses, many of them masterpieces of Inigo Jones, sent their servants dashing off to their Fire Insurance offices to get the engines out. When they arrived the flames from the chapel were leaping high into the night sky, but while the mob allowed the engines to play on the adjoining houses they would not permit the firemen to do anything about the chapel itself, which by one o'clock in the morning was almost completely burned out and all its contents with it; including a magnificent reredos valued at £2,500.

The chapel of St. Anselm and St. Cecilia was not the only one to be

[1] One poor man, for instance, had been arrested as he had tried to push his way out of the chapel with some cushions which were needed to dam the water for the fire engines which were said to be on their way.

ransacked that night. The chapel attached to the Bavarian Embassy in Warwick Street, Golden Square was another place where English Catholics were known to join the foreign congregations for Mass on Sundays and here too sometime before midnight a crowd had collected. Windows were smashed; ornaments, chairs, prayer-books and vestments were brought out and burned in the street. An old German blacksmith horrified by this wanton waste of valuable property decided to rescue some from these senseless drunken rioters and hurried home for his wheelbarrow. Stolidly and openly, apparently as if about his normal business, the old man made journey after journey backwards and forwards from the chapel to his house with loads of furniture, mass-books and other more unlikely commodities, including quantities of contraband tea. For the eighty-years-old Bavarian Ambassador, Count Haslang, who had represented his country at St. James's for over forty years, had for most of that time been carrying on a sideline business as a smuggler—'a prince of smugglers' Walpole called him—and had been using the cellars beneath his chapel as a warehouse for contraband goods.

Although completely stripped of its contents, however, the chapel itself was not, like that in Lincoln's Inn Fields, burned to the ground. And the rioters after making a brief expedition into Count Haslang's own house, where they contented themselves with a few token pieces of furniture and some more contraband groceries, went after more culpable game.

This they conceived to be old Bishop Challoner who had, in fact, hindered rather than encouraged the passing of the Catholic Relief Bill. One of the rioters, however, said that the bishop used sometimes to say mass in the chapel and that was enough for the more enthusiastic of them who marched off to Bloomsbury, where Challoner lived, with the expressed intention of roasting the frail old man alive. When they arrived at Gloucester Street they discovered that none of them was quite sure which was the bishop's house. They wandered up and down the street two or three times, shouting curses and obscenities at 'Papishe bishops'. But Bishop Challoner did not hear them, for he had taken shelter at Finchley with Mr. Mawhood a wealthy, kindly Catholic who had a country house there.

Disheartened by not being able to find their proposed victim, and tired for it was now well on into Saturday morning and they had had an energetic and exciting night, the rioters began to break up into small groups and to disperse. The reporter of *The London Courant* said that as he wearily went home at 'about two o'clock everything was perfectly over and quiet'.

And so it seemed. But in the streets the bonfires, those warnings to the 'papishes', still smouldered. Beneath the soft white ash the embers were burning yet, waiting for a wind to fan them into flame. In one of these ashen heaps of hot embers in Black Eagle Street, a scarred and blackened cross stood apparently unsupported in the air, and was standing there still, strangely upright, at dawn when a bookseller began his long journey to Bath. He went up to it and touched it with his stick and it fell with a fluttering thud into the now cold cinders, and because it had not been burned and had stood upright in that curious, seemingly impossible way, it appeared to him in some way significant so that he remembered it long afterwards.

5

DENS OF POPERY

B y noon on Saturday the trouble seemed all to be over. In some parts of the town Roman Catholics took care to remain as much as possible out of sight and to give no grounds for offence when their business brought them into contact with those who might resent them. And Irish labourers on the advice of their priests were unusually conciliatory and docile. But these precautions as the day wore on appeared unnecessary. Life after yesterday's violent upheaval had returned to normal and although there were arguments and fights and quarrels this was nothing out of the ordinary, for there always were, and today they developed into nothing worse.[1]

Many Members of Parliament armed themselves with sticks to protect themselves in case of renewed trouble on their way to the House and some peers took clubs and even blunderbusses in their coaches. But they passed through the streets unmolested and scarcely noticed.

In the Lords the main business of the day was naturally with what the Lord President of the Council termed 'the great fall from dignity which their Lordships had suffered the preceding day'.

The Duke of Richmond, as was to be expected, was one of the chief partakers in the debate which followed Lord Hillsborough's remarks, and was in his usual astringent if prolix form as he told the House of the Government's incompetence in not ensuring that the Justices of Peace took adequate precautions to prevent the riots which had occurred. 'The cause of the present disturbances and discontents', he said, 'originated in Government itself. The whole of yesterday's business was

---

[1] One sturdy Roman Catholic woman in Spitalfields, however, despised this cautious attitude. She stood at the door of her house and said in a loud voice that she 'still hoped to see the day when she should be enabled to wash her hands in the blood of Heretics and the churches run with their blood'. Later for saying this her house was stripped and burned down. Undeterred, she repeated it.

53

ascribable to the Quebec Act . . . and not the repeal of the Acts relative to popery. . . . The Quebec Act absolutely established the
Popish religion in Canada, by sending a Popish bishop there and allowing every part of the exercise of that most dangerous and intolerant
religion.'

The Marquis of Rockingham thought the Duke's suggestion that the
trouble was caused by the Quebec Act was absurd. He had heard the
mob call out 'No Popery!' but 'clapping my hand to my watch to
secure it, I felt several hands directed to it. It is pretty obvious, therefore, what the mob came for'.[1]

Lord Shelburne agreed with Lord Rockingham in thinking the
Ministers might save themselves the useless trouble of bothering about
the repeal of the Quebec Act. He had no doubt, he said, that 'Canada
as well as every foot of ground we possess in America at present, will
at a very short period follow the fate of the thirteen United Provinces'.
Having dismissed the Quebec Act with a practised pessimism, he took
up, with a more constructive approach to the lessons of the day, the
Duke's other point about the Government's failure to impress upon
the Justices the need for vigilance, and doubted that they would have
been effective in any event. For 'it must be evident', he thought, 'that
the Police of Westminster is an imperfect, inadequate and wretched
system. The commission of the peace is filled by men, base to the last
degree, and capable of every mean act derogatory and opposite to the
justice of the laws which their office obliged them to administer with
truth, equity and wisdom. The miserableness of the Westminster Police
was so obvious that the example of yesterday points it out as the fit
object of reformation and shows most forcibly that it ought to be
entirely new-modelled and that immediately. . . . Recollect what the
Police of France is. Examine its good but do not be blind to its evil.'

This reference to the French Police, a professional force alien to the
Englishman's fundamental concept of freedom, as a possible model,

[1] Lord Rockingham was quite right. The advertisements appearing in the Press
from Monday show what many of the rioters came for and got away with. The
following from *The Gazeteer and New Daily Advertiser* is typical of many:
'PUBLIC OFFICE, Bow-Street, June 5th, 1780. PICKED out of a Gentleman's
pocket, near the House of Commons, on Friday last, a small plain gold
watch, maker's name Lindgreen, Stockholm; with a steel chain and cornelian seal,
impression, arms argent on a fess gules, between two lions passant guardant sable
a flower de lis, or, between two crescents argent. If offered to be pawned or sold,
stop it and the party, and give notice to Sir John Fielding, and you shall receive
Two Guineas reward from the Gentleman robbed.'

deeply shocked most Members present and induced the Duke of Northumberland to speak up in defence of the Justices so disparagingly referred to by Lord Shelburne. The office of a Justice of the Peace for Westminster was, his Grace said, 'an exceeding troublesome office. Those who execute it get very little thanks for their pains. It is for this reason impossible to persuade gentlemen of family and fortune to undertake it, but notwithstanding the popular prejudices to the contrary, if the House would give themselves the trouble to enquire into the characters of many of the gentlemen now in the commission for Westminster they would find the greatest part of them very liberal-minded, honest worthy men.'

It was an unjustified compliment. The following week was to show that Lord Shelburne's Justices 'base and miserable' were more common figures than· the Duke of Northumberland's 'honest worthy men'. When the need for firm action became imperative, only a handful of Justices, Magistrates and Aldermen could be found to carry out their unpleasant duty; the rest hid at home or fled in panic to the country. The Lord Mayor himself gave the worst possible example. The soldiers on the other hand and the officers in command of them behaved with a calmness, patience and restraint which was as remarkable as it was pacifying.

The first example of this self-control was given at about three o'clock in the afternoon when the thirteen men arrested during the previous night were marched under a sergeant's guard, to the Public Office in Bow Street, to be examined by Sir John Fielding. Until that time the streets had been unusually quiet and uncrowded but as soon as the procession of soldiers and prisoners came out of the Savoy a hostile and 'vast concourse of people' appeared in that sudden, alarming, inexplicable way which was to become so familiar.

They jeered and shouted at the soldiers and pelted them with mud and filth. But the soldiers marched on calm, determined and unprovokable. Once a Guardsman, irritated beyond endurance by a man who pranced up and down beside him and then hurled a stone in his ear, threatened his tormentor with his musket. An officer marching at the rear of the column ran forward and knocked the barrel of the musket into the air in case the man should be tempted to fire it.

When the procession reached Sir John Fielding's house in Bow Street, the crowds had reached such threatening proportions that the soldiers were ordered to form a half-moon round the house to hold them back and to prevent them carrying out their shouted threats to break the door down and release the prisoners. Although the guardsmen were pushed and jostled, pinched and kicked they stood their ground with patience and good humour until the time came for them to march off to Newgate with those prisoners committed for re-examination. The restraint and calm determination of these well disciplined and forbearing guardsmen had a sobering effect of great consequence. The crowd at first so hostile and so contemptuous was at last moved to admiration and respect, so that when at about five o'clock the little procession reached Newgate, it was not only allowed to pass down the street unmolested but was even greeted as it stopped in front of the Lodge gate with a cheer which was more deferential than derisory. The people went home, a journalist thought, in high good humour, laughing and talking among themselves, apparently willing to leave the prisoners to their fate and giving the Government cause to believe, as one of its supporters said in the House, that 'the riots are all over. The town is quiet again and will, God willing, remain so.'

There was indeed some justification for this view. The morning had passed uneventfully, the afternoon had ended happily. Nowhere had any Roman Catholic been ill-treated or threatened. The jeering and pelting of a prisoner's escort was not after all an uncommon occurrence. The Protestant Association was rather ashamed of itself, while its 'ruffian apostle,' to quote Walpole's indignant phrase, 'who preached up this storm' remained quietly at home.

And then at about nine o'clock the trouble began.

It started in Moorfields and that it did so there was not fortuitous.

Moorfields was one of the poorest districts of London, just to the east of the ragged tumbling slum quarter of St. Giles's, portrayed in Hogarth's 'Gin Lane', and north of Bedlam. It was a part of London where many Irish labourers had lodgings and where the doss-houses were frequently full of Irish vagrants who paid a penny a night to sleep on the lousy, rat-ridden straw. In that part of Moorfields near Finsbury Yard, a merchant of Irish extraction named Malo carried on business as a silk merchant. He employed in his workshops and warehouses over a thousand men amongst whom were many Irishmen and Catholics. A Catholic himself Malo was always ready to give work to members of his own religion and, as of Irish blood, always willing to employ emigrants from that impoverished country where many of his own relations were still living. But there was perhaps another and less tender reason which prompted him so readily to employ Irish labour and that was its cheapness. An Irishman, it was well known, would work for less money than an Englishman. Starving and unemployed in Ireland, he was prepared when he came to London to work for as little as half an Englishman's usual wage. The results of this were obvious. Throughout the eighteenth century in London the Irish were resented and hated by the English workers and fights between the two were frequent occurrences. These fights as often as not ended in pitched battles, for whereas when two Londoners began a fight a circle was formed around the two contestants so that they could settle the matter undisturbed, if an Irishman was involved other Irishmen immediately came to his assistance and declared war on all Englishmen.

Although most Irish immigrants were unskilled labourers or self-employed street-hawkers, porters, chairmen, milk-sellers, publicans and doss-house keepers there were also in various parts of London small Irish colonies of skilled or semi-skilled workers, mainly bricklayers and weavers. Everywhere in London where vacant land was being developed there could be seen groups of huts surrounded by potato patches where these Irish bricklayers lived, working for a shilling a day and subsisting almost entirely on a diet composed of potatoes and gin. And in Spitalfields and Moorfields there were whole streets and courtyards occupied by Irish weavers.

It was against this Irish colony in Moorfields, more than against Mr. Malo himself, that the attentions of the mob were directed on Saturday night. It was true that the threats had been made against Mr. Malo's house and the Catholic chapels, those 'Dens of Popery', but as Defoe had observed some years earlier, there were 'ten thousand stout fellows that would spend the last drop of their blood against Popery that do not know whether it be a man or a horse'.[1] But they knew all about Irishmen.

Mr. Malo had fortunately been warned of the mob's intentions and had been to Sir James Esdaile, the alderman of the ward, who called out all the constables in the district. The crowds in the street that night, however, were more rowdy than dangerous. They shouted and jeered

[1] An acquaintance of Charlotte Burney said that he heard some people expressing their approval of 'having the Catholic chapels destroyed, for they say it is a shame the Pope should come here'.

at the constables but they seemed, for the time being at least, unwilling to carry out their threatened destruction of the mass-houses.

Mr. Malo was, nevertheless, well aware that as soon as a leader appeared in the vast, milling, shouting mass of people the danger would be very real and he went to the Lord Mayor to ask him for more protection from the rioters, should they decide to attack, than the doddering old watchmen and frightened constables would give him.

Alderman Kennet, Lord Mayor of London, had started life as a waiter in a brothel, an occupation which he found sufficiently profitable for him to buy his own brothel before he was thirty. Developing ambitions to enter public life and supposing that brothel keeping was not an enterprise likely to endear him to the more respectable among his potential supporters, he sold his interest in the brothel and invested the money in the business of a wine and spirit merchant which, although without doubt less lucrative, was certainly more reputable.[1]

Mr. Malo was given evidence of his extreme rudeness. 'You do not know anything of the business', the Lord Mayor told him brusquely when he had asked for his protection. 'I have orders to employ the military if necessary, but I must be cautious what I do, lest I bring the mob to my own house. I can assure you that there are very great people at the bottom of this riot.'

At a later meeting Kennet would not even answer when Malo implored him for protection for his wife and children but left the room. He returned immediately to ask, 'Surely, Sir, you are a Papist?' Mr. Malo said that he was of the religion in which he had been educated, the Roman Catholic faith.

'I always thought so', said his Lordship, and again left the room, this time for good.

The Lord Mayor could not justly complain, as later in fact he did complain, that he had no warning, that the riots took him so much by surprise, that he was seized with a fit of 'temerity which made him not know what he was about'.

---

[1] He was as ill-mannered as he was ill-bred. Joseph Brasbridge, a convivial silversmith, who knew him slightly, said that one evening at the Alderman's Club he went up with an empty glass in his hand to Alderman Pugh, a soap merchant, who was playing whist.
'Ring the bell, Soap-suds', he said, insolently drunk.
'Ring it yourself, Bar', Alderman Pugh replied, turning the insult. 'You have been twice as much used to it as I have.'

Some hours before Malo's visit he had received a letter from Lord Stormont:

> My Lord. As information which I have received gives me reason to apprehend that tumults may arise within your Lordship's jurisdiction, I think it is my duty to convey to you immediately this information. I cannot too strongly recommend the matter to your Lordship's attention.

The next day, learning of the Lord Mayor's grossly inadequate preventive measures, Lord Stormont again wrote to him:

> My Lord. Information which I have just received makes me think it my indispensable duty to recommend the contents of the letter which I had the honour to write to your Lordship yesterday, to your *most serious consideration*.

This letter, like the first, was ignored.

But eventually late on Saturday night Kennet was persuaded to take some sort of half-hearted action against the crowds still milling, noisy, alarming but as yet undirected, in the streets and alleys around Moorfields. He sent a message to the Tower for military assistance and after a long delay seventy-three soldiers arrived in Moorfields under command of an officer with very little idea of what he was expected to do. Fortunately, by this time many of the demonstrators had gone home and those that remained were, without much difficulty, persuaded to do the same.

It was no more than a temporary success. The next day when the crowds again collected in Moorfields they meant, a lively woman among them shouted, to do 'some good business'. Yesterday was just a warning to get the 'Papishes on the hop'.

But it was a hot day with not a breath of wind in the air, and the people seemed content to sit idly around on doorsteps and in the streets and to lie on the hot dry ground in Middle Moor Fields and the Tenter Grounds. They seemed unwilling, a Guards officer noticed, to wander far away from the district and the Artillery Ground usually crowded on a Sunday afternoon was strangely quiet.

As the evening cooled the excitement mounted. At about eight o'clock the crowds converged, as if instructed during the day to do so, on a Catholic chapel in Ropemaker's Alley. Some women who lived next door to the chapel leaned out of a first floor window and begged the people below to be careful. Their entreaties were greeted with a hail of stones and brickbats, which had been collected to smash the windows of the chapel, and the women hastily withdrew and fled in terror from the back door of their house.

The intoxicating sound of smashing glass was the awaited signal. Hundreds of street-boys and girl prostitutes ran excitedly up and down Ropemaker's Alley and the courts adjoining, shouting that the fun had started.

It continued unabated in Moorfields for two horrifying and long-remembered days and nights. Every Catholic chapel in the district was burned to the ground; Irishmen were attacked with sticks and knives whenever they were recognized; quiet and inoffensive Catholics were insulted, spat upon and their clothes torn off their backs; their houses were broken open and their furniture and books and pictures and carpets were tossed on to raging bonfires in the middle of the streets. Cellars were invaded and food and wine were brought up to be consumed in Bacchanalian parties around the fires; while the Pope and St. Patrick were burned in effigy on the sites of burned-out chapels and Irish taverns.

In the midst of the devastation the Lord Mayor and the magistrates looked idly and helplessly on. On Sunday night when the mob had demolished one house and were setting off to attack another, Joseph Brasbridge heard Kennet call out in a nervous voice, half deferential, half jocular: 'That's pretty well, gentlemen, for one day. I hope you will go to your own homes.'

As he stood contemplating the burning of another house, Ensign Gascoyne of the Coldstream Guards who had at last been called out to quell the riot, went up to him for orders. Kennet told him to be quiet and to leave him alone. Gascoyne persisted and Kennet turned on his heel and strolled away. The young Ensign, not knowing what else he could profitably do without authority to act offensively, gave his troops orders to form a close half circle round the fire, in order, as he later reported, 'to prevent their adding much to it which we were not able to do as the mob flung wood, doors, chairs, etc., over the heads of the soldiers from a window'.

Lord Beauchamp, who was present at this exhibition, angrily went after the Lord Mayor and said to him, 'This might be prevented. It is your duty to do something.'

Kennet replied with the same affectation of indifference he had assumed in his conversation with Ensign Gascoyne, 'The whole mischief seems to be that the mob have got hold of some people and some furniture they do not like and are burning them and what is the harm in that?'

Lord Beauchamp told him that he would report this reply to the House, whereupon the Lord Mayor turned his back on him and sauntered off.

He was apparently as equally unconcerned at the destruction of Mr. Malo's house which the mob, as if saving up the best property to the end, did not attend to, until all the smaller offending buildings had been ransacked or demolished.

Poor Malo, insulted by the Lord Mayor, had been no more successful in his frantic appeals to help, subsequently directed at the Government and then direct to the army. Unwilling to leave his house until the last minute, he was obliged in the end to escape over the roof with his wife and daughters. His son, who had thoughtlessly left something precious behind, rushed back for it before it was too late. Just as he got back into the house, the rioters burst in through the front door and at the sound of them he fell to the floor in a faint.

In a moment the rioters, now experts at the job, were wrenching his bedroom door, together with all the other doors in the house, off its hinges. They tore up the floor-boards with chisels, ripped off the shutters and panelling, pulled out the skirting boards and bookshelves and piled the lot, with all the furniture from the house, in the street. On the top of the enormous bonfire were placed several of Mr. Malo's treasured canaries in their cages. Some bystanders horrified by the sight and sound of the poor birds screeching in their cages, offered to buy them from one of the leading demolishers of the house. But no, the man said, for they were 'Popish birds and should burn with the rest of the Popish goods'.[1] And so although some were rescued the others were left twittering in their cages until the fire had burned them up.

By now the fires which had at first been confined to the Moorfields district could be seen in several other parts of the town. For the riots were spreading. Encouraged by trouble-makers, prostitutes and runaway apprentices and led by criminals, ordinary, normally quiet and honest people were no longer either willing or able to stand idly watching but felt compelled to join in, forced on by the excitement of violence, the satisfaction of destruction and the chance of loot. Protes-

[1] The following day a similar excuse was given for the demolition of the house of a Roman Catholic brewer in Turnstile. 'The mob said he was a papish and sold papish beer.'

tantism was no longer a cause but an excuse. On Monday evening Susan Burney who was waiting at home in St. Martin's Street for her father and mother to return with Charlotte from a visit to Mrs. Reynolds, was startled when the door suddenly opened and 'William came into the parlour with a face of alarm'. He told her, she wrote in her journal-letter to Fanny who was staying in Bath, that

> There was terrible rioting about the streets and that the mob were breaking several windows in Queen Street and threatening to set fire to some of the houses because they were inhabited by Roman Catholics. . . . However, we were to have some of this horrid work before our own eyes, for very shortly after my father and the others returned we heard violent shouts and huzzas from Leicester Fields, and William who went to see what was the matter returned to tell us that the populace had broke into Sir George Savile's house and were then emptying it of its furniture. They had piled up the furniture in the midst of the Square and had forced Sir George's servant to bring them a candle to set fire to it.

By the time the troops arrived the furniture was blazing so furiously that the Burneys looking out of their observatory[1] window could see the whole of Leicester Fields illuminated as brightly as if it were day. The troops moved into the house and the rioters having broken all the windows ran away to other houses where they could carry out their work of destruction undisturbed.

The troops in Savile's house were soon joined by many of his friends who sat at the broken windows with sticks and pistols to protect what remained of his belongings and property. But the rioters, otherwise occupied, did not return to Leicester Fields that night.

One of the houses thought to be marked out for destruction after Savile's was Edmund Burke's in Charles Street, St. James's Square. Both Mr. and Mrs. Burke were away from home when, at about nine o'clock, Burke was given this information by someone who had overheard the rioters discussing their intended victims for that night. He rushed home and began packing up his most important papers which was all that he considered he would have time to save. At ten o'clock there was a rattle at the door and coming downstairs he found sixteen soldiers in the hall.

> Government had, it seems [he explained to his friend Shackleton some days later] 'been apprised of the design at the time when they were informed of the

[1] Their house had formerly belonged to Sir Isaac Newton.

same ill-intention with regard to houses of so much more consideration than my little tenement; and they obligingly afforded me this protection, by means of which, under God, I think the house was saved. The next day I had my books and furniture removed and the guard dismissed. I thought in the then scarcity of troops they might be better employed than in looking after my paltry remains.'

Soon after the peremptory entry of the sixteen soldiers Joshua Reynolds came over, having himself heard that Burke's house might be in danger, and offered his services. Burke thanked him but pointed out that the Government had accorded him its protection, and so leaving the soldiers in possession they both went to Savile's house and joined the now formidable garrison there. When it seemed unlikely that Sir George's house would be attacked again that night Burke went to his wife at General Burgoyne's, where he was offered and accepted hospitality for the rest of the week.

Other intended victims of the mob's vengeance were less fortunate. Sampson Rainforth, the King's tallow chandler, who had helped to quell the riot at the Sardinian Chapel and whose name had appeared in the Press as giving evidence against the arrested rioters, was dragged from his bed and forced to watch as his house and warehouse were ransacked and all his possessions burned in Clare Street. His stocks of fat were brought up in their tubs from the cellars and placed around the bonfire where as they melted they gave off the most poisonous fumes. Some tubs too close to the flames caught fire and the liquid fat spilled out and ran down the street in hot, stinking streams. A gang of street boys, delighting in the cries of excited disgust from a group of maid-servants looking out of an attic window, tipped up all the remaining tubs and barrels to swell the river of boiling fat.

As at Savile's house; as at Mr. Maberly's, which was burned to the ground a few hours later; and as at two Catholic chapels in Spitalfields, the troops arrived when the damage was done and the rioters were about to move on to new territory. But had they arrived earlier they would have been of little use for no magistrate could ever be found to give them orders to act or even to read the Riot Act. And for an officer to act against the rioters, without the sanction of the civil authorities, was unthinkable and, so far as the army was concerned, illegal. This view of the law was afterwards questioned by Lord Mansfield, but there is no doubt that at the time there were few officers who did not believe it to be the right one.

And so the army was constantly exposed to ridicule. A contingent of troops would be ordered by the commander-in-chief to the scene of a riot and when it arrived the soldiers stood helplessly by, waiting for orders which never came, while the rioters laughed and jeered at them, threw mud and stones at them, daring them to use their muskets; until their officer, unwilling to take the responsibility of giving the order to fire and yet seeing how pointless it was to remain only to be insulted, marched his men away again to the derisory cheers of the crowd.

Indeed more than one observer, noticing the soldiers smiling in simple red-faced and good-humoured sympathy upon the rioters, doubted that they would obey the order to fire even if given it. For they had no time for Catholics either. The Frogs were Catholics and the Spaniards too and the enemy in more wars than any of them could remember. Mrs. Kenyon, one of those who noticed this sympathetic attitude, heard one guardsman say as he complacently watched a mass-house burning: 'Great fools! Why don't they pull down the buildings? Fire might hurt their neighbours.'

There was, James Hutton thought, another reason also for the soldiers' apparent indifference. 'The doctrine, said to be got among the soldiers', he wrote to Lord Stormont, 'is that having sworn to preserve the Protestant succession, it would be a breach of their oaths to assist the Catholics, and that therefore they would not fire on any persons destroying Romish chapels. This must have been put in their heads, for it never could have arisen from a soldier's reasoning.'

Who put this doctrine in the soldiers' heads, James Hutton did not say, but there were many who during the next few weeks were ready to swear that it was the magistrates and aldermen themselves, business men hating the Government and willing to lend their support to any cause which might lead to its downfall.

Alderman Frederick Bull, who had seconded both Lord George's motions in the House on Friday, was a man typical of many of his colleagues. He was by trade a tea merchant and controlled a large and very successful business in the City. Before the outbreak of the war with America much of his profit had been made out of the export of China and Indian tea to the American colonies, but now as a result of the war enormous stocks of tea remained unsold in his warehouses. Knowing this, his enemies and rivals had reason to doubt that his support for the Protestant cause and Lord George Gordon was entirely altruistic. Certainly after the members of the Protestant Association had thought it necessary publicly to dissociate themselves from the rioters by newspaper advertisements, the constables in Alderman Bull's ward continued, as they had done from the first, to wear blue cockades and to protest their faith in the rioters as national heroes.

Alderman Bull's constables were not the only ones to refuse to interfere with the rioters' activities. At the burning of the mass-house in Ropemaker's Alley on Sunday night one marshalman voiced the feelings of most of the others when he said that he would 'not go to protect any Popish rascals'. And at Sampson Rainforth's house the following night a constable told a journalist who had come out to report on the conflagration that he thought it his duty and that of his colleagues to see that 'no honest Protestant got hurt by Popish conspirators'. These were not exceptional men. Everywhere that constables or magistrates, watchmen or justices were wanted they were not to be found, or being found were not to be persuaded to use their authority. Only 'Sir John Fielding's people' made a real and concerted effort to do their unpleasant and dangerous duty, and this they did with terrible consequences for the 'blind beak' himself.

6

SO MANY INFERNALS

ON Tuesday morning George Crabbe put his work away early and left his lodgings to go down to Westminster. He had come to London from his native Aldeburgh the year before with three pounds in his pocket and a burning ambition to make his name as a poet, and he was anxious not to miss any scene which might excite his sensitive imagination.

He found line upon line of Horse and Foot Guards standing shoulder to shoulder in the middle of the streets, and forming clear lanes for the Members to ride down on their way to the House. 'But this martial appearance far from intimidating the mob, only rendered them more insolent: they boldly paraded the streets with colours and music.' Most of them carried sticks, some had bludgeons and even naked cutlasses. All wore a blue cockade—the badge of insurrection—in their hats or tied with a ribbon in their hair.'[1]

The number of persons [*The General Evening Post* reported] was the greatest ever known. . . . The people advanced upon the Guards several times and at one time almost drove them back, which occasioned Justice Hyde to order the Horse Guards to advance upon them which they did, but with some difficulty at first for the people with sticks kept them off for some time; but

[1] Several of them carried in their hands copies of an inflammatory handbill, entitled 'England in Blood!' an advertisement which had appeared on the streets that morning publicizing *The Thunderer* which was to be published on Thursday and which would be 'addressed to Lord George Gordon and the glorious Protestant Association, showing the necessity of their being united as one man against the infernal designs of the Ministry to overturn the religious and civil liberties of this country in order to introduce Popery and slavery. In this paper will be given a full account of the bloody tyrannies, persecutions, plots and inhuman butcheries exercised . . . by the see of Rome. . . . To which will be added, some reasons why the few misguided people now in confinement for destroying the Romish chapels should not suffer, and the dreadful consequences of an attempt to bring them to punishment.'

at last the Horse broke through and rode furiously among them. Soon after they came down in a body, with colours flying and staves in their hands but did not attempt to interrupt the Guards any more.

At last a Justice with courage had been found. Riding up and down the lines of soldiers on an immense white horse, apparently unconcerned for his own safety, Justice Hyde not only gave orders to the troops but seemed determined to make it obvious that he was doing so. With the help of his energy and example the Members were able to find a way through to both Houses which by three o'clock were well attended. Only Lord Sandwich was once again unable to get through. Not turning back soon enough as he had done on Friday he was pulled headlong out of his coach and rolled over in the dust of Parliament Street; the windows of his coach were broken in and a jagged corner of glass used to cut open his cheek before the Guards came up to his rescue and he was able to escape into a coffee house.

But he was the only casualty in the House of Lords and in the House of Commons not one of the two hundred and twenty Members present had received anything worse than insults.[1]

They were, nevertheless, as on Friday, in an understandably indignant mood, to which many of them were anxious as always to give fluent and passionate voice. When these outbursts of Parliamentary indignation had been expressed, four resolutions were put to the vote. The first: that it was a dangerous breach of privilege to insult or attack Members coming to do their duty. The second: that a committee be appointed to inquire into the outrages and discover their authors. The third: that the Attorney-General be ordered to prosecute those charged with destroying the foreign chapels and the Ambassadors' houses. And the fourth: that compensation should be paid to the sufferers.

All these resolutions were passed unanimously, even Lord George Gordon voting in their favour. He, in fact, seemed a changed man. He had admittedly come to the House that day with his blue cockade still in his hat but when a Member objected to it as an 'ensign of riot, his Lordship very readily pulled it out'. Well aware that the riots of the

[1] 'Before I went to Lady Hales this morning', wrote Susan Burney, 'Mr. Burke had passed through our street, when he was beset by a number of wretches, who wanted to extort from him a promise to vote for repealing the Act in favour of the Catholics. My mother saw him and heard him say, "I beseech you, gentlemen; gentlemen, I beg. . . ." However he was obliged to draw his sword ere he could get rid of these terrible attendants.'

week-end had done great and irreparable damage to his cause, he was anxious to do all he could to disassociate himself and the Protestant Association from them.

The day before, shocked by the appearance of the men who had paraded past his house, cheering lustily and carrying on their shoulders relics and ornaments looted from the chapels at Moorfields, which they afterwards burned in an open space nearby, he had given orders for the distribution of handbills 'recommending peace' and had written for publication in the Press a condemnation of the rioters. This notice had appeared in *The Morning Chronicle* and other papers that morning:

PROTESTANT ASSOCIATION [it ran]. WHEREAS many riotous persons on Friday last after the Petition of this Association was presented to the Honourable the House of Commons, did tumultuously impede the passage to both Houses of Parliament, and grossly insulted the persons of many of the Members; and afterwards proceeded with violence to destroy the chapels belonging to Foreign Ambassadors (so sacred in all countries) to the great breach of the peace, the disturbance of private persons and families, and to the disgrace of the best of causes.

RESOLVED unanimously, that all true Protestants be requested to shew their attachment to their best interest, by a legal and peaceable deportment, as all unconstitutional proceedings in so good a cause can only tend to prevent the Members of the Legislature from paying due attention to the united prayers of the Protestant Petition.

                                    By order of the Committee.
London June 5. 1780.   G. GORDON, President.

And so Lord George behaved in the House that Tuesday afternoon with exemplary correctness and restraint. When General Conway moved that the House should take the various Protestant petitions into consideration when the tumults had subsided and not before, his only comment was that if the House named a day for this debate he felt sure that the 'populace would soon disperse'. For most of the time during which the House was sitting he sat silent and apparently absorbed in thought.

At about five o'clock it was suggested that the House should adjourn until Thursday after a Member had given it as his opinion that 'no Act of theirs could be legal while the House is beset by military force'. But although it was a simple matter to adjourn the House it was by now a very difficult one to get out of it. For the rioters, Romilly told Roget, 'were become so outrageous that there was no possibility of awing them but by reading the Riot Act, which, you know, gives a right to fire upon the mob if they do not disperse'. They had got to 'such a pitch of confidence', the Earl of Jersey told Countess Spencer, 'that I cannot conceive any way of bloodshed being avoided'.

Once again it was left to Justice Hyde to expose himself to the anger of the rioters. He rode across to a commanding position in Palace Yard and in a 'loud clear voice' he read the proclamation from the Riot Act and then ordered the Horse Guard to charge the mob to clear a way for the Members to get out of the House. At six o'clock the first Members were able to make their way out.

Sir Philip Jennings Clerke, however, did not like the look of the 'prodigious crowd' beyond the doors and going up to Lord George he said to him: 'Come, Lord George. You must be my protector.'

The two men left together but by the time they reached 'The Horn', the mass of people surrounding them had become so dense that they could get no further. There was a coach standing outside the tavern which Lord George recognized as belonging to Mr. Wiggins the publican, who fortunately at that moment was looking out of an upper window at the crowds below. Lord George called up to him.'

'Wiggins', he shouted above the din, 'I am in sad distress, will you lend me your chariot?'

'Yes, my Lord', Wiggins shouted back, 'with all my heart.'

Lord George and Sir Philip climbed gratefully inside. But no sooner had they done so than a great cheer went up for 'Lord Gordon' who had been followed all the way from the House by these excited, pestering, unwanted supporters. 'Let's take Geordie off', one of them shouted, and began to unharness the horses. Several others ran forward to help him and within a minute the horses had been taken off the shafts and the carriage, pulled by a cheering, shouting, screaming gang of demonstrators was rattling up Parliament Street.

Sir Philip, now more nervous than ever, leaned over and called in Lord George's ear: 'Can you contrive any way in the world to let me out, for I have a friend waiting for me to dinner at Whitehall?'

Lord George put his head out of the carriage window and shouted at his supporters to stop and 'go peaceably home'. But no one heard him, or having heard paid no attention, and the jolting coach was borne faster than ever along its furious headlong way. 'It went as fast', Sir Philip said afterwards, 'as if we had a pair of very good horses drawing us, and it ran over twenty people I suppose.'

It went on past Whitehall, through the Strand and Fleet Street, down Cheapside and Poultry, stopping for a moment at the Mansion House to give three cheers in honour of the Lord Mayor, and then rattled on again down Lombard Street 'quite to the further end of the City to Alderman Bull's house'.

Now at last Lord George and Sir Philip were permitted to alight but even when they had with difficulty got into Bull's house, the demonstrators outside would not disperse. Finally one of the Alderman's servants came out on to the front door-step and shouted to the crowd that his Lordship had left by a back door. But still they would not go away and it was two hours before the unwilling hero could get out of the house and make his escape for home.

By this time most of the demonstrators had been drawn away by other and more thrilling sights, the roaring crackling sound of fire and the smell of smoke.

The first house to suffer that night was Justice Hyde's in St. Martin's Street.

Earlier that afternoon when the Horse Guards had charged the crowd to clear a path for the Members leaving the House, a giant of a man had been seen riding a cart-horse and waving an immense black and red flag, like the standard bearer of an opposing army. He shouted abuse at the soldiers and encouraged those who had fallen. His name was James Jackson and he had a voice that 'boomed like the crack of doom'. Holding his flag high above his head on a long pole he rallied his supporters behind him and shouted out in his deep, resounding voice: 'To Hyde's house a-hoy!'

Susan Burney on her way back from dinner with Lady Hales met these hopeful, excited incendiaries as they flowed in a great wave across Leicester Fields to St. Martin's Street. They surrounded her coach, laughing and shouting as they marched and formed such a compact mass all around it, that the coachman could not turn round into St. Martin's Street and had to get down from his seat and leave the coach where it was at the corner of Long's Court. He helped Susan out and pushed his way through the crowd, leading her by the hand to the front door of her house. She was, she confessed, 'terrified to death' and when at last she got into the house she found her 'mother and Charlotte half out of their wits'. They told her that 'about half an hour before, many hundred people came running down our street huzzaing and shouting with blue flags—tha t their particular spite here was against Justice

Hyde, who has a house towards the bottom of the street, and who had been active in endeavouring to quell the rioters. He was fortunately not in his house, for had he fallen into their hands, I believe he would have been torn to pieces. However, they broke into his house and acted the same part that they had at Sir George Savile's.'[1]

Watching from an upper window Susan and her family saw the rioters break into the house and throw everything which it contained, furniture, clothes, carpets, books and curtains, into the street. And as there was too much stuff to make one bonfire of convenient size, they made several and fed each of them, when they had emptied the house of all its furniture, with window frames, floor-boards, shutters and panelling.

> There were [Susan counted] six of these fires, which reached from the bottom of the street up to the crossing which separates Orange and Blue Cross Streets. Such a scene I never before beheld! As it grew dusk, the wretches who were involved with smoak and covered with dust, with the flames glaring upon them seemed like so many infernals. . . . At last the ring-leaders gave the word and away they all ran past our windows to the bottom of Leicester Fields with lighted firebrands in their hands like so many furies.

About half past six a young ensign marched into the street, at the head of about thirty Foot Guards. 'But the daring populace appeared not the least alarmed; on the contrary, they welcomed them with loud shouts and huzzas.' The ensign tried to find a magistrate to give him an order but as usual no one in authority could be found and the young man felt obliged himself to make a speech to the rioters. The speech was greeted with ribald laughter and cat-calls until the ensign, with a gesture of irritated despair, gave the order for his men to march away which they did with 'the mob shouting and clapping the soldiers on their backs as they passed'.

Encouraged by this minor triumph over the military, the rioters ran up and down the street exulting in their uncontrolled freedom to do as they liked. They insisted that every window in the street should be illuminated 'for this victory over all law and government'. Any inhabitant who refused to show a light in his windows, had them all broken, the ground floor ones by poles, the upper ones by rocks and brickbats. But it was difficult for the rioters to see which windows were

---

[1] The next day the mob pulled down his country house at Islington.

illuminated and which were not, for all of them brightly reflected the leaping, scorching flames of the fires on the hot glass.

All this Charlotte and Susan, now joined by their father, saw from their first-floor window, thankful to be spared the attentions which the mob paid to their neighbours. And then across the street opposite the house Susan saw

about ten men and women in a group looking at our windows. 'No Popery!' cried they, and repeated this two or three times. We had no idea that we were ourselves addressed till one of the men said to the rest, pointing to us, 'They are all three papists!' 'For God's sake', cried poor Hetty, 'Mr. Burney, call out "No Popery" or anything!' Mr. Burney accordingly got his hat and huzza'd from the window. It went against me to hear him, though it seemed no joke in the present situation of things to be marked out by such wretches as papists. 'God bless, your honour!' they then cried, and went away very well satisfied.

The street was quieter now. The fires still blazed as fiercely as before and every unbroken window shone with light, but the crowds had 'greatly diminished'. Unheard and unseen by the Burneys, James Jackson, still waving his flag aloft and sitting astride his heavy horse, had been busy directing the rioters at the far end of the street, until believing that Justice Hyde had been sufficiently punished, he boomed out in that terrible, gong-like voice: 'A-hoy for Newgate!'

This was a new and exhilarating instruction. The rioters threw their last bits of fuel on to the fires, picked up their crowbars and axes and joining in the general shout 'To Newgate!' they ran off down Green Street and into Castle Street, towards the Strand.

A party of them filed off down Bow Street to attack Sir John Fielding's house, where the day before the thirteen arrested rioters had been examined. It was, like Hyde's house, stripped of its furniture which was tumbled out of doors and windows and was blazing fiercely in a matter of minutes. Floor-boards and doors and windows, wrenched loose with expert speed, followed the furnishings and soon great tongues of flame and billows of smoke were belching out of the holes in the wall where once the window-frames had been.

Refreshment for the hot and thirsty demolishers was provided opposite the burning house by the landlord of 'The Brown Bear' who, afraid of what might happen to his own premises if he did not hold open house, was offering free drinks in the street to all comers. Thus encouraged and fortified, the rioters left Bow Street to join the now enormous crowd of demonstrators and spectators in front of Newgate.

The news that the biggest prison in London was about to be assaulted swept all over the capital and drew thousands of people into Newgate Street and Old Bailey. Henry Angelo who had been to dinner with Albany Wallis was walking home past the Admiralty when he came across several groups of people hurrying in the opposite direction. 'What's the matter?' he called out. 'They are going to burn Newgate', was the general buzz. He ran back to Norfolk Street to tell Wallis and his guests, who included Parson Bate and Richard Brinsley Sheridan, what he had heard. 'They all laughed', he remembered, 'and no one would believe me. However, away I ran to Newgate. . . . Having placed myself at the corner of the narrow lane facing the debtors' door, I had a full view of what was going on. Fortunately, whilst I was standing facing a door, an offer was made me, that upon paying sixpence I might place myself at the garret-window, which I readily accepted . . .'

7

THE SKY LIKE BLOOD

NEWGATE was the oldest and the largest of the London prisons. There had been a gaol on the site since the twelfth century and for generations of Londoners the word Newgate had meant more than the name of a prison; it was a symbol of oppression, a closed-in world of hunger and despair behind walls whose grandiose heaviness brought a shudder to the heart. It had some years before been enlarged and parts of it had been rebuilt in a style as externally ornate as that which had been favoured by the architects commissioned to design the new building after the Great Fire. It was, as George Crabbe told his friend Sarah Elmy, 'very large, strong and beautiful', and it was partly because of this elaborate beauty, embellished by ornamental stone figures in niches in its outside walls, which seemed to stand there as a mockery of the squalor within, that Newgate was hated more than all the other London prisons; some of them indeed more terrible even than this.

Behind these walls on Tuesday evening were four of the thirteen men arrested on Friday night and it was the rioters' intention, so they announced, to get these men released; and with them as many other convicts as they could.

They set about their task with a curiously military discipline. 'They did not proceed to storm', *The Gentleman's Magazine* reported, 'until they had given their terms like regular assailants' and had placed sentinels at every approach to the prison so that any prisoners who escaped could not be taken off to other gaols.

Their terms were shouted by one of the ring-leaders outside the front door of the Keeper's house. Mr. Akerman, a much respected man and an admired friend of Boswell, put his head out of a first-floor window. He was, he told the fire-raisers with that polite but firm respect with which he treated his prisoners, quite unable to accede to their

74

request. He was the Keeper of the Prison and in duty bound to hold any prisoners committed to his charge. 'They must be aware it was a question he could not answer to their satisfaction and as it was his wish to do his duty without offending any person, he hoped they would not reduce him to the necessity of refusing their request.' If the gentlemen outside would be so good as to wait, however, he would send for the sheriffs for further instructions.

Quite naturally unwilling to wait for a second opinion, and having fulfilled what they took to be their obligations as 'regular assailants' they began the more satisfying part of their attack and hurled a cascade of stones at Mr. Akerman's windows, while he, his wife and daughters rushed up to the attic and escaped over the roof.

In spite of the hail of stones a tall, strong young man in a white coat, with a pickaxe in one hand and a scaffold pole in the other, went forward and thrust his pole like a battering-ram through one of the ground-floor windows. Encouraged by the cheers of the crowd, this young man, subsequently discovered to be a mad Quaker, the 'infatuated son of a rich and respectable corn factor', shattered the other ground-floor windows; and helped by a hysterical youth who climbed on his shoulders armed with handfuls of tow dipped in turpentine and who battered at the cracked first-floor windows with his head, he had soon broken all the windows in the house.

As this was being done several ladders were brought up and put against the walls and a few moments later the spectators were treated once again to the now familiar and exhilarating sight of furniture, doors and floor-boards hurtling through the broken window-frames, to crash and splinter on the cobblestones beneath. This time the mob did not make a bonfire in the street but piled the furniture and what *The Morning Chronicle* called 'a nice collection of pictures', in an enormous heap against the sides of the house. To the Keeper's relief, as they were setting fire to it, a column of nervous constables, about a hundred in number, marched up.

The rioters, on instructions from some enterprising and experienced soldier, opened up a lane for them so that they could pass through to the house, and when the last constable had marched unsuspectingly into the ambush, the rioters fell upon them with shouts of triumph and beat them up 'with great fury'. They wrenched their staves from their hands, broke them in two and ignited them at the now crackling fire, hurling them about as brands 'wherever the fire appeared but faintly kindled'.

By eight o'clock the house itself was in flames. George Crabbe went
close to it and

> never saw anything so dreadful. The prison was, as I said, a remarkably
> strong building; but, determined to force it, they broke the gates with crows
> and other instruments, and climbed up the outside of the cell part, which
> joins the two great wings of the building where the felons were confined; and
> I stood where I plainly saw their operations. They broke the roof, tore away
> the rafters, and having got ladders they descended. Not Orpheus himself had
> more courage or better luck; flames all around them, and a body of soldiers
> expected. They defied all opposition.
>
> The prisoners escaped. I stood and saw about twelve women and eight
> men ascend from their confinement to the open air, and they were conducted
> through the streets in their chains. Three of them were to be hanged on
> Friday. You have no conception of the phrensy of the multitude. This being
> done, and Akerman's house now a mere shell of brickwork, they kept a store
> of flame there for other purposes. It became red-hot and the doors and win-
> dows appeared like the entrance to so many volcanoes. With some difficulty
> they then fired the debtor's prison—broke the doors—and they too all made
> their escape.

About three hundred prisoners in all escaped within an hour, helped
out by guides who had broken open all the different doors of the
warren-like prison 'as if they had all their lives been acquainted with
the intricacies of the place'.

Henry Angelo, from his sixpenny seat in a nearby attic, was also
watching this 'new species of gaol delivery'. 'The captives marched
out', he wrote, 'with all the honours of war, accompanied by a musical
band of rattling fetters. Whilst listening to the noise of the hammers at
one house, I narrowly escaped being knocked down for my curiosity and
had anyone called out, "There's a Papist!" it might have been worse.'

Frederic Reynolds who with his schoolboy friends had been
enormously enjoying himself by rushing up to groups of rioters and
making them scatter by screaming: 'The Guards! The Guards!', described how these fettered convicts were taken away to the different
blacksmiths of the neighbourhood, 'blaspheming and jumping in their
chains' and how he followed one of them, 'who was to have been
hanged the following Monday. On some sudden alarm the mob hastily
brought him to the door, with a fetter still on one leg; then quitting
their hold on him, and receding, they cried, "A clear way and a clear
run!" "Swifter than an arrow from a tartar's bow", flew the rogue.'

As these prisoners rushed away to freedom or hobbled off as best they could in their chains, others less fortunate, in deeper and more inaccessible parts of the burning prison could be heard screaming in terror, 'expecting an instantaneous death from the flames' or from the 'thundering descent of huge pieces of building'. Showers of sparks and pieces of red-hot metal shot up into the sky as iron bars and flaming beams and great hunks of elaborate masonry tumbled with 'a deafening clangor . . . on to the pavement below'. While all the time the scream-ing, wild, triumphant figures of the 'demoniac assailants' added the final touch of horror to the inferno-like scene.

Many of these figures could be seen standing perilously, in postures of arrogant, abandoned recklessness, on ledges, the tops of walls and astride window-sills on those parts of the building not yet too hot to touch. Now hidden by gusts of black sulphurous smoke, now brightly lit in a cascade of sparks, they shouted obscenities at each other and made vulgar gestures as they urinated into the flames, seemingly un-conscious of their danger or at least heedless of it.

Below them in the street their companions were dancing with de-light as they brought up buckets full of gin and wine which they had looted from Mr. Akerman's cellar. They took it in turns to drink the liquor from the buckets or from their hats which they passed round, sodden and dripping, from hand to hand.

A gang of these men, having gulped down as much gin as they felt inclined for the moment to stomach, marched away to Bloomsbury Square, raging drunk and ringing a great bell they had found in the cellar, shouting their intention of roasting alive Lord Mansfield and the Archbishop of York, who had escaped so lightly on the way to the House of Lords on Friday afternoon.

In a letter to his young son in the Navy, the Archbishop gave a description of the terrifying scene that followed. He was next door with the Lord Chief Justice when three magistrates called to give them warning of the mob's intentions. Lord Mansfield was at first incre-dulous.

'What had you and I', he said, appealing to the Archbishop, 'to do with the Popery Bill?'

The Archbishop told him that this at the moment seemed to carry little weight with the mob. The business 'lies deeper', he said. 'You and I are marked men.'

What then asked Lord Mansfield did he intend to do?

'To defend myself and my family in my own mansion while I have an arm to be raised in their defence.'

This, Lord Mansfield acknowledged, was bravely said. But 'while an Archbishop like a true church militant is strong enough to protect himself, a feebler and an older man must look up to the civil power for protection.'

It was eventually agreed that the magistrates should collect forty guards under command of an ensign and that half the force should garrison the one house, and half the other. But when the troops arrived Lord Mansfield, advised that their presence in his house might provoke an attack, would not let them in and the Justice who accompanied them eagerly marched them away to Bloomsbury Church, promising with patent insincerity to return immediately he was wanted.

Not long after midnight, the drunken gang from Newgate, ringing their bell, 'with great shouts and flags' and carrying a rope with which to hang the Lord Chief Justice, marched into the square followed by hundreds of supporters. They had decided to attack Lord Mansfield's house first but on their way they stopped outside the Archbishop's to shout that he 'was next and when they had done their business at the corner they would return'.[1] 'Oh, my dear Jack', he wrote to his son remembering this moment. 'I had many wishes that you were by my side'.

He tried to get his wife and eldest daughter to escape, as the younger children had already done, but they would not leave and stayed with him as he distributed arms to the servants who still, in spite of the intimidating threats of the mob, 'seemed hearty'.

Soon they heard the shouts of the rioters rising to a crescendo of excitement as the furniture next door began flying out of the windows and splintering on the pavement below. Looking out of the windows of their own house they could see Lord Mansfield's precious library of rare books and manuscripts, legal reports and notebooks, falling and fluttering down into the street; the collection of a long lifetime hurled through gaping holes in the wall where the library windows had once been, to be destroyed in a few crackling, delirious moments in the bonfire now raging beneath.

---

[1] A similar threat had been made in the afternoon to the Archbishop of Canterbury by five hundred rioters who had paraded round Lambeth Palace. When these rioters did return, however, they found the Palace and grounds heavily guarded by troops. A guard of 150 men was still there two months later.

Watching in helpless anger and pity his old friend's valued collection and fine furniture so wantonly destroyed, the Archbishop begged the ensign in command of the troops in his house to act on the authority of a constable, as the Justice who had gone to Bloomsbury Church could not be found and nor in fact could any other. But the ensign told him with great respect that he could not act on such authority and that if no proper authority were given him he very much regretted being quite unable to do anything. And so nothing was done; and the ransacking of Lord Mansfield's house went on undisturbed. Nearly three hundred soldiers were now drawn up in the square and stood there 'tame spectators of the conflagration, no one magistrate daring to command their services'.

The Archbishop looked out at these soldiers in the square and wondered what protection they would give him when the rioters decided to attack his own house, which he felt sure now they soon would. As he and his family nervously awaited the expected attack, in other parts of the town also, the havoc continued unchecked.

Soon after one gang had left Newgate for Bloomsbury, others had left to 'burn up some Irishmen', while still more had gone to the other London prisons to release, so they threatened, all the prisoners in the Metropolis, sending regular notices, *The Gentleman's Magazine* said, at what time the convicts 'might expect enlargement'.

The first two gaols to be attacked were Bridewell and New Prison which adjoined each other in Clerkenwell.

The doors of Bridewell were forced open with such ease and the prisoners released with so little trouble that the rioters did not stop to burn the building, but immediately went on their way to New Prison, the doors of which, they found, had already been thrown open by the terrified gaolers anxious at all costs to avoid a fight. 'Now', one of the rioters shouted, having pushed some of the more nervous prisoners out of the cells, 'now for Northampton Chapel.'

Northampton Chapel in Clerkenwell, had formerly belonged to Mr. Maberley who had helped Sampson Rainforth in his efforts to disperse the rabble in Lincoln's Inn Fields on Friday night. And it was presumably for this reason marked out for destruction by the rioters, who did not know it had changed hands and was the property of Lady Huntingdon, who lived next door to it and who had founded a Methodist sect which sometimes met there. One of the rioters, however, said that his mother went to the Northampton Chapel on Sun-

days and that it must be a 'No Popery place'. Another said that they
had better burn it anyway.

While the discussion continued friends of Lady Huntingdon and of
Lady Anne Erskine who lived with her, flew to the house with warnings of the mob's 'immediate approach'. Lady Anne was frankly terrified and wrote to the Earl of Buchan afterwards to tell him of her
ordeal.

> Such a scene I never beheld [she told him]. And I pray never may again;
> and the situation of this place which is very high and open, gave us an awful
> prospect of it. We were surrounded by flames! Six different fires—with that
> of Newgate among the rest towering to the clouds—being full in our view at
> once, and every hour in expectation of this house and beautiful chapel making
> the seventh. . . . The flames all around had got to such a height that the sky
> was like blood with the reflection of them. The mob so near we heard them
> knocking the irons off the prisoners; which, together with the shouts of those
> they had released, the huzzas of the rioters, and the universal confusion of the
> whole neighbourhood make it beyond description! Every moment fresh
> reports coming in of fresh fires being broke out—some true, some false; some
> that the Parliament House was on fire, others the Archbishop's Palace at
> Lambeth; but all agreeing in our danger.

But the danger for the moment was averted when a rioter, tiring of
the profitless argument about the Northampton Chapel, shouted out,
'Why there? Better go to the Fleet Prison and let us make another
gaol-delivery.'

This was a popular suggestion and most of the rioters ran off towards
the Fleet. At one o'clock in the morning, standing in front of the prison,
they shouted their demand that the doors should be thrown open. And
a moment later the vast gates were pulled back on their hinges by the
frightened turnkeys and a crowd of prisoners ran ecstatically out.
Others, however, were more cautious. They had been in the prison
for years, they said, and had nowhere to go and 'no wish to be turned
out so late'. Would the rioters be so good as to give them till tomorrow
at the same time to get all their belongings out and to find somewhere
to take them to. The request was granted by the 'compassionate mob'
and for that night at least the prison was spared.

There were now, it was estimated the following day, more than sixteen hundred convicts at large in the capital. Some of them were debtors and innocent enough, others were poor helpless and harmless creatures who had fallen foul of the harsh bewildering criminal code, but

there were many who were hardened ruffians waiting until that night for the ride to the gallows or the transportation ship, and now released into a town at their mercy and open to their vengeance.

To men such as these and their hangers-on and companions, Popery meant nothing. They were those who, in Defoe's phrase, did not know whether indeed it was a man or a horse and did not care. They joined in the rioting, not because it was said to be against the Papists but because it offered them a chance to get free food and drink, free women perhaps, and an opportunity to get their own back on society in a wild, exciting, satisfying orgy of destruction. They attacked the houses of Justices not because these men were anti-Papists or had attempted to quell the riots, as in fact hardly any of them had, but because they represented the law which had put them and their friends in those stinking prisons. They walked around the town carrying iron bars wrenched from Lord Mansfield's railings or stolen from the shops of ironmongers, threatening to knock down anyone who did not contribute to their 'Rioters' Fund'. But more than a few of them did not even know what the riots were meant to be about.

There were also still in the streets hundreds of fanatical Protestants whose pathological hatred of Roman Catholics was fanned into new life by the heady, thrilling atmosphere of violence and vengeance. These 'Puritans', as Gibbon called them, 'such as they might be in the time of Cromwell . . . started out of their graves', reminded by the smoke and flames and screams of the never-to-be-forgotten fires of Smithfield and the stories of the past.

In alliance with these criminals and fanatics were the thousands upon thousands of ordinary, poor working men and women and children, flowing out of the slums of Shoreditch, Spitalfields and St. Giles's and the unpaved, unlit, decaying warrens of streets and courtyards down by the river. Pale and forgotten people, ill, hollow-cheeked and hungry they poured from doss-houses, brothels, crowded cellars and workshops to watch the houses burning; to run forward to grab a leg of mutton from a larder, a bottle from a cellar, a scorched blanket from a bonfire. Sometimes getting drunk and joining in the fun; easily led, easily persuaded, having nothing to lose, with generations of hardship, indifference and bitterness behind them, they wandered about in large groups and in small, converging like a sea upon any place where excitement seemed to be offered and there joined with the others and became a mob. And thus spontaneously created a mob, they were urged to violence by that sensual, reactive impulse which brings a mob together and which forces it on to devastation, losing their identities in a fusing welter of destruction.

They shouted 'No Popery!' but it was no more than a war cry now. At first it had been only the Catholics, the Irish and a few unfortunate public figures who had suffered; but now it was to be anyone in authority, anyone who might be held responsible for their poverty and discontent, their dangerous malaise. They struck out in irrational, unthinking desperation, unconsciously hoping to release in their uproar the frustrations and irritations of years of neglect. Any reason for violence would have done. Only the spark was needed. Popery was as good an excuse as any other.

For more than three hours after the prisoners had hobbled in their clanking chains out of the open doors of the Clerkenwell gaols, this frustrated mob scurried unchecked back and forth through the streets; now in little groups, now coagulating in an amorphous mass; swelling up in one place and then breaking off in twos and threes to form up again in some other; parts of a violently purposeful whole but having no life of their own, like bits of amoeba.

Faced by these ubiquitous enemies, the troops called out to deal with them moved about the town in useless admonitory patrols, unsure of what was expected of them and knowing only that whatever happened, however much they might be provoked, they were not to fire or to use their swords without specific orders to do so from the civil authority.

Henry Angelo hurrying away from the burning ruins of Newgate came across one of these helpless patrols 'walking their horses towards the spot as if returning gently from a review'.

And then, at about half-past three that morning, the situation suddenly altered.

An hour earlier a determined magistrate, Mr. Burden, had marched into Bloomsbury Square with Colonel John Woodford and a platoon of Foot Guards. Standing on the corner of Hart Street he had read the proclamation from the Riot Act and had been ignored. The rioters had heard all that stuff before and had continued undeterred to run in and out of Lord Mansfield's house collecting more fuel for the fires. Mr. Burden gave Colonel Woodford authority to open fire. Colonel Woodford, a popular and respected officer and by a strange ironic chance the husband of Lord George Gordon's devoted sister, passed on the order to his men. According to *The London Chronicle* only about half of them obeyed him and some of these deliberately fired high. Several balls crashed through the parlour windows of Mr. Dubois's house, ricochetting round the walls, but fortunately injuring none of the eight occupants of the room. But in that dense mass of people outside in the square some of the shots found their marks. In the brief, shocked silence that followed the first surprising, terrifying volley, four men and a woman were found to have been killed and seven others wounded. Those who had not been hit and who had tried to run away at the threat of violence, stared back at the soldiers in a sort of vacant, dazed amazement, seeming neither afraid nor angry.

As if appalled by what he had done Colonel Woodford immediately marched his men off. And within a few minutes most of the rioters had gone away too. By five o'clock Bloomsbury Square was almost deserted. The bodies of two of the dead rioters, left by their companions where they had fallen, lay sprawled on the flame-lit cobbles and here and there in doorways and propped up against walls and railings could be seen the drunken figures of men and women who had come up from Newgate, full of Mr. Akerman's gin and wine, to watch the fun and had passed out in alcoholic stupor. But of the jumping shouting mob into which Colonel Woodford's men had fired there was no sign.

The respite, however, was a short one. Within a quarter of an hour of the firing the rioters returned.

This time they carrried with them boxes of wood shavings, buckets of turpentine and tow, and lengths of tar-soaked rope; and they marched into Lord Mansfield's gutted house and set fire to it, shouting that although Lord Mansfield himself had escaped, his neighbour, the Archbishop, should not.

The patches of hot thick tar, spilled across the floor of Lord Mansfield's house, caught fire in a quick succession of explosive roars, shaking the ground of the square, as a fire engine rattled up Southampton Street. Intrigued apparently by these explosions, the platoon of Guards from the chapel marched over to the fire engine, more, an observer thought, out of curiosity and to watch the blaze, than with any intention of helping the firemen to prevent it. Certainly neither Mr. Burden nor any other magistrate gave them orders to interfere with the rioters who were now crowding round the engines, refusing to allow the firemen to operate them. One of the ringleaders said that they would let the engines play on neighbouring houses if the soldiers went away. So after a short argument the soldiers moved off, and when they had gone, the rioters pushed the engine over on its side and laughingly pulled the firemen's hats down over their ears.

The Archbishop, looking out of his window, had noticed that one of the rioters in front of his neighbour's house was a well-dressed man, presumably a gentleman.[1]

He seemed to be directing the mob in its activities and giving advice as to how the operation should be conducted. While watching this man, the Archbishop was alarmed to hear him call out, 'You stay too long here! You forget the Archbishop. Come, my lads, that one house more and then to bed.'

Hearing the dreaded threat again, the Archbishop changed his mind about defending his 'own mansion' to the end and decided to make a retreat from it. He had by now persuaded his wife and daughter to escape, but to escape himself was more easily decided upon than done.

The way into the stable yard was blocked by a crowd of angry rioters who were holding above their heads, as a sort of battle standard, the corpse of a woman shot by Colonel Woodford's men. Unable to get out of his house this way, the Archbishop eventually escaped by a back door into the house of Colonel Goldsworthy, his neighbour on the other side.

Anxious not to implicate Goldsworthy, he refused his offer of sanctuary and wearing his brother's hat and concealing his purple archiepiscopal robes under a long greatcoat, he walked out of the house and into the square as a sudden blaze from Lord Mansfield's distracted the attention of the mob. He ran over to the other side of the square, to the house of Mr. Wilmot who was fortunately at home and who lent him his coach to take him away to a friend of his in another part of the town. As the coach was turning round, however, a rioter pressed his face against the glass window and, peering under the blind, he recognized the Archbishop inside. 'The Archbishop of York is in that coach', he yelled as it rattled away past him. 'He has got another hat and the blind up but I saw his face.'

[1] This was no doubt Henry John Maskall, a rich and dissolute young man, who was tried at the Old Bailey on 3 July. A witness at his trial deposed that he had seen the prisoner abet the mob and that a party of twelve men had gone up to him and asked, 'Where next?' Maskall had replied, 'The Duke'. The witness had followed Maskall to Russell Street where a man had approached him with a paper in his hand and asked: 'Why leave out Peterborough and Bristol?' Maskall had said, 'They are not left out. I have not scratched them out, but don't stay long in Devonshire, but go to the Bank. There is a million of money to pay you for your pains and at the excise office £40,000 not paid in.'

The Burning of Newgate on the night of 6 June, 1780

The Riot in Broad Street

Immediately several others ran up and tried to stop the coach but the coachman whipped up the horses for all he was worth, and they galloped away too fast to be caught, and the Archbishop was able to make his escape to Baron Skynner's house in the Adelphi.

Although it was not yet dawn the streets through which he passed were so light and warm that groups of people were sitting about playing cards or dice as if it were already day. Almost every window was illuminated by command of the mob and in front of several houses were lanterns shining on notices which read: 'This is a Protestant House', or 'No Popery' or even 'God blast the Pope.'

The sky was a sultry, glowing, incandescent, red, reflecting the blaze of a hundred fires and irradiating the buildings and streets and squares with a strangely disturbing light—sombre yet luminous.

This satanic, unreal light seemed to make it possible for the people to believe the wildest rumours. The King, it was said, was burned in the ruins of Buckingham House; Lord North was hanged by the mob in Downing Street; the Queen was murdered; thirty thousand Protestant labourers were on the march from the country to join their comrades and another thousand Cornish miners were coming to reinforce them; the rioters were going to release the lunatics from Bedlam and the lions from the Tower. The presence of well-dressed men amongst the mob at the scenes of destruction gave support to the theories of those who insisted that there was 'more in this business than met the eye'. As to who these well-dressed men were opinions differed, but that they were in some 'dark and dangerous' plot against the Government or the country, few people doubted. Two of them were 'dug out of the ruins of a house where they ran from the military although the house was burning. One had ruffles with a large diamond at his shirt breast, the other very well dressed with a plan of London in his pocket. It was publicly talked of at The Hague, Amsterdam and Paris that London would be in ashes on the 8th of June.'

The expectation of the sack of London was lent curious emphasis by the report that Colonel Scott, an American prisoner of war, had said that his countrymen were sick of the war but had been 'buoyed up by Spanish gold and by French promises of the conflagration of London'. Was not Benjamin Franklin himself in Paris obtaining French support for the American colonies in their war against the British? Was not Samuel Adams one of the leaders of the American rebellion also there? And was it not likely that the most active rioters were, as later Justice

Barrington insisted they were, 'lads well trained by some of Dr. Franklin's people in the diabolical practice of setting buildings on fire and abetted by French money'.

Those who did not yet believe in the activity of French and American *agents provocateurs* thought that the leaders of the mob were in the pay of the Opposition. Frederic Reynolds was one of those who thought so. 'It was reported', he wrote, 'that several great oppositionists were aiding and leading the mob, in disguise; and, strange as it may now appear, many, and I among them, believed this wild rumour.'

One of the better known Opposition peers, Lord Effingham, was widely believed to have been an active rioter. He was seen at the burning of Newgate. He was recognized by his ruffles—which he never wore—leading a mob on Blackfriars Bridge. His dead body was identified, disguised as a chimney sweep, in Fleet Market. Frederic Reynolds, so shocked by this last account, 'ran home with the greatest speed' to tell his father who was Lord Effingham's most intimate friend.

> I found my father, [he wrote] alone in his office; where, having deliberately heard my extraordinary communication, he told me, with a strange expression of countenance (which I conceived to be the effect of the intensity of his grief), to go up stairs, and cautiously break the sad tale to my mother, and to the family.
>
> I entered the drawing-room, and, though a large party, waiting for dinner, was assembled there, I commenced, without prelude, my affecting narrative; when, one of the guests advancing as if in the ardour of attention, I caught a view of his countenance, and suddenly stood aghast—it was Lord Effingham! He advanced, and taking me by the hand, I trembled as if I had been guilty of perjury; but, my father entering the room at that moment, somewhat abated my confusion, by withdrawing the attention of the company from me to the story, which he continued to their great amusement. When he had concluded, his Lordship patting me on the head, to encourage me, said, 'If everybody were as anxious about my life as you are, I should be sorry, for their sakes, to be killed so often; for you might have heard, Fred, this is my *third* death, during these riots. However, to cure you of your fright, and to prove to you, I have yet some remnants of loyalty, here, my boy, take this *little portrait* of his Majesty', at the same time giving me a guinea.[1]

[1] In view of all these rumours having gained such wide publicity Lord Effingham was surprised some time after the riots to be offered the appointment of Treasurer of the Household. His appearance at Court, Walpole said, 'caused much amusement and some Tory remarked on the coat he wore', whereupon Burke commented, 'It is the same in which he was killed at the riots.'

As these reports of English treachery and foreign plots circulated about the town, the Government was energetically calling in more troops. At least seven thousand soldiers from the Home Counties arrived in London before dawn on Wednesday and thousands more were on the march. This reliance upon military force was strongly condemned by the leaders of the Opposition. Burke attacked the Ministry for 'establishing a military on the ruins of the civil government'. The rows of soldiers he had seen on his way to the House earlier that day had made London, he said, seem more like 'Paris, Berlin or Petersburg than the capital of a government limited by law'. It was, he thought, 'a mistaken idea to imagine the people of this country could be bullied by legions of armed men'. Fox agreed with him and for his own part would 'much rather be governed by a mob than a standing army'.[1] It was the old familiar cry for the freedom of the individual; the belief for so long cherished that even lawlessness was better than oppression.

It was a view which the Government, in their responsibility, could not possibly accept. Without help from the Magistrates and Justices, faced with the complete collapse of those limited methods of law enforcement which were all that the contemporary concepts of freedom would allow, the Ministry began to listen with reluctant attention to the arguments for martial law.

[1] 'Mr. Wilkes', *The Gazeteer and New Daily Advertiser* reported with laconic scepticism of the sincerity behind the protest, had already in the Court of Aldermen 'made a speech as usual decrying the use of military force'.

8

UNDER MARTIAL LAW

IT was going to be another hot, still day. By eight o'clock the sun, warm and inviting, and the promise of spectacles of devastation had brought from their beds crowds of sightseers, from all over London and the villages around, who did not normally rise till much later. The streets, one of them thought, where the rioters had concentrated their attentions were like the scenes of recently and fiercely fought battles. Piles of charred and blistered furniture still smouldered before the gutted, blackened ruins of once elegant houses. Here and there lay the huddled bodies of men and women, as if dead, too drunk to move or to wake. In the poorer districts whole alleys and courtyards and whole camps of Irish immigrants lay in tumbled, smoking confusion. Hundreds of people inspected the ruins of Newgate which was 'open to all; anyone might get in, and what was never the case before anyone might get out'. Dr. Johnson was one of them. He had gone out to see the ruins with Dr. Scott, he told Mrs. Thrale, and found them 'with the fire yet glowing. As I went by the Protestants were plundering the sessions-house at the Old Bailey. They were not, I believe, a hundred; but they did their work at leisure, in full security, without sentinels, without trepidation, as men lawfully employed in full day.'

Lord George got up and went out early too, in order to call at Buckingham House and offer his services to the King. On Monday evening he had made a similar offer to the Court of Aldermen at Guildhall. But the aldermen, although willing to profit by the results of the riots were anxious to dissociate themselves from the instigator of them, and greeted him with extreme coldness. Several members insulted him and 'finding his presence rather obnoxious', *The Gazeteer* reported, 'he retired'. The next day in Parliament he had offered to 'go out to pacify the associators . . . but he was held down in his seat by several Members who insisted on his not quitting the House'.

On Wednesday morning he was again rebuffed. Lord Stormont, who was at Buckingham House that morning, described how 'a page came and scratched at the door' and said that Lord George Gordon was outside and wanted to see the King. Lord Stormont told the page to see that Lord George was shown into a room in the colonnade and then he joined him there. 'What do you want?' Lord Stormont asked him. 'His answer to me was that "he desired to see the King because he could be of essential" or "material service" or "do great service in suppressing the riots". I went with the message to the King' whose answer was: ' " It is impossible for the King to see Lord George Gordon until he has given sufficient proofs of his allegiance by employing those means which he says he has in his power to quell the disturbances and restore peace to the capital." To that his Lordship answered that "if he might presume to reply he would say that his best endeavours would be used".'

On several occasions after this abortive attempt to see the King, Lord George did in fact use his best endeavours to 'quell the disturbances' and took it upon himself to go out amongst the rioters and try to persuade them to go home. But they looked at him in amazement, laughed and carried on with their work of destruction. Some of them, he felt sure, did not even know who he was.

The King also used his best endeavours and to better effect. On Monday he had written to Lord North:

I think it right to acquaint Lord North that I have taken every step that could occur to me to prevent any tumult tomorrow, and have seen that proper executive orders have been sent to the two Secretaries of State. I trust Parliament will take such measures as the necessities of the time require. This tumult must be got the better of or it will encourage designing men to use it as a precedent for assembling the people on other occasions; if possible, we must get to the bottom of it and examples must be made. If anything occurs to Lord North wherein I can give any farther assistance, I shall be ready to forward it, for my attachment is to the laws and security of my country, and to the protection of the lives and properties of all my subjects.

Having arranged for the Members to get to the House in a more dignified way than had been possible on Friday, the King was annoyed by their apparently forbearing attitude when they had arrived there.

Lord North cannot be much surprised [he wrote that evening] at my not thinking the House of Commons have this day advanced so far in the present business as the exigency of the time requires; the allowing Lord Geo. Gordon, the avowed head of the tumult, to be at large certainly encourages the continuation of it; to which is to be added the great supineness of the civil magistrates; and I fear without more vigour that this will not subside; indeed, unless exemplary punishment is procured, it will remain a lasting disgrace and will be a precedent for future commotions.

There was something at least that the King could do on his own authority. From Tuesday onwards there appeared daily in the Press a Royal Proclamation offering a reward of £500 and a 'pardon if necessary' to anyone who would 'discover any other person or persons who, directly or indirectly, were concerned in pulling down . . . the chapel of any Foreign Minister so as that the person or persons may be prosecuted for the same'.

By noon on Wednesday not a single informer had taken advantage of this offer and it was obvious that some more drastic measures would have to be adopted. During the morning threatening messages had been delivered not only at the houses of numerous Catholics who had so far escaped the attentions of the mob but also at the houses of almost all the leading members of the Government, warning them of destruction that night. 'Wedderburn and Lord Stormont', Walpole wrote to the Countess of Upper Ossory, 'are threatened and I do not know who. The Duchess of Beaufort sent an hour ago to tell me Lord Ashburnham has just advised her that he is threatened and was sending away his poor bedridden Countess and children.'

The Commander-in-Chief was receiving frantic messages every minute. Mr. Wilmot who had lent his coach to the Archbishop of York sent one such communication to Lord Amherst. 'Mr. and Mrs. Wilmot present their compliments to Lord Amherst and acquaint his Lordship that the mob threaten their house the next in Bloomsbury Square, and beseech instantly a party of Horse Guards (as the mob do not mind the Foot) to come to their assistance directly. 7th June.' Another arrived from the Mansion House: 'I have this moment received information that the mob intend making an attack upon the Bank. The civil power of the City being insufficient to prevent it, I must entreat your Lordship will immediately send a sufficient number of Horse and Foot to assist the civil power on this occasion. I am, etc. B. Kennet, Mayor.'

With so many regiments in America, Lord Amherst found it impossible to attend to every such request, and even when he was able to send troops to a danger spot, the officers in charge of them could find on arrival no magistrate to give them any orders. The Commander-in-Chief was naturally enraged by this utter collapse of civil authority. 'It is the duty of the troops, my Lord', he explained in an angry letter to Lord Stormont, 'to act only under the authority and by direction of the Civil Magistrate.' 'After the troops had marched to the places appointed for them', he went on to complain, 'several of the magistrates refused to act . . . I leave it to your Lordship to judge in how defenceless and how disgraceful a situation the military are left, and how much such conduct as this tends even to encourage Riots, and how much the public services as well as the troops must suffer by it.'

Well aware of the dilemma in which the troops were placed by what he had referred to as the 'great supineness of the civil magistrates', the King was determined to do something to help them. 'There shall be one', he told a meeting of the Privy Council on Wednesday, 'that I can answer for, that will do his duty' and threatened to head the Guards himself if the military authorities were not given more extensive powers. And undoubtedly he would have had the courage to do it. 'I am persuaded', Topham, a captain in the Horse Guards whose duties brought him into close touch with the Royal Family, told Frederic Reynolds, 'that the King does not know what fear is'.[1]

The supposed legal disability of the troops to fire on a lawless mob without specific instructions from the civil magistrates to do so, even after the Riot Act had been read, rested on the much-quoted opinions of Sir Philip Yorke, one of the most admired attorney-generals of the eighteenth century, and of Lord Raymont another great and earlier legal authority. This was not, it subsequently transpired, Lord Mansfield's interpretation of the law, and the Archbishop of York, no doubt having discussed the matter with his next-door neighbour, expressed the opinion in a letter to his son that the respect for Sir Philip Yorke's opinion was 'a fatal error'.

Fatal error or not, it was undoubtedly the opinion that 'prevailed among the military' until the King insisted upon a new reading of the law at that urgent meeting of the Privy Council on Wednesday. The Councillors were in general in disagreement with the King; only the old Earl Bathurst and one or two others supporting him. The Council

[1] 'No person can doubt', Wraxall thought, that the King 'would have given on that occasion, had it been unfortunately necessary, the strongest proof of courage.'

was about to break up in irritated dissatisfaction when, very late, Wedderburn, the Attorney-General, arrived. Immediately the King asked him to give his opinion as to whether officers could use their own discretion in firing on the mob. Wedderburn said that he thought they could. 'Is that your declaration of the law as Attorney-General?' the King asked him. 'Yes', replied Wedderburn. 'Then', said the King, standing up and dismissing the Councillors, 'so let it be done.'

A few hours later a Royal Proclamation giving effect to Wedderburn's momentous declaration was published.

This was not a declaration of martial law in the strictest sense of the term but its effects were not much less far-reaching and it was evidently interpreted as such. *The London Chronicle* reported: 'The Privy Council having issued an edict for putting the cities of London and Westminster under martial law, Lord Amherst as Commander-in-Chief received orders to make such a disposition of the military as seemed most conducive to put an end to the present alarming insurrection.' And Amherst lost no time. The King's Proclamation was immediately followed by an order issued to all officers in London:

> Adjutant General's Office. June 7th 1780.
> In obedience to an order of the King in Council the military to act without waiting for direction from the Civil Magistrates and to use force for dispersing the illegal and tumultuous assemblies of the people.
> Amherst.

The civil authorities, however, treated the Royal Proclamation with less respect. At the same time that the Privy Council had held their meeting a Common City Council meeting had been held in the Chamber of the Guildhall. A resolution was put to the meeting 'that this Court doth agree to petition the Honourable the House of Commons against the Act of Parliament lately passed in favour of Roman Catholics'. In spite of the horrors of the preceding night and the threats of worse horrors to come, this irresponsible resolution was passed unanimously.

Shortly after it had been passed, a breathless messenger arrived to tell the Council of the Royal Proclamation. Scarcely had he gasped his message out than Jack Wilkes, in high good humour, laughingly proposed that he should be arrested. But it was apparent that he did not want to be taken seriously. Astute and calculating as the likeable and brilliant old reprobate was, he realized now that it was time to dissociate himself from Bull and Kennet and those other aldermen who still, either through fear or the hope of advantage, had done and intended to do nothing to suppress the riots. Wilkes, unhappily married to a Nonconformist and brought up with strict severity by a father who was almost a Puritan, was himself a man of easy tolerance and had a sincere sympathy for Roman Catholics. 'I think it would do honour to our Church', he once said, 'to treat with tenderness all those who are unhappy enough not to be in her bosom.' But it was not so much from a belief in tolerance as from reasons of expediency that he decided now to show which side he was on. He had done nothing on Tuesday and he realized quite well what further inaction might mean. He talked the unwilling Kennet into a promise to call out the *posse comitatus*. And he himself went back to his ward to form a force which he could put, with himself at its head, under the command of the officer in command of troops in the City.

The town was now full of soldiers. 'The Military', *The Morning Chronicle* told its readers with some apprehension, 'are pouring into town at every avenue.' There were by the late afternoon over fifteen thousand men under arms 'each regiment having its field pieces loaded with grapeshot'. The militia regiments had come in from the country to help the regular regiments already stationed in and around London. The Royal Palaces, the Bank, the Royal Exchange, the Guildhall and the Inns of Court were all heavily defended. The Museum and the Government offices were like barracks. The drawbridges of the Tower were kept up and water was let into the moat. Hyde Park resembled 'the field of Malplaquet before the battle'; tents were going up everywhere; lines of men marched backwards and forwards sweating in the heat; idle groups sat in the grass, dozing or cleaning their muskets, talking, smoking, laughing, playing cards, drinking; their buttons undone, their sore, bare feet steaming after the long march. They had come from as far as Canterbury, Coventry and Newbury. For many of them this was their first sight of London and they sounded, a Londoner thought, hearing them talking in their outlandish yokels' accents, like so many foreign peasants at a festival. They laughingly referred to each other as 'your Worship' having been told that they were now the only effective Justices of Peace. When the orders came to fire on their own countrymen would these red-faced, kindly, rough, awkward, cider-squeezing, bog-trotting, slubberdegullions obey? Many doubted it. 'The panic which had seized upon the people', Samuel

Romilly wrote, 'gave birth to a multitude of reports; at one time it was said that none of the soldiers would do their duty but were all ready to join with the rioters'.

Hearing these and other even more disturbing reports Walpole, who had stayed at Strawberry Hill until today because the house next door to his was to be auctioned and he wanted to know who would buy it, decided that 'there was no bearing to remain philosophically in the country and hear the thousand rumours of every hour, and not know whether one's friends and relations were not destroyed'. As he drove past Hyde Park Corner he saw a squad of Guards on duty at the door of Apsley House, the home of Earl Bathurst who had encouraged the King in his firm and uncompromising attitude. In Piccadilly he met his friend George Selwyn and 'the signorina[1] who I wondered be ventured there'. George Selwyn climbed into his chaise 'in a fury' and told him 'Lord Mansfield's is in ashes and that five thousand men were marched to Caen Wood' to pull down his Lordship's country house and raid his cellar.

Walpole, who had no great love or respect for the Lord Chief Justice, was not much disturbed by this, but the report that the rioters in preparation for their night assaults had invaded the Artillery Ground and provided themselves with stolen firearms, really alarmed him. All afternoon they had been trying to buy or steal pistols and muskets from gunsmiths' shops but the gunsmiths had wisely locked up their stocks in secret hiding places or sent them to the Tower and shut up their shops. Now the rioters had found as many muskets as they wanted.

It was not only the gunsmiths who had put up their shutters. By the middle of the afternoon there were few shops of any kind still open. Across the closed shutters of almost all of them were chalked the now sickeningly familiar words 'No Popery' or 'This is a Protestant house and shop.' From the windows hung bits of blue silk[2] and from the hanging signs dangled blue ribbons and blue cockades and decorated Presbyterian pamphlets. Even many of the houses of Jews and Roman Catholic foreigners had signs outside protesting that the occupiers were good Protestants. Grimaldi, the dancing master and father of the famous clown, refused to put out such a sign and when the mob passed by

[1] Maria Fagniani, Selwyn's adopted daughter.

[2] 'I shall most willingly allow blue flags to be put on my house', Mrs. Montagu said. 'I have learned by sad experience that in the land of Liberty one must illuminate and inscribe and wear the livery imposed not by Government indeed but by the ungoverned.'

his house, Angelo, who was a pupil of his, said that 'being a foreigner they thought he must be a papist; on hearing that he lived there they all stopped, and there was a general shouting. A cry of "No Popery!" was raised and they were just going to assail the house, when Grimaldi who had been listening all the time and knew their motives, put his head out of the window from the second floor; making comical grimaces he called out, "Genteelmen in dis hose dere be no religion at all!" ' They laughed and went on giving him three cheers. Another Italian, Pacchierotti, was equally fortunate in escaping the wrath of the mob. He told Susan Burney 'he was not in the least frightened. I dared not tell him', Susan wrote, 'how frightened I was myself for him. I begged he would not expose himself by walking about at such a time as this when the city seemed to be inhabited by wild beasts, not human creatures. "Why should I fear?" said he smiling. "I have commited no fault. To say the truth I am not alarmed because the English nation, it seem to me, is composed of good-natured mild people." He told me that Mr. Bertoni was terribly frightened. "He trembles", said he, "like a leaf, as a littel child! I could not persuade him to come here with me!" Pacchierotti told me many people had advised him to take his name off his door, but he said he did not intend to do it.'

The passers-by, Catholic and Protestant alike, wore blue cockades and plumes as a sort of passport and to avoid the insults and attacks of the mob. 'I am decking myself with blue ribbons', Walpole wrote from what he called his 'garrison in Berkeley Square', 'like a May Day garland. I am sorry I did not bring the armour of Francis I to town. . . . It will probably be a black night.'

Already although it was still bright daylight gangs of youths and women were parading about the town armed with railings and chains and cutlasses, drunkenly shouting: 'No Popery!' and 'exacting contributions which they called mob-money from everyone they met'. In Holborn one gang, encouraged by free drinks of gin and brandy given to them by a Catholic distiller as a bribe to stay out of his premises, knocked threateningly at every door and refused to leave until they had been paid to do so. Gangs of bullies broke into houses with the excuse that they had come to search for Popish books. A chimney sweep picking over books in a house in Newgate Street came across a Bible and told his comrades· that this house at any rate was a good Protestant one. 'This is the right religion', he said spitting on the book in evident approval. 'It is Lord Gordon's religion by God.' A man named Thomas Taplin, who was subsequently executed, led on horse-back a gang of about fifty ragamuffins. At his trial an apothecary deposed that a boy had come up to him and said 'God bless your honour. Some money for your poor mob.' The apothecary told him to get out of the way and the boy said, 'I'll go get my captain.' Taplin then rode over and exclaimed with threatening jocularity, 'God bless this gentleman. He is always generous.' And the apothecary thought it sensible to give him half a crown. Another man on horseback, holding his reins in one hand and a blunderbuss in the other, politely declined to accept anything but gold. 'The pious insurgents', Walpole thought, learning that Charles Turner had been robbed in the street of five guineas, 'will soon have a military chest.'

These self-appointed collectors were little troubled by the troops, whose officers were besieged with orders from Whitehall to march contingents here and there, to be in position at nightfall at each new threatened danger spot. 'The houses of the Secretaries of State', wrote Wraxall, 'of every bishop, of every Catholic, of every Justice of the Peace and of all the King's tradesmen were marked out for destruction. The Catholics and many other persons moved all their effects. Their neighbours as well as themselves fled into the country or waited in the utmost terror the approach of evening.'

And when at last the light began to fail Robert Smith, who was in Cheapside, remembered how curiously quiet it suddenly became.

9

A BLACK NIGHT

IN Cornhill, as in Threadneedle Street and all the other streets around the Bank, the soldiers waited in nervous, excited silence for the threatened attack. Around them the warehouses and offices, the shops and taverns were locked and shuttered. Across the quiet streets thick ropes, brought up earlier in the day by sailors from Deptford, were tied between the stone posts that marked the edge of the pavements. In the courtyard of the Bank itself were several cannon.

As the sun went down the rioters mustered on the corner of Old Jewry and Poultry, and just before it set they charged towards the Bank. But coming up against the ropes and other barricades stretched across Poultry in front of the Mansion House their 'impetuous course' was halted and they broke up into small detachments. As the first of these detachments reached the bottom of Threadneedle Street the order to fire was given. There was a sudden crackle of fire and about twenty people fell dead or wounded and were dragged by their comrades into the church of St. Mildred and into the doorways in Scalding Alley.

At the same time two other groups of rioters clambering over the barriers in Princess Street and Bartholomew Lane were fired upon, but the aim of the militiamen was so inaccurate that two innocent bystanders watching the scene in a doorway of St. Christopher's Church were shot through the neck.

Robert Smith himself narrowly escaped the same injury.

I had the curiosity [he wrote] to walk out from Frederick's Place, and to stand at the south-west corner of the Old Jewry, from whence I could observe all that passed. Shortly afterwards, four or five drunken fellows with blue cockades in their hats came reeling down Cheapside, bawling out 'No Popery!' As they approached, the eyes of the volunteers were intent upon them, and the commanding officer called out 'Attention!' All was silent, and the drunken fellows, without offering any violence, were about to pass the corps, by walking on the foot pavement, as if to make towards the Compter, when the officer told them to 'fall back'; and at the same time a few muskets were pointed towards them to prevent their passing. They retreated a few paces to the spot where I stood, and there made a halt, muttering curses at the soldiery, when all of a sudden two or three muskets were discharged at them. One of the balls lodged in the door-post of the house against which I stood, not half a dozen inches from my right shoulder; another passed between my legs, and shattered the brickwork against the calves of my legs.

I lost no time in making good my retreat down the Old Jewry; and the rioters taking the same direction, the soldiers discharged their pieces plentifully, without distinguishing the guilty from the innocent. The balls whistled along by me before I could turn into Frederick's Place, but I providentially escaped. The rioters too were all untouched; but a poor fellow who had just come out of Schumaker and Hayman's counting-house with a bill his master had sent him for, was shot through the heart. He fell, gave a convulsive kick or two, and died. Another in crossing the Old Jewry from Dove Court with a plate of oysters in his hand was shot through the wrist.

All over the town the war had now started. 'The streets', Thomas Holcroft reported, 'were swarming with people and uproar, confusion and terror reigned in every part.'

As promised the previous night the prisons which had so far escaped were all attacked and before it was dark, the King's Bench and Fleet Prisons,[1] the Borough Clink and Surrey Bridewell were all in flames and their convicts gone. Only the New Gaol was saved by its tough keeper who stood at the gate his eyes flashing with anger and holding a blunderbuss in his hand shouting 'as many as will may enter but none may return alive'.

At the attack upon the Poultry Compter three men were killed when the troops sent to defend it opened fire. The rest retreated but said they would return later with reinforcements. Unwilling to run the risk of a pitched battle so close to the Mansion House, however, the Lord Mayor sent an order across Poultry for the inhabitants of the Compter to be released.[2]

The burning of the King's Bench Prison was witnessed by the ener-

---

[1] *The London Gazette* reported that the amount of the debts of the prisoners released from these two prisons alone totalled £700,000.

[2] In order to open a clear avenue to the back of some of these prisons the rioters burned down any buildings which stood in the way. Two taverns in Southwark, 'The Ship' and 'Simon the Tanner', were burned to the ground to open up a straight route to the New Gaol in Long Lane.

getically ubiquitous Angelo. About six o'clock, on his way to Charing Cross after dinner, he

> heard that the Park facing the Horse Guards was full of soldiers, and that the gate of Spring Gardens was shut; when meeting with one of the officers of the Guards, Captain Boswell, he took me with him inside. The Hertfordshire Militia was there under arms standing quietly at ease; and also the Foot Guards. I had not remained there long, when a black smoke made its appearance, passing towards us over the Horse Guards, the wind blowing from the eastward. The news soon spread that the King's Bench was on fire; and though all seemed to credit it, not a soldier stirred, waiting for orders; whilst the officers were all the time busy in conversation. The King's Bench on fire, and I not there! This was too much at such a time to be kept stationary. I soon hurried away, and arrived near the obelisk in St. George's Fields, the space then before the Bench being quite open with no houses. On seeing the flames and smoke from the windows along the high wall, it appeared to me like the huge hulk of a man-of-war, dismasted, on fire. Here with amazement I stood for some time gazing on the spot; when, looking behind me, I beheld a number of horse and foot soldiers approaching with a quiet step. Off I went in an instant, in a contrary direction; nor did I look back till I was on Blackfriar's Bridge.

Five men who had been sitting on top of the prison calmly smoking and drinking while flames shot out of the windows below them, gave warning of the soldiers' approach and asked their commander below to hold out a blanket into which, one after the other, they all safely jumped and then ran away.

Meanwhile another contingent of infantry had been ordered to the Fleet Prison where the rioters, not content with burning the building down, were trying to push into the flames a fire engine belonging to the Royal Exchange Fire Insurance Office. Encouraging them from the roof of the Market House were four men who were jumping up and down, waving and cheering with phrenetic energy. On refusing to come down after being ordered to do so by the officer in charge of the troops, they were suddenly fired on from three directions at once. Immediately they all fell down on the roof, flat on their faces and the soldiers congratulated themselves on their good marksmanship. But after a little while one of the four raised his head a little 'and instantly clapt it down and lay still again; he repeated this manoeuvre two or three times', while the soldiers unsuccessfully fired volley after volley at him. After every discharge he playfully popped up his head again and threw tiles at the soldiers' heads; and then at last 'he ventured to slide down and ran away with great celerity. He was by far the genteelest in appearance of the four.'

As the infantrymen fired at these men on the roof, a contingent of cavalry rode up to reinforce them. Captain Gardner, of the Light Dragoons, reported that 'I read to them the King's orders but to no purpose and after having had my horse struck by fire brands several times I ordered the quarter rank in front to charge them. I cannot ascertain the number killed. I believe twelve of them to have been cut down.' Colonel Leake in command of the entire force at the Fleet believed that altogether no less than a hundred rioters were killed there.

Nathaniel Wraxall who had set out with three friends at about nine o'clock 'in order to view the scene' could not get very near the Fleet Prison for the showers of sparks and pieces of flaming wood which came falling down around him. He had made his way to the Fleet from Holborn where he had seen the beginning of the attack on Langdale's distillery.

Langdale, a Roman Catholic with twelve young children, owned one of the largest distilleries in London[1] and it was because of his trade more than because of his religion that he had been repeatedly threatened with invasion by the rioters since Monday afternoon. At last, just before dusk on Wednesday evening, at a time when his distilleries, warehouse, offices and the several private houses occupied by his family and work-people were undefended, owing to his garrison having been called off to the Bank, the assault began. It followed the usual pattern. The doors were forced, the windows smashed in, the rioters rushed into the house and the furniture, office books and equipment flew out through the broken windows. A bonfire was soon raging in the street and the premises themselves, less than half an hour later, were burning fiercely too, expertly ignited by the rioters, now thoroughly efficient as incendiaries.

As the buildings leapt with a roar into flame, a gentle wind came up. Until now the fires had not spread as the air was so calm and still, but tonight in Holborn gushes and eddies of wind took the flames this way

[1] Thrale's distillery was saved by the 'astonishing presence of mind' of Perkins, the manager, 'in amusing the mob with meat and drink and huzzas'. 'Our brewhouse', Mrs. Thrale told Johnson, 'would have blazed in ten minutes when a property of £150,000 would have been utterly lost'. In fact, after Mr. Thrale's death in 1781, it was sold for £185,000.

The Riots in Moorfields

At Langdale's Distillery

Two illustrations from *Barnaby Rudge*

Israel bar Abraham Gordon

and that wrapping the street in fire and setting alight houses further down Holborn towards Fleet Market, until the whole district looked, as Wraxall said, 'like a volcano'.

The fire was given an added and ferocious life by a fire engine pumping through its hose not water but gin from the stills in Langdale's cellar. Another engine, captured from its operatives by an enterprising old cobbler, was pumping up gin into buckets, while the cobbler did a good trade selling it to the spectators of the havoc at a penny a mug.

Others, unwilling to pay for what they could get for nothing, ran into the raging building and down the stone steps into the cellar and came up choking with blackened faces and bloodshot eyes, carrying untapped casks of gin, or pails and jugs, bowls and even pig-troughs overflowing with this most valued anodyne. Soon, even this effort was unnecessary for as the heat below ground became intense the stills burst and overflowed and the gin came gushing up into the streets and ran in warm streams in the gutter and between the cobbles, joining a flow of rum pouring out of a pile of enormous staved-in rum casks. Delirious with excitement, the people knelt down and dipped their faces in the river of fiery spirits and gulped as much of it down as they could before it made them choke and burned their throats like acid. For the gin was in its raw state, unrectified. Wraxall saw men and women lying down prostrate in the streets incapably drunk; some of the women had babies in their arms or struggling near their insensible bodies, screaming in terror or in pain. Several staring, wide-eyed figures lay on their backs in grotesque postures, their faces blue, their swollen tongues still wet with the poisonous liquid.

Below them in the cellars, trapped now by the fire, were the scorching bodies of men and women overcome by the fumes and the smoke, burning to death. And in the warehouse, too drunk to get out when the flames leapt in, other men and women could be heard screaming and shouting and giggling, scarcely aware of what was happening to them or too drunk to care.

At length the Northumberland militia arrived. They had come by forced march from the north and were so exhausted, one of their officers thought, that their dulled senses could not take in the full horror of the scene. They wearily obeyed an order to open fire on a group of pickpockets who had been threading their way between the prostrate bodies, picking off them anything worth stealing and shouting obscenities at the officer who had called to them to give themselves up. The shots scattered the pickpockets who ran away from a scene which when they had gone presented little life. The flames still crackled, the spirits still bubbled in the street but most of the people who remained were motionless, and the others seemed only able to crawl or stumble about in delirium.

The militiamen marched off to the Bank, where hundreds of troops were needed to repel a new and more dangerous attack.

This second impetuous assault was led by a man, afterwards recognized as a brewery drayman, who rode a cart-horse decorated with chains and fetters stolen from Newgate the previous night. He rode up and down Poultry and Threadneedle Street shouting hoarsely and waving handcuffs and fetters above his head, unconcerned by his danger and glorying in his conspicuousness.

Wave after wave of rioters rushed towards the Bank to be met by the fire of Colonel Holroyd's hard-pressed militiamen, now reinforced by Lord Algernon Percy and the contingent of the Northumberland Militiamen just come from Holborn. At each volley a few fell but the others re-formed and came on again. Jack Wilkes, who had formerly commanded the Buckinghamshire Militia, was also by this time at the Bank and was as energetic in defence of it as anyone. He fired with determination into the packed ranks of the oncoming rioters, at the sweating, shining faces and the rushing bodies caparisoned with their blue cockades once the badge of his own supporters in former and less savage riots. 'Fired six or seven times', he noted briefly in his diary, 'at the rioters at the end of the Bank. Killed two rioters directly opposite to the Great Gate of the Bank; several others in Pig Street and Cheapside'.

When the havoc was at its height a breathless and agitated Lord George Gordon appeared.[1] He ran up the steps of the Bank and shouted at the rioters with frantic, distracted gestures, beseeching them ingenuously to go home. The sight of so much bloodshed for which he felt responsible, seemed to have driven him out of his mind. His vehement, incoherent speech merely encouraged the mob to further bravado. At length, persuaded of this, he went up to Lord Rodney, whom he knew slightly and who was then an officer in the Guards, and offered to stand shoulder to shoulder with him and 'expose his person to the utmost risk to resist such proceedings'. His offer was declined,

---

[1] He had already been seen that evening at two different places in Moorfields and again in Coleman Street 'haranguing the multitudes' and trying to persuade hem to disperse.

t

he was pushed out of the way, and the battle went on with renewed vigour around him.

In this battle, as in others, the presence of so many well and fashionably dressed men among the rioters was as alarming as it was suspicious. Wraxall reported that several dead bodies, expensively dressed, were carried off and thrown into the river for fear that they might be recognized; and Colonel Stuart, writing to his father Lord Bute, told him that

Colonel Twistleton, who commanded the party at the Bank, informed me that they [the mob] were led by a person in a Navy uniform with his sword drawn, that many decently dressed people encouraged them till they were near the Guard, but that they then retired and pretended to be spectators.

One very singular circumstance he likewise told me; a very well dressed man was killed whose face they took great pains to hide, but after most of them dispersed a curious watchman looked at the body, expressed some surprise, and said he knew the Person. Upon which they seized the watchman and dragged him to Moorfields, where they swore him in the most sacred way to secrecy. As they also took off the body, nothing has been discovered.

I would not have mentioned this had not the Sheriff related verbatim the same story.

The same strange stories of well-dressed gentlemen among the rioters were told of the mob which attacked the toll-houses on Blackfriars Bridge later on that night.

For generations the halfpenny toll charges incurred by pedestrians crossing Blackfriars Bridge had been resented by the hundreds of Londoners who were obliged to cross the river there every day, and while so many obnoxious houses were being burned it seemed a good opportunity to destroy the toll collectors' houses also. They were built mainly of wood and were soon burning so fiercely that the flying sparks and billows of smoke could be seen from as far away as St. Paul's Churchyard. Revealed in the bright light and caught in so narrow a space, the rioters presented an easy target for the troops. The slaughter here, Wraxall thought, although not nearly so many rioters were involved, was as great as at the Fleet Prison and the Bank. The dead and wounded bodies tumbled over into the river, made foul at that point by the revolting effluent of the Fleet Ditch, or fell headlong on to Blackfriars Stairs, hated for so long as the place from which felons under sentence of transportation used to sail in closed and stifling lighters, to join a ship sailing for the York or Rappahannock Rivers in Virginia.

Once again the maligned Lord Effingham was recognized as one of those expensively dressed figures who were to be seen at every trouble spot. This time, so it was afterwards reported, he had been thrown into the river, severely wounded but not quite dead, by a friend who was anxious that such a prominent member of the Opposition should not be shown to have been so compromisingly involved. The cold water had revived him, he had been fished out and had made his escape to Grange Hall in Yorkshire where he was now convalescing in secret, hiding his wounds even from his doctor.

He was thought not to be alone in this. Wraxall was confident that 'numbers concealed their wounds in order to evade discovery of the part which they had taken in the disorders of the Capital'. Certain it was that scores of dead bodies, even though Lord Effingham's was not one of them, were pushed over into the river from Blackfriars Stairs, Queen Hithe Dock and Dowgate Wharf that night, and some of those which were not burned or carried out to sea on the morning tide, were found next day lying in the streets, some, it was said, with *louis d'or* in their pockets.

As the corpses fell like rats into the river beneath Blackfriars Bridge, another violent assault was being made in a different part of the City, in Broad Street. Several troops had to be called off from Blackfriars to meet this new threat and others from the area of the Bank which was itself not yet out of danger. A volunteer in the London Military Association, till then defending the Bank, reported how 'the King's troops could not move from their positions near the Bank, therefore it fell to the lot of part of our corps to march to Broad Street where was a large mob ransacking a house and burning the furniture in the street. They would not disperse and bid us fire and be damned. There was soon exhibited a scene of killed, wounded and dying. We were very merciful to them by firing only one gun at once, instead of a volley, thereby giving time to many to get off.'

The main object of attack was the house of a rich Irishman named Donovan; and Mrs. Samuel Hoare, the wife of the Quaker banker, who lived just opposite, was able to view the scene from her windows much more closely than she would have wished. Broad Street, she had told her mother, had been a nightmarish place to live for some days. 'I must own', she had written on Friday, 'I have never felt my fears equally awakened.' The cry of 'No Popery!' on the Tuesday evening was to be heard 'from every corner. . . . There is now such a tumult in the street I cannot proceed.' This evening when the troops marched into the street to help Mr. Donovan, the children's nurse had a fit and Mrs. Hoare and her husband were obliged to hold her down for an hour. 'Think how much the horror of the scene was heightened', she told her mother, 'when a large party of the Horse Guards attended by a company of volunteers arrived. They halted exactly opposite our house. Three times the commanding officer exhorted the people to disperse, but they obstinately refused. Then advancing but a few paces, they fired near a hundred pieces and left four unhappy men dead on the spot and fifteen wounded.'

The commanding officer of the London Military Association, Bernard Turner, a sugar refiner, deposed in Court how he had marched into Broad Street to disperse the mob 'destroying Mr. Donovan's house'. He had argued with them and then been obliged to fire. When most of the mob had been forced back by the shooting he had marched his men off to St. Catherine's where the rioters were destroying the house of another Irishman, Mr. Lebarty. Some of the mob 'had iron bars, some had spokes of wheels, and some few had cutlasses. There were one or two odd pieces of firearms among the mob at Mr. Donovan's house, but they were chiefly armed with bludgeons, spokes of wheels and iron bars.'

The London Military Association, which distinguished itself by its patience and courage in Broad Street, was one of several voluntary associations which had by now joined the regular troops and militiamen in defence of the city. At first these military associations, never in the best and safest of times encouraged by the authorities, had been frowned upon. On Monday, after two Catholic chapels, one in Aldgate and another in Wapping had been destroyed, the Irishmen of Wapping decided that they did not intend to lose their chapel in Virginia Street 'without a blow in its defence. They went to their priest and proposed to enrol themselves in a body to defend the remaining Catholic chapels'. The priest went to one of the Secretaries of State and put his congregation's proposition to him, but the Secretary of State refused to consider the idea and said that the military would be sufficient to deal with any threat. The priest returned to his disappointed flock and told them that their suggestion was not acceptable and that on no account must they interfere in an unofficial way and advised them to stay out of mischief. That night when the troops turned out to guard the northern approaches to Virginia Street, the mob came into the street from an alley on the south and ransacked the chapel. The troops turned round but there was no magistrate to give them any orders so they did nothing.

Other applications to the Government to form military associations received no more encouragement than that of the Irish in Wapping, but provided they did not come from Irishmen they were not actually refused, although it was generally left to the applicants to provide themselves with arms.

Many communities by Wednesday evening had followed the example of Mr. Thorpe of the Globe Tavern in Fleet Street and had, without authority, formed themselves into vigilante patrols. One such patrol was formed by Mr. Seddons, an upholsterer, who mustered his hundred employees and marched them off to fight a mob attacking the house of a friend of his. Another formed by a young nobleman, and comprising nearly four hundred gentlemen and their servants, patrolled the area around Lincoln's Inn Fields. The Inns of Court themselves were protected, not very effectively, by the lawyers who had chambers there. In Barnard's Inn twenty-two sets of chambers were burned down before the troops came to the assistance of the beleaguered lawyers, who were doing their unaccomplished best to defend them. Writing from 'Barnard's Inn—what remains of it' after the attack, Doctor Warner begged George Selwyn to give him leave to 'lodge the shattered remains of my little goods in Cleveland Court for a time ... The staircase, in which my chambers are, is not yet burned down, but it could not be much worse for me if it were. ... There can be no living here, even if the fire stops immediately, for the whole place is a wreck.'

The officer in command of the soldiers sent to protect the Temple, which was particularly marked out for destruction as the Bishop of Lincoln was its Master, refused help from the lawyers who had dutifully collected there. On receiving an order to move out to deal with an uproar in the street, he marched his men out through the Temple gates and the lawyers, young and old, hopefully and cheerfully followed, with an alarming collection of weapons and firearms over their shoulders. As the last soldier passed out, however, the gate was locked behind him. The officer returned at the howl of protest which greeted this treatment and told his would-be supporters through the ironwork: 'Gentlemen, I am much obliged for your intended assistance, but as I do not choose to allow my soldiers to be shot, so I have ordered you to be locked in.'

One young lawyer, however, determined not to be humiliated, climbed over the wall and ran after the soldiers, a little unsteadily for he had had a good dinner, shouting that he was as good a shot as any of them. But when he caught up with them, a sergeant turned round and knocked him out with the butt-end of his musket. A journalist, standing on a nearby roof, saw him fall quite clearly by the light of a raging fire a little further down the street, but before climbing down to help him, he took a final look round at the holocaust, at the bright fires where the King's Bench and Fleet Prisons still roared fiercely, at the fires in Broad Street and around the Bank, at the dully glowing embers on Blackfriars Bridge, and at the scores of lesser unidentified fires all round him.

'London offered on every side', as Wraxall said, 'the picture of a city sacked and abandoned to a ferocious enemy.'

Surveying the terrible scene from the top of Gloucester House with the Duchess of Beaufort and her daughters, Walpole also saw the 'two vast fires' which he took to be 'the King's Bench and Lambeth; but the latter was the New Prison and the former at least was burning at midnight. Colonel Heywood came up and acquainted His Royal Highness that nine houses in Great Queen Street had been gutted and the furniture burned.' Later on Walpole went to 'Lord Hertford's and found him and his sons charging muskets. Lord Rockingham had two hundred soldiers in his house and is determined to defend it. Then I went to General Conway's (in Warwick Street, Charing Cross) and in a moment a servant came in and said there was a great fire just by. We went to the street door and thought it was St. Martin's Lane in flames, but it is either the Fleet Prison or the Distiller's. . . . After supper I returned to Lady Hertford finding Charing Cross, the Haymarket and Piccadilly illuminated from fear . . . lines being drawn across the Strand and Holborn to prevent the mob coming westward. Lady Hertford's cook came in white as this paper. He is a German Protestant' and had refused to illuminate his windows. 'On coming home I visited the Duchess Dowager and my fair ward.' His fair ward was the Duchess's grand-daughter, Lady Elizabeth Compton, and although it was now past two in the morning he found it impossible to go to bed ('for Lady Betty Compton', he said, 'has hoped I would not this very minute, which, next to her asking the contrary is the thing not to be refused') and so he sat down to write a long letter to the Countess of Upper Ossory.

There will, I fear [he wrote] be much blood spilt before peace is restored. . . . The Justices dare not act. . . . Yet I assure your ladyship there is no panic. Lady Aylesbury has been at the play in the Haymarket, and the Duke of Gloucester and my four nieces at Ranelagh this evening. . . . As it is now three in the morning I shall try to get a little sleep if Lord George Macbeth has not murdered it all.

But if he did sleep poor Susan Burney did not.

On going into the Observatory [she wrote in her Journal] we saw a yet more lamentable and shocking appearance than that of the preceding evening. Such a fire I never beheld as one of four that was burning with violence at that time. We afterwards found it was the house of a great distiller on Holborn Hill, which, as he was a Papist, was set on fire, and that the flames communicated very quickly to a prodigious number of small houses adjoining.

 We now found that we were in the most imminent danger ourselves, that our house would be burned or pillaged, in all probability, and that inevitable ruin must follow to my beloved father, and to all that belong to him. The Chapel on one side of our house, Porter's house at the back of it, the Pawnbroker's on the other side, Mr. Drummond's in Leicester Fields, and the house nearly opposite to us, at the corner of Blue Cross Street, were all destined to the flames, and there was not the slightest reason to hope that our house encircled by so many fires, should escape.

All these fires 'and more', Susan's father wrote in a letter to his friend Twining the following Sunday, 'furnished a sight from my Observatory, particularly that of the distillery, which surpassed the appearance of Mount Vesuvius in all its fury.'

 Viewing the same horrifying scene from the top of his house in Downing Street, Lord North was in his usual imperturbable good humour. 'I am not,' he said nodding at one of his heavily armed dinner guests, 'half so much afraid of the mob as of Jack St. John's pistol.'

 The mob had made an attack on Downing Street a few hours earlier, but had been furiously charged out of the way by a troop of the Queen's Light Dragoons under command of Lieutenant David Howell who had reported that 'three men were cut by the Dragoons under my command but I believe no lives lost'. And the Prime Minister's house since then had been safe.

 Lord North had asked to dinner that evening Sir John Macpherson, a future Governor-General of India who had passed on to him a warning of the intended attack upon the Bank which Macpherson had received from Count Maltzan, the Prussian Minister. After dinner the Prime Minister, Macpherson, St. John and three other guests, Mr. Eden, General Simon Fraser and Colonel North, had gone up to the roof to get a better view of the fires which were reflected so luridly in the panes of the dining-room windows.

'You see, Macpherson', said Lord North with cheerful understatement, 'here is much confusion.' And then a little later in more serious mood he asked him: 'What is your opinion for the remedy of this evil?'

'I should try, my Lord, to effect a junction with the Heads of the Opposition for the protection of the Country.' But this suggestion did not please Lord North. 'It is not practicable', he said; and they went downstairs to finish their port.

Others, however, less well guarded than the Prime Minister found it difficult to take so calmly philosophical a view of their predicament.

It was true, as Walpole said, that there was no panic. Charlotte Burney writing to Fanny at Bath told her that on Wednesday evening there were 'a number of exceedingly genteel people at Ranelagh, though they knew not but that their houses might be on fire at the time'.

But most families, and the Burneys among them, thought of leaving town and many did.[1] 'My mother', Susan Burney wrote, 'who looked jaundiced with terror, wanted us all to set off instantly for Chessington.' But they decided not to go since their house, they thought, 'had it escaped the flames, would then have been probably emptied of its contents by the late Newgate prisoners and their friends.'

Frederic Reynolds's father, however, was one of those who joined this 'largest exodus since the plague'.

> On Wednesday [his son wrote] he put one hundred and fifty guineas into his pocket, and took us all with him to Southbarrow; where, after dinner, he said if the rabble continued to rule, he would in a day or two, depart for France—'A wise country', he added, 'where the Government was not in the people!'

> Jack agreed with him, and both he and my father continued vehemently to inveigh against a democracy, until the former unluckily hinted that he

[1] 'You cannot conceive', Lord Jersey wrote, 'how families have been leaving this hazardous spot.' It became almost impossible to hire a coach. Five guineas was refused by one coachman for taking a family less than ten miles. Many of those who did not leave town spent the nights in houses less exposed, they thought, than their own. The Duchess of Devonshire left Devonshire House every night and slept on a camp bed at Lord Clermont's in Berkeley Square.

thought the cause of the riots had commenced with the cry of 'Wilkes and Liberty!' My father felt the rebuke and rising abruptly from his chair, cried angrily to Jack, 'Either you or I leave this room.'

'I know my duty, Sir', replied my eccentric brother and walked out humming 'God Save the King'.

Those families who did not, like the Reynolds, go to the country, did at least send away their more valuable belongings. 'There was not, I believe', Doctor Burney thought, 'during this day and night, a thinking or sober inhabitant in any part of the town who was a housekeeper, or in possession of anything valuable, that thought himself safe. Everyone moved his papers and most valuable effects to the dwelling of some friend, whose situation was equally dangerous; for what street or quarter of the town could be found without a Justice of the Peace, a Judge, a Minister of State, an Ambassador, a Bishop or a Roman Catholic!'

The Burneys decided to send their things, Susan wrote,

to the Boyles', my sister's and Mr. Kerwan's which all seemed less exposed than our own. . . . Accordingly our plate was packed up and my father himself went in a coach with it to the Boyles. When he returned home I assisted him to pack up his MS. papers in large bags, which we sent by William in our coach, to my sister's where they were taken in.

We now sent a second coachful with my father's cloathes, my mother's and some other portable things. But William soon came back with all the things he had taken in the second journey and told us that Tavistock Street was so full of rioters, who were knocking at several doors with great fury, that he thought it was not safe to carry them into Mr. Burney's house.

The rioters, whom William had seen in Tavistock Street, were making a compulsory collection among the householders for the 'poor prisoners' they had released from Newgate and the other gaols. 'Everybody gave half-crowns and some more.' In other streets where gangs of rioters went from door to door levying donations for the prisoners, they marked the doors with symbols like those used by tramps and gipsies to indicate the sort of reception they had received. O meant that the contribution had been poor; Ŏ that a contribution had been refused and that the house should later be destroyed; ✓ that the donation had been generous and that it might be worth while returning; ⊙⊙that there was a woman in the house.

Many of the poor prisoners, for whom allegedly the money

collected was destined, were indeed in a sorry way and could well have found a use for it. The more hardened among them made the most of their freedom and the opportunities for plunder and violence it afforded them, but others wandered aimlessly about, hungry, homeless and afraid. Hundreds tried to give themselves up but could find no one who would be responsible for them.[1] Hundreds more, so drunk they scarcely knew what they were about, attacked with screams and yells the shells of their former homes; in the streets around Newgate were scores of convicts. who would not have been out of place in Bedlam, waiting to be divested of that freedom which had come so suddenly and frighteningly to them. Newgate may have been the 'foulest place on earth' but outside its familiar walls that strange, unwelcoming world was now more terrifying than ever.

At just before four o'clock in the morning the Bank was attacked for the third time. The rioters had got hold of some muskets and rushed up Threadneedle Street with a wild and desperate courage, firing as they ran. The defending troops waited until the last moment and then opened fire with a deafening volley. About eight of the attackers fell dead and many more were wounded. The second rank of rioters stood hesitantly for a moment behind their writhing comrades. Making use of this momentary advantage the Horse Guards from one side and a platoon of Light Infantry from the other charged the uncertain and shaken rioters with so obvious a determination that they, although so confident and so reckless a minute before, fell back and ran for their lives.

As the retreating rioters raced down Fish Street Hill towards the river they were beaten back into the side streets by heavy fire from St. Magnus's Churchyard and Globe Alley. For by now Lord Amherst had followed the advice of several officers under his command and had stationed strong forces on the bridges across the Thames. Colonel Stuart was one of those who had appreciated how essential this step was. Criticizing Lord Amherst's conduct of the operations he mentioned in a letter to his father the advisability of securing the bridges.

[1] The keepers of prisons whose accommodation was not completely burned out and who could have accepted prisoners back refused to accept even those who voluntarily surrendered themselves. A press gang which had caught a murderer in the very act of sawing up the trunk of his wife's body, off which he had already sawn the head and hands, could not persuade the Keeper of New Prison, Clerkenwell to take him in. Eventually they persuaded him, but he sulkily told them he would not have accepted any of his former inmates.

You will think it strange [he wrote] that Lord Amherst out of near 12,000
men should have only 300 men in the City, besides those stationed at and not
to leave the Tower; but such was the case, and so alarming did it appear to
me that I could not help proposing a Plan to my Uncle for the Defence of
this side of the River, and he insisted on my stating it to Lord Hillsborough.
That these three bridges should be held with considerable Detachments and
a Cannon, that the Tower should cover the right Flank, the Parks the left; in
the Parks two thousand men; on the six stations between, a thousand men at
each.

Other officers strongly urged Lord Hillsborough to pass on this
suggestion for London's defence to Lord Amherst. And eventually,
with some reluctance, for he was interfering in matters not properly
his concern, he was persuaded to write to the Commander-in-Chief.
'It is recommended to your Lordship', he had told him, 'to secure the
Surrey ends of London and Blackfriars Bridges directly. . . . Securing
these two passes would effectually prevent the Junction of the Mobs.
. . . I submit this from Colonel Onslow.'

Lord Amherst had taken the advice and in the early hours of Thursday morning had ordered large numbers of troops to move into positions on both London and Blackfriars Bridges and a smaller force to
secure the approaches to Westminster Bridge. It was a turning point
in the battle.

10

ONCE again on Thursday morning the sightseers were out in their thousands as soon as the sun was up. One of them was William Hickey who rode out after breakfast in the carriage of his friend Bob Pott, accompanied by Pott's mistress, the cold and beautiful Emily Warren.

Emily Warren's first lover had found her at the age of twelve, and extremely beautiful even then, leading her blind father through the streets begging. She was now one of the most famous courtesans in London. She could neither read nor write; she was greedy, selfish, calculating, vain and irritable; and in bed she was passionless. But she was intelligent and amusing. She could talk well and her overwhelming loveliness assured her the constant devotion of her admirers. Bob Pott who, at the moment, kept her, paid for her house and let her use his carriage with his coat of arms emblazoned on the doors, was the only man for whom she had much cared. He was at the time away on business in Bengal and knowing that Hickey was her lover's close friend she had consented, after repeated blandishments, that he should go to bed with her. And it was with a consequent sense of pride that Hickey ventured out that day in her well-advertised company 'to view the scenes of desolation and enmity committed by the rioters'. He found them 'dreadful and shocking to behold'. He saw the ruins of Langdale's distillery[1], the King's Bench, Fleet and Newgate Prisons and the toll houses on Blackfriars Bridge. 'The city and suburbs', he noticed, were filled 'with the military'. Everywhere he went there were soldiers. There was a large camp now in St. George's Fields in addition to the ones in St. James's Park, Hyde Park and in the gardens of the Museum.

London, in fact, was beginning to look like a strongly defended

[1] Langdale's loss was subsequently estimated as being more than £100,000.

garrison. 'What!' exclaimed Reynolds's father when he heard of these military camps and had forgotten his sentiments of the night before. 'Do we live in Turkey? Are the free people to be *dragooned* out of their independence?'

Others were not so full of this conscientious 'patriotic enthusiasm', and were thankful enough to be surrounded by soldiers, whatever constitutional precedents might be involved. Doctor Burney was one of them. He went out early, Susan wrote,

> into the city on foot and visited every spot where the Rioters had been most busy. He saw the ruins of Newgate, where everybody went in and out as freely as they walk under the Piazzas in Covent Garden—went to the Bank, which had been attempted to be broke into three times the preceding evening but was fortunately preserved by the soldiers. He took some money in order, dear soul, to pay everybody to whom he owed anything while he had anything to give them. For this purpose he went to Mr. Bremner's and Mr. Coutts's. 'If we must be ruined' said he, 'at least I will have the satisfaction of not owing a guinea in the world.' He then visited Lord Townshend and freely spoke his opinion as to the necessity of some spirited exertion in the King or Ministers to put a stop to the horrid proceedings of a set of lawless, daring and inhuman ruffians.

Henry Angelo was also out early. He went to see the ruins in Bloomsbury Square and then went to Holborn

> where one shocking sight followed another. The first appearance of the ravages of the preceding night, was at Langdale's distillery, in Holborn; the inside of the house was consumed, and several dead bodies were lying near; the greater part of those who had made themselves drunk in his premises. As I walked on towards Snowhill, I saw several bodies on each side of the street, whether dead or drunk, I did not stop to inquire, the crowd behind pushing all before them.

These piles of bodies lying about in Holborn, with blackened, roasted faces caked with dry blood, fascinated the excited, pushing crowds of people who looked at them with that glint of horrified satisfaction which comes to the eyes of those who contemplate the twisted, sickening aspect of corpses caught in the unnatural postures of violent death. 'Some hundreds,' Walpole wrote, 'are actually dead about the street with the spirits they plundered at the distiller's; the low women knelt and sucked them as they ran from the staved casks.'

Down by the river, scores of inexplicable bodies, which had fallen
or been thrown into a boat beneath Blackfriars Bridge the previous
night, and had been prevented from floating out to sea by a waterman
at Puddle Dock Stairs, were laid out in rows on Dung Wharf. Nearby
hundreds of men and women were frantically rummaging for half-
pennies amongst the ruins of the toll gatherers' houses on the bridge up-
stream, under the eyes of a platoon of militia too weary to prevent them.

Occasional shots could be heard in different parts of the town,
where gangs of desperadoes had made strongholds among the ruins or
on roof-tops, from which they opened fire whenever the red coat of
a soldier appeared; but apart from this sporadic firing and the infre-
quent shout of a military command, all seemed strangely and un-
nervingly quiet as the sightseers continued their grisly perambulation
among the bodies and the softly smoking ruins.

Remembering how similarly quiet it had been during the morning
of the day before, the Privy Councillors came to attend a meeting at
St. James's in anxious mood. Many of them immediately and strongly
advocated the proclamation of unconditional martial law. It was, however, eventually decided not to take so drastic and uncompromising a
step but to affirm the soldiers' authority to act entirely upon their own
discretion. The difference between this and martial law was a small
one, but there was a difference in law and thus no unfortunate precedents for the casual enforcement of military rule were created. The
Courts of Justice were theoretically to stay open.

Few people doubted, nevertheless, that the fatal step had been taken.
So general in fact was the belief that within a few hours the Government felt obliged to put out handbills on the streets proclaiming their
innocence of having committed so unconstitutional a sin.

Whereas [the handbills read] some ill-designing and malicious persons
have published, for the purpose of disquieting the minds of His Majesty's
faithful subjects, that it is intended to try the Prisoners now in custody by
martial law; Notice is given by authority that no such purpose or intention
has ever been in the contemplation of Government; but that the said prisoners
will be tried by the due course of law as expeditiously as may be.[1]

[1] Another handbill circulated in the town on Thursday 'earnestly requested of
all peaceable and well-disposed persons (as well Protestants associated as others)
that they will abstain from wearing BLUE COCKADES as these ensigns are now
assumed by a set of miscreants whose purpose is to burn this city and plunder its
inhabitants'. Employers were asked in another handbill not to employ men
wearing blue cockades.

Although this may well have been the Government's intention, more than one newspaper reported that on Thursday afternoon several rioters were court martialled before a Military Judge Advocate and ordered to be executed; and a man was seen hanged from a lamp-post in Cheapside and two others in Southwark. More angered than intimidated by the excessive zeal now displayed by the military, a gang of rioters refreshed by a morning's rest collected at about five o'clock on Fleet Bridge, shouting curses and threats at the murdering soldiers. Some carried cutlasses, others bars, nearly all of them held bottles and were more than a little drunk. They swore they would cut to pieces the next lot of soldiers they saw.

Soon after six a troop of Horse Guards, under command of a young ensign named Marjoribanks, trotted down Fleet Street towards the Bank to relieve the guard which had been on duty there all day. At sight of them bobbing proudly and complacently along, the rioters gave a ferocious cheer and charged headlong down Fleet Street towards them. The Horse Guards issued with muskets which were strange to them were not given time to load before the rioters were upon them, but they lashed out so furiously with their bayonets that twenty of the rioters fell dead almost at the moment of impact. Thirty-five others were wounded and were taken off to the hospital where several died within the hour. Of the soldiers, only Marjoribanks himself and three of his men were wounded. Mrs. Conway's footman who was delivering a message at Lord Amherst's saw the Guards when they came back to make their report and told Walpole that their bayonets 'were steeped in blood'.

The news of the short ferocious fight spread quickly and by half-past six a crowd had gathered to see the Fleet Street cobbles 'awash with fresh blood'. Expecting that this latest clash heralded another night of violence and destruction, the standing guards at the Palaces and public buildings were alerted and told to stand to. In addition to the buildings threatened on previous days, on Thursday, Greenwich Hospital, the Customs House, the Navy Pay Office, the South Sea House, and the offices of the East India Company all received warning of destruction and had consequently sent messages to the Commander-in-Chief earnestly begging for protection. Lord Amherst with more troops at his disposal than on former days, and relying on civilian vigilante patrols to safeguard the streets, was able to send troops wherever they were thought to be needed. By eight o'clock there was scarcely a building of importance in London which was unguarded. Private houses as well as public buildings were full of soldiers. Lord Rockingham's house in Grosvenor Square, Burlington House, Bedford House, and Marlborough House resembled barracks 'with a soldier's hat at every window'. The courtyard in front of Leicester House was like a drill ground.

In the streets detachments of the London Military Association and other voluntary civilian bands patrolled about, some silent and grim, others laughing, but all 'animated by the example of the regulars', with a determination which was unmistakable. Most of these patrols were small, but a few were almost the size of a regiment.[1]

The larger of the patrolling bands undertook not only to fire on 'any four persons collected together who will not instantly disperse' but also to search any buildings where it was thought rioters or escaped prisoners might be hiding. A member of one of these patrols searching the higgledy-piggledy, ramshackle warren of slum tenements and courts and alleys between Field Lane and Union Court north of Holborn Bridge discovered how easy it was for an escaped prisoner to avoid detection in this part of London.

> The houses [he wrote] are divided from top to bottom into many compartments with doors of communication in each and also with adjacent houses, some having two to four doors opening into different alleys. In many of the rooms I saw eight to ten men in bed, in others as many women. The peace-officers and the keepers of these houses appeared to be well acquainted with each other and on terms which rather shocked us. Our jealousy increased the more as these officers insisted there could be no motive for going into certain houses, although from them we brought away the most suspected persons.

In spite of the reluctance of the peace-officers to give these irregular bands any help or encouragement they had by nightfall taken into their custody several hundred suspected men and women. And it was undoubtedly due to the obvious determination of the ordinary citizens

---

[1] In Cripplegate Ward, *The General and New Daily Advertiser* reported, two thousand inhabitants were under arms and in Clerkenwell there were even more. The borough of Southwark according to *The Morning Chronicle* was protected by a posse of over three thousand men, some of whom were on horseback. The parishioners of St. Sepulchre's, close to Newgate Prison, formed a patrol of their own and marched up and down singing hymns while the inhabitants of St. Paul's, Covent Garden 'unanimously resolved each man with his servants to defend his own and his neighbour's house'.

of London, who, after a week of nervous uncertainty, were now resolved to defend not only themselves and their property but also the
lives and properties of their fellow Londoners, whoever they might be
and whatever their religion or race, that the young Pitt was able to
assure his anxious mother that 'everything seems likely to subside'.

There were, of course, disturbances on Thursday night. A gang
broke into the premises of a silk dyer in Spitalfields and stole four
hundred pounds worth of silk; twenty sponging houses were burned
down in Southwark and at Newgate a hundred men were arrested as
they were setting fire to those cells which had escaped the fire on
Tuesday. But these were minor affairs. There was nothing on Thursday
night to compare with the horrors of the night before. 'A sudden calm'
had come over the town, Lord Jersey reported with relief to the
Countess Spencer the following day, 'and the night was perfectly
quiet'. *The General and New Daily Advertiser* went further and suggested that the calm would now be lasting. 'From appearances last night',
it commented on Friday morning, 'we have reason to hope that no
further depredations will be committed.'

The hope was largely justified. Throughout Friday and the following days, the Government took steps to tighten the grip which it had
at last, and at such cost, regained. Troops were still coming into the
town to maintain and intensify its 'war-like appearance'. 'The patroles
of cavalry', Wraxall wrote, 'stationed in the squares and great streets
throughout the West End gave London the aspect of a garrison.' And
Coutts, the banker, remembered with regret how military the City
looked with 'soldiers instead of merchants on the Royal Exchange;
red coats instead of black in St. Paul's'.

Encouraged by this display of military power, and their fears apparently dispelled by what the *Public Advertiser* termed the 'silence,
decency and tranquillity' of the streets, more and more people wished
to associate themselves for the preservation of the peace. Lord Amherst
received numerous applications from such now conscientiously public-
spirited people, wishing to form authorized bands to enjoy a little brief
authority and to protect themselves and their 'neighbours against a
renewal of the mischiefs so recently experienced from a lawless and
licentious banditti'.

The Commander-in-Chief who would have been thankful for the
help of more irregular volunteers during the rioting was not convinced
that the necessity for them any longer existed. He was already having

difficulty in collecting the arms issued to those voluntary patrols already formed and was for that reason, if for no other, anxious to avoid the formation of others. 'No person', he wrote to Colonel Twistleton, 'can bear arms in this country but under officers having the King's Commission. The using of firearms is improper, unnecessary and cannot be approved.'

The regular troops and the militia were, he thought, quite strong enough to maintain the peace and to organize the capture of the escaped convicts. And he was right. For although on Thursday morning there were nearly two thousand convicts at large, they were, during the following days, arrested without trouble in their hundreds and imprisoned in sheds, which had been quickly erected for their benefit amidst the ruins of the King's Bench and in St. Paul's Churchyard. Several hundred people who were suspected of having taken a leading part in the riots were also arrested, but Colonel Stuart who saw some of them in Wood Street Compter, the Poultry Compter and the Artillery Ground doubted that they could be considered ringleaders.

'I have seen the prisoners', he told the Earl of Bute, 'and am sorry to add that they all appear too wretched to have been the schemers of so deep and well conducted a project.' They were mainly petty thieves and burglars who had seen in the riots an opportunity for the exercise of their slender talents and many of them were arrested as they were actually dividing up the plunder. A gang of over forty men were taken in St. Giles's as they were quarrelling over their spoils and were chained together arm to arm and marched off to Tothill Fields, Bridewell.

The rumours that these men were all to be tried by courts martial, and the reports of bodies already hanging from lamp-posts, alarmed the liberal-minded to such an extent that Lords Amherst, Hillsborough and Stormont were besieged with protests.[1] Although there is no evidence to suppose that the Government authorized these executions, or in fact any unassailable evidence that they took place at all, there is no doubt that the apprehension of those who feared there might be truth behind the reports was very real. George Cumberland wrote to his brother on Friday to tell him that there were strong rumours that more of the ringleaders were 'to be executed in different parts of the

---

[1] The public was further alarmed when *The General and New Daily Advertiser* reported on Saturday 'four out of fifteen prisoners taken to the Guard Room at St. James's were hanged in Hyde Park yesterday and the remainder are to be executed this morning on the parade in St. James's Park'.

city'. And Lord Amherst thought it necessary to write to Lord Stormont to tell him that 'the Recorder has been here to express his hopes of there being no intentions of trying the prisoners by Military Law; as report goes they are to be tryed and hanged immediately in the Park, and that he has most dreadful apprehensions of the consequences of it'. The Speaker also called on Lord Amherst to express his hope that there would be no 'necessity of military executions'.

Any ideas which might have been entertained were dropped. After Saturday no more military trials or executions were reported, and apart from the sight of soldiers everywhere and the blackened gutted ruins, the town began to return to normal.

As was to be expected after such a dangerous and frightening week, the people greeted its ending with that excited, bubbling enthusiasm which is near to hysteria. The conduct of the inhabitants of Farringdon Ward Without was typical of the extravagant behaviour of most Londoners, boisterous in their relief. At a rowdy meeting, called to discuss the methods which should be adopted to make life comfortable for the soldiers stationed in their ward, the people of Farringdon, happy and generous, resolved that the military should not only have every assistance but should be 'properly accommodated and entertained' at the Ward's expense. A table was ordered for the officers in a tavern near to St. Paul's, while every soldier was to have each day a pound of meat and two pints of porter in addition to his ordinary ration. When the meeting broke up at six o'clock, bread and cheese and porter were ordered for all. At eight o'clock 'The Rev. Doctor Douglas', so *The Morning Chronicle* reported, 'waited upon the officers and showed them into several appartments of the church which were allotted them for their accommodation.' He ordered 'a handsome supper' from an adjoining tavern which the officers, 'some of the principal inhabitants and the Reverend Doctor sat down to under the Great West Portico. The Light Horse were assembled within the rails in the front of the church and every man had some cold meat and some porter given him.' And when it was dark and everyone was full of food and a little drunk the festivities were marked by the formal firing of two rockets, followed by a display of fireworks.

So general, in fact, did these firework displays and illuminations become during the next week, that when on the 15th news was received from America that British forces had won a minor victory in South Carolina, the Government thought it necessary to publish in the papers notices in which it was 'earnestly recommended to all persons to forbear such demonstrations as they might tend to affect the Public Peace'.

Nevertheless the following day the newspapers reported a night of celebrations and the firing of rockets from Blackfriars Bridge.

The rejoicing, however, was far from general. For many the news of a success in America served only as a saddening reminder of a disastrous war temporarily forgotten, while victory over the rioters gave to many others not so much a reason for celebration as a cause and opportunity for anxious thought. For who, after all, were the rioters, and what had they really been rioting about? There could be no doubt, it was agreed, that after the first few days religion had become no more than a pretext and later on not even that. The frightening ease with which the 'scum', as Edward Gibbon called them, 'boiled up to the surface in the huge cauldron' and took over the town was the more alarming because who could say that it would not happen again? Suggestions to introduce a paid police force were met, in spite of all that had happened, with a horrified reception by 'your true Englishman' who as Doctor Burney perspicaciously remarked was 'never so happy as under a bad government' and who would undoubtedly agree with Fox's contention that it was better to 'be governed by a mob than a standing army'.[1] 'I will lay you a wager', Burney told Twining, 'that when the House meets you will have fine orations against calling in the military'. And, of course, there were.

For days the arguments in both Houses went on. 'There is', Walpole told Mason, 'a universal anarchy of opinion; no three men agree on any three propositions. Lord Shelburne and Lord Rockingham are bitter enemies. Burke is mad for toleration. The Duke of Richmond and Charles Fox agree with him on that point; while the Duke is as violent for annual parliaments as the Rockinghams against them. Lord Shelburne and Lord Camden are as strongly anti-papistic.'

When during a debate the Duke of Manchester attacked the Government for authorizing the military to fire on civilians, Lord Mansfield rose and although, according to Stormont, quite unprepared to speak that day, made a long, fluent and uncharacteristically emotional speech in justification of the Government's action.

[1] Although the riots had made obvious the necessity for an efficient police force it was not for many years that these prejudices were overcome. In 1796 there were still only 149 full-time paid peace officers.

My Lords [he said] we have not been living under martial law but under that law which it has long been my sacred function to administer. . . . It has been imagined that the military cannot act, whatever crimes may be committed in their sight, until an hour after . . . the Riot Act has been read. But the Riot Act only introduces a new offence—remaining an hour after the proclamation—without qualifying any pre-existing law or abridging the means which before existed for preventing or punishing crimes.

He pointed out that all citizens have a right and a duty to suppress riots and to do what they can to prevent the rioters committing felonious acts such as the burning of houses. Soldiers, he insisted, 'had this power and were bound by this duty as well as other men'. His sad excuse that he had not consulted his books for he had now 'no books to consult' brought from Walpole the disdainful comment that 'Lord Mansfield has risen like a phoenix from the flames, and vomits martial law, as if all law books were burned as well as his own'.

There is no doubt, however, that Lord Mansfield was voicing the opinion of most conservatives in London who felt that the Government had been fully justified in what it had done. 'Of what consequence', George Cumberland asked his clergyman brother in a letter written at the end of the week, 'is the destruction of twenty or thirty houses or the loss of fifty ragamuffins if the civil authority is strengthened by it?' Several former members of the Opposition also came round to this view. Lady Townshend, for instance, 'was so terrified by the times', said Walpole, 'that she talked the language of the Court instead of opposition.' This put Selwyn 'in mind of removed tradesmen who hang out a board with "Burned out over the way"'.

As the debates about the legality of the Government's action were continued day after day, the conversation in clubs and coffee houses, taverns and drawing-rooms came back again and again to that far more diverting topic—the riots themselves and what had caused them and most intriguing question of all, who had been behind them.

It was well known that at the beginning most of the more active and violent rioters were apprentices and girl prostitutes with 'plunder and drink their chief objects' and that 'half a dozen schoolmasters might have quelled the insurrection'.[1] It was also agreed that the self-confessed

[1]'If one could in decency laugh', Edmund Burke told Champion in a letter dated 7 June, 'From what was London' 'must not one laugh to see what I saw, a single boy of fifteen years at most in Queen Street mounted on a pent house demolishing a house with great zeal but much at his ease, and throwing the pieces to two boys still younger, who burnt them for their amusement; no one daring to obstruct them.'

Protestant Martyrs were fired more by brandy than by religious enthusiasm. 'The Pope need not be alarmed', Walpole told Sir Horace
Mann. 'The rioters thought much more of plundering those of their
own communion than his Holiness's flock.' And as the Reverend
Richard Cumberland quite rightly said, the frantically voiced 'fears
and dread of Popery' were often nothing but a 'Pretence for Violence'.

But after the first few days there was 'a different species of rioter' to
be observed. The young bullies and the street boys, the girl prostitutes
and the rowdy brothel maids were still there but amongst them, directing them and encouraging them were mány professional criminals,
and, more alarmingly, those well-dressed men who had so much disturbed the Archbishop of York. 'No mob', he told his son with sweep-
ing exaggeration, 'acted without a number of well-dressed men to
direct them.'

Exactly who these well-dressed men were was a matter of violent
debate. Many had no doubt that they were agents paid by the Opposition to bring down the Government with accusations of anarchy. 'De-
pend on it', Richard Cumberland wrote to his brother, 'the rioters were
encouraged and supported by that abandoned Party who have long
been diffusing the Seeds of Insurrection.' Many others were certain
that the French and Americans were to blame. 'I am convinced', Lord
Mountstuart wrote to his brother, 'that tho' the beginning of the
tumults was entirely owing to the Fanaticks, yet they had no notion of
the outrages being carried so far, and that the American emissaries took
the advantage of the mobbery once begun to carry their diabolical
purposes to the great extent they did.'

Lord Hertford's suggestion that the responsibility for the havoc
could be attributed in equal shares to the Opposition and 'foreign
enemies' was one which found much agreement.[1] 'I am convinced',
Mrs. Montagu wrote, 'our Ministers will not care to lay open the

---

[1] The notion that the French were responsible was kept alive by the assiduous
distributors of handbills. One of these headed 'NO FRENCH RIOTERS' circulated in
large numbers on Thursday and Friday read: 'This is to give notice that it now
appears that the horrible riots which have been committed in the City have been
promoted by French money. If the French are suffered by these means to prevail,
Popery will certanly be introduced.' That at least one member of the Government shared the general fear is shown by an order given to Admiral Geary
Commander-in-Chief at Portsmouth, on Wednesday night. The Admiral was
ordered to put to sea immediately 'for fear the enemy should take advantage of
our intestine commotions and attempt to land a body of troops on the Island'.

treachery of Persons of Consequence, but will content themselves with
hanging a few loose wretches. . . . As for the design to do mischief at
Woolwich, that must have had Americans and French for its author.'
Mr. Batt, a King's Counsel with Chambers in Lincoln's Inn, agreed
with her. 'American treachery and English treason', he told a Member
of Parliament, 'I believe are at the bottom of it, and religion is the pretext. However', he added nervously, 'say nothing of this beyond your
own family.'

Mr. Batt's fear that he might live to regret so damaging an accusation
was quite general.

Like many others he was certain that several influential City merchants, rich, unscrupulous and hard headed, bore a greater responsibility
for encouraging the riots than was ever proved. Believing the Government to be entirely out of sympathy with their business interests they
had been prepared to let hundreds of people be killed in their attempts
to bring about its downfall. Now that they had failed they were willing
to go to any lengths to prevent any proof of their responsibility coming
to light, and to follow the example of Wilkes in demonstrating a
change of heart.

> The fear that passes among the better sort of people in the City [Colonel
> Stuart told his father] surpasses description: they talk of whole streets where
> there are none but disaffected people. They mistrust one another and those I
> have conversed with generally agree that many very principal men among
> them are deeply concerned in the business; notwithstanding which we have
> not been able to make any discovery. . . . More and more are my apprehen-
> sions of the deep designs of artful people, but strange to tell the People well
> affected are so alarmed that they will not give any information lest their
> houses and property should suffer.[1]

As time went by the early fears and panic subsided. Mr. Coutts, the
Banker, sensibly wrote that although there was a 'notion prevailing
that there were many dark and dangerous plots at the bottom of these
riots', he did not really 'think there is any foundation for such ideas'.
James Boswell came to the same conclusion. 'Whatever some may
maintain', he was satisfied that 'there was no combination or plan either
domestic or foreign'. *The Gentleman's Magazine* decided that 'a blind

---

[1] Curious announcements in the Press lend emphasis to the reports of general
nervousness and distrust. The printer of *The Morning Chronicle* apologizing for the
'palpable defects of his paper' asked that nothing inflammatory in the way of
letters or articles should be sent to him in case they should 'inadvertently get into
his paper'.

and ignorant fury inflamed by drunkenness and seconded by the interested views of thieves and housebreakers has in fact been the cause of the whole commotion.' And Romilly concluded that there seemed 'no possibility that these momentous excesses were concerted beforehand, or that they formed part of any regular plan to overturn the Government. They appear to me to have been only the accidental effects of the ungovernable fury and licentiousness of a mob, who gathering courage from their numbers and who, having ventured on one daring act, found their only safety to lie in universal havoc and destruction.' 'It is impossible', Wraxall wrote, 'for the most prejudiced person without violating truth to accuse the Opposition of having had any participation as a body direct or indirect in these outrages.'

Walpole too agreed that there was no evidence to suppose that there had been a plot.

> The Court at first [he wrote to William Mason] had a mind to bestow a plot on France, Spain and the Americas, but now seem to abandon that plan. ... Some Americans, perhaps, taught by the lessons we have given them of burning houses, joined in the opportunity. ... France solicited by American agents might, as she used to do when teased by the Jacobites, contribute a little money or a few arms and some rogues, of whom she was willing to disburthen herself, but I do not imagine it was a branch of her political schemes to burn London. She would have had some force ready to pour in or distract us in some other quarter, while the army should be all drawn to the capital.

A week later he had decided that even this opportunist and underhand support by France and America was unlikely. 'Not a Frenchman, not an American', he told Sir Horace Mann, 'appears to have had a finger in a single outrage.'[1]

So the evidence of foreign guilt, so eagerly awaited was not forthcoming. Nor has it ever been discovered. There were hints certainly. The week after the riots ended the Master of the Dover Post Office reported to Sir Stanier Porter: 'In times of tumult like the present I think it my duty to inform you that not long since a passage vessel under the command of Mr. Sharp (who pretends to be a burgher of Holland tho' an inhabitant of this Town but a few weeks ago) sailed

---

[1] Benjamin Franklin, at one time supposed to have been involved, wrote a letter to the Secretary to the American Legation at Madrid on 17 June in which it appears he knew no more of the riots than he had been able to learn from newspapers and eye witnesses.

from Margate to Calais with a great number of people on board.' A similarly cryptic implication appeared in a letter to Lord Amherst from an officer who said that he had discovered in a house in Lambeth Butts, a group of suspicious-looking men 'in company with a French waterman and packed up for a voyage'. Hints like these, encouraged by rumours and embroidered by gossip and conjecture, were all that a sensation-hungry public had to go on for its proof of 'dark and dangerous plots' and its accounting for the behaviour of these curious well-dressed men and the attacks on public buildings.

The reasons for the appearance of these obvious gentlemen amongst the mob were undoubtedly less sinister than was generally supposed. The excitement of violence and the contemplation and encouragement of destruction, are not instinctive pleasures peculiar to the lower orders of society. Cock fights and dog fights, bull baiting and cat dropping afforded as much enjoyment to the rich as to the poor, as much sensual satisfaction and amusement to the well-bred as to the vulgar and indeed would do so still. Violence knows no frontiers of class or money. Education may train the mind but it cannot control the emotions. To insist that the assault on the Bank and other public buildings was proof of foreign influence was nonsense. The mob attacked the Bank because there was gold in it and because the rich both Catholic and Protestant had stored their valuables there, and the gentlemen joined in for the sheer thrill it afforded them. They were well-dressed and had presumably no need for money and so, the Archbishop of York and the others concluded, there must be some deep plot behind their actions. But they were not only well-dressed, they were also bored and idle, irresponsible and mostly drunk. They had no need for money but they felt an urgent need for the exhilaration of danger and for the satisfaction of a hunger for violence.

But if not then a foreign plot; if not a traitorous scheme of the Opposition which got out of hand; if, as Walpole said, religion and Lord George Gordon had only been godmothers to 'the shocking affair', what *had* caused it all? What had turned a relatively harmless religious demonstration into the most savage riots in English history? It is a question which has never been completely answered.

There is no single answer. One clue is afforded by the names of those whose houses were burned or who claimed compensation for the loss they had suffered. Murphy, Donovan, O'Hara, Flanagan, McNamara, Lebarty, O'Reilly, McCarthy and Conolly are all names which appear more than once in the records. The areas which suffered most extensively in the poorer districts were those which were known to be Irish quarters. 'I suppose', Burke said in a speech to his constituents later on in the year, 'there are not in London less than four or five thousand of [the Roman Catholic persuasion] from my country who do a great deal of the most laborious work in the metropolis; and they chiefly inhabit those quarters which were the principal theatre of the fury of the bigoted multitude.' This demonstration of prejudice against the wage-cutting, blacklegs of Irishmen, arose principally from economic causes rather than religious ones. There were also, however, prejudices which were more recognizably religious.

The English Catholics as well as the Irish were suspect, not only as members of a foreign and superstitious religion but as members of an exclusive and restrictive club, a sort of secret trade union, a closed shop. In hard times the Protestant employees of a Catholic employer were the first to go. When Langdale's and Malo's premises were attacked it was not as Roman Catholics that they were hated but as employers who were thought to be prejudiced in favour of Catholic labour.

When the mansions in Bloomsbury Square were attacked, it was not so much because Markham and Mansfield were believed to have shown undue sympathy for Catholic relief, but because the Archbishop of York and the Lord Chief Justice were representatives of a detested order. The prisons, the Inns of Court, the Bank and the houses of magistrates were all hated and assaulted as symbols of oppression, riches and dishonest power.

In later centuries historians were able to detect in the riots, a violent symptom of that quasi-revolutionary movement which was to end the political system of George III. But the rioters themselves were, of course, only indirectly concerned with this. They were interested in destruction, not reform.

The poor were in revolt against authority. For as long as any of them could remember they had been insulted, frustrated and ignored; the victims of laws specifically directed against them; the lower orders in a society which shamefully abused them. They rose up incoherently in protest, unprepared and inarticulate, unsure even themselves of what they wanted or hoped to attain. Encouraged by fanatics and criminals, reckless and drunken, they themselves became criminals, and died to no purpose which they could name, rebels without a cause and without a leader.

11

LOOK UPON THE PRISONER

THE man whom many of them had called their leader was in the Tower.

On Friday afternoon two King's Messengers, Mann and Stanley, had called at Lord George's house in Welbeck Street.

'If you are sure it is me you want', he had told them politely, 'I am ready to attend you.'

'They sealed the boxes containing his papers', Colonel Stuart told his father, 'and upon searching his person found a pocket pistol, and a large knife: the officers asked why he carried such weapons; he replied, "to defend myself against the Roman Catholics".'

Outside in the street, *The London Evening Post* reported, were 'the biggest number of guards ever to attend a state prisoner'. He was taken to the Horse Guards in a hackney coach, with the blinds drawn and with two guardsmen sitting on the roof and two officers in the coach with him. In front of the coach marched a company of infantry; behind it rode a whole regiment of Dragoons followed by a Colonel's Guard of the Horse Guards; at either side were three ranks of militiamen.

In the War Office he was examined by Lord North, Lord Amherst, the Secretaries of State and several Privy Councillors. 'He kept a tolerable good countenance', Lord Jersey said, 'and answered with great cunning all their questions.' The examination lasted more than four hours, and at half-past nine he was committed to the Tower.

The King's Messengers returned to his house to collect all the loose papers and letters they could find but, remembering what Wilkes had done with the men who had searched his house under authority of a general warrant, they dared not break open any drawers or cupboards and contented themselves with sealing the escritoires and bureaux.

Before they left they arrested the butler and old Mrs. Yond, the housekeeper on a charge of 'constructive treason' and took them back with them to Whitehall. The next morning they brought in for questioning before the Privy Council more likely traitors.

The first of these was Alderman Kennet. Lord Beauchamp, true to his angry threat, had complained of the Lord Mayor's conspicuous inactivity during the riots in Moorfields and his complaint was supported by Mr. Foley, a Member of Parliament who had also been present. Mr. Foley, called to repeat his complaint before the Privy Council, said that 'his Lordship appeared more like a spectator than a magistrate' and that he had done absolutely nothing to disperse the rioters. He was also charged with having released the prisoners taken during the riots without proper authority. A copy of the Bill of Releasement was produced and read out to the members of the Examining Committee. 'Whereas', the Bill announced, 'the undermentioned people were taken for a *supposed* Riot, the Mayor and Council think proper to release them.'

When Kennet was called to answer these charges he could not at first be found. 'Ring the bell', a Privy Councillor who knew of the Lord Mayor's origins suggested, 'and then Mr. Kennet will come as a matter of habit.'

He was eventually discovered dozing in a chair, as the morning was 'exceeding hot', and he came into the Councillors' presence, yawning and smelling of brandy. He excused himself by saying the 'rioters were so violent' that if he had interfered 'death would have been his portion'. He seemed to have 'no pain at declaring he thought fear a very sufficient excuse for his want of activity'.

The Privy Councillors, feeling that they had not sufficient grounds upon which to hold him dismissed him with contempt and he left them apparently quite unconcerned by their hostility and scorn.

James Fisher, the Secretary of the Protestant Association, was next examined but he too was dismissed after having tired the Councillors by long, evasive answers to the simplest questions. He had taken the precaution of destroying all his correspondence as soon as he heard of Lord George's arrest, and when his house was searched no evidence could be found upon which either he or the Treasurer of the Association could be held.

Unlucky in their search for likely and important scapegoats, apart from the 'lunatic apostle' himself, the Government began to advertise for less important culprits. Day after day advertisements appeared in the Press offering rewards of a hundred pounds each for information leading to the conviction of anyone who had encouraged or directed the rioters either by money or by 'Bells, Flags, and other Signals and Devices', or who had given warnings of 'Attempts and Preparations to suppress, resist or interrupt the said Riots'.

By these and other means the Government were able to swell the already large number of prisoners awaiting trial. The work of restoration and rebuilding of the burned-out prisons had scarcely begun and new sheds had to be erected in the courtyards of the King's Bench, the Fleet and Bridewell to accommodate the new arrivals. Anxious to begin the trials without delay, the Government instructed the Prosecution to treat the documentation of their evidence as a matter of extreme urgency. By 29 June the Old Bailey sessions had opened.

And once begun, the trials were rushed through at a speed which, even by eighteenth-century standards, was remarkable.

Within twelve days forty-four prisoners received sentences of death. The Old Bailey sessions ended on 11 July and during the Southwark Sessions which followed a further twenty-four prisoners were capitally convicted.

The trial reports reveal the Government's inability to find any of those 'very great people at the bottom of the riots', a single worth-while scapegoat. The prisoners, as Walpole said, were just a pack of boys and ruffians and 'a regiment of street walkers'. Among the pathetic motley of those condemned to death were two gipsies, a West Indian slave, a demented cross-eyed beggar, three abscess-covered climbing boys and a negro prostitute.

George Bawton, 'a poor drunken cobbler', was sentenced to death with William Brown for extorting money by threats. A witness deposed that he offered Bawton twopence when a contribution for the mob was demanded from him and that Brown, brandishing a knife, had said, 'I'll rip you up if you don't give us 6d.'

Denis Reardon was found guilty of murder. His wife had come home 'drunk as a lord', wearing a blue cockade and shouting 'No Popery!' He confessed to having been so enraged by her that he had cut off her head with a carving knife.

Enoch Foster, a strong man in a circus, was sentenced for having demonstrated his strength by throwing floorboards through the windows of a house in Whitechapel.

Edward Dennis, the hangman who plays so large a part in *Barnaby Rudge*, made a brief and contemptible appearance on 3 July when he was tried for having helped to pull down the house of Mr. Boggis in

New Turnstyle. Dennis admitted the charge but pleaded compulsion as the mob had threatened to burn him if he refused to help them. When he was arrested the Keeper of Tothills Bridewell refused to take him in, as he said the other prisoners would cut him up as soon as he got inside.

John Geary had raped two servant girls in a burning house in Moorfields and had left them there to roast while he had walked out wearing nothing but their bodices.

It was with the conviction of such creatures as these that the Government had to be content. Within a week of the end of the sessions eighteen of them were hanged, most of them upon the scenes of their crimes. All of them behaved well except a man who was drunk and kicked his boots off into the indignant faces of the people who had come to watch him swing, and a youth who screamed hysterically when the hangman pulled his blue cockade out of his lapel before fixing the rope round his neck.[1]

The case against the chief State prisoner did not proceed as quickly as that against his so-called 'minions'. The date of his trial was fixed for August and then postponed to September. When September came the Prosecution were still not ready and the date was again postponed.

While waiting in the Tower he was treated well enough. At first he had been kept in a 'dark dirty little apartment' and was not allowed either books to read or pen with which to write. All letters addressed to him were opened and read before being passed on to him. For the first fortnight he was allowed no visitors apart from members of his family, and they were permitted to stay for no longer than an hour at a time. During these visits his gaolers remained within earshot of every conversation. When he was ill his doctor was refused admittance until the Governor of the Tower received instructions from Lord North to allow him in.

Later on these strict rules were relaxed and although his visitors were still searched before being permitted to enter his cell, he could receive

[1] It is impossible now to say how many people in all lost their lives because of the riots. Twenty-one people are known to have been executed and the Government admitted that 285 rioters were killed by the troops and 173 wounded. It was subsequently acknowledged that these numbers were an under-estimate. Wraxall believed that in all over seven hundred people were killed. Allowing for the exaggeration in the accounts of eyewitnesses and journalists and taking into account the military reports in the Public Record Office the figure seems probably to have been not less than 850.

whom he wished for as long as he liked. Frequent visitors were John Greenwood, an auctioneer whose sale-rooms in the Haymarket had been used by the Protestant Association for their meetings, and William Bailston an American who had taken a prominent part in the Boston Tea Party. Both Greenwood and Bailston were friends of Dr. Franklin and both were known to carry secret letters for him, a circumstance which once more sent the rumours flying that Lord George was an American agent and the riots an American plot. In view of these rumours, the Governor of the Tower thought it advisable to forbid his prisoner to talk to 'Citizen Laurens who had been President of the American Congress and who on his way to Holland in quality of Minister Plenipotentiary had been taken prisoner' and also committed to his charge. Lord George had met Laurens one evening while taking his exercise round the ramparts and had had a long conversation with him, but after that one meeting he was not allowed to see him or to talk to him again.

Another visitor less suspect than the Americans was John Wesley. On one occasion 'I spent an hour with him at his apartment in the Tower', Wesley wrote in his Journal. 'Our conversation turned upon Popery and religion. He seemed to be well acquainted with the Bible and had abundance of other books, enough to furnish a study. I was agreeably surprised to find he did not complain of any person or thing, and cannot but hope his confinement will take a right turn and prove a lasting blessing to him.'

Ten days later Wesley saw the indictment of the Grand Jury against him and 'stood aghast. What a shocking insult upon truth and common sense! But it is the usual form. The more is the shame. Why will not the parliament remove this scandal from our nation?'

The sentiment was not exceptional. It was now nearly the end of December. Lord George had been in the Tower for more than six months. Tempers were cooling and memories beginning to fade. 'I believe Lord George Gordon has prevented infinitely more mischief than he has done', Mrs. Montagu wrote to her sister. 'I look upon him as a Political conductor, he has brought down the electrical matter which threatened our whole state.' And in another letter she repeated the simile. 'I consider Lord George as a state electric conductor. . . . His Lordship has wonderfully purged the ill-humour of his fellow subjects and I hope in a great degree cured the epidemical democratick madness. The word petition now obtains nowhere, the word association cannot assemble a dozen people. We are coming to our right senses. . . . The gathering storm which threatened our strongest, noblest and most venerable edifices has by him been brought down and sunk into the earth before it burst on our heads, he has indeed buried it under the gallows.'

Even Walpole, who did not 'care a straw about Lord George Gordon', admitted that he could not find it in his heart to exclude him from his invariable pity for a man on trial for his life and wished, as always, that the 'condemned man might escape'.

In spite of the change in public opinion, however, few people supposed that Lord George would in fact escape. He 'will probably suffer', Lord Hillsborough thought, expressing the general view.

Being a relatively poor man[1] he could not himself afford a famous and expensive counsel, but sympathetic friends and relations, anxious to do what they could to secure an acquittal, contributed over £3,000 towards the costs of his defence. And by adding to this sum part of his own capital he was enabled to choose a man at the top of his profession.

The natural choice was Lloyd Kenyon. Kenyon was a lawyer whose quick and brilliant mind and whose remarkable knowledge of the law were the admiration of his profession. He was one of the most highly paid barristers of his generation. His income in 1780 was well over £6,000 and his services were constantly and increasingly in demand. He had, however, little experience of criminal courts and his 'utterance thick and hurried' and his cold detachment made his speeches to the jury ineffective. A Junior more passionate, more human, would, it was felt, have to be found to counterbalance this hard and vaguely suspect brilliance. The man to instruct was clearly Thomas Erskine, Lord George's cousin.

Erskine like Gordon had been in the navy but he had transferred to the army when he was nineteen and had, in fact, not long resigned his commission when he accepted his countryman's defence. He was extremely good looking,[2] popular, elegant and witty but he had beneath this superficial gaiety and charm a mind of acute shrewdness and a

---

[1] He received, of course, no salary either as a Member of Parliament or as President of the Protestant Association. He had an allowance from his brother of £500 a year and about £5,000 capital.

[2] His features and complexion were so delicate that when his regiment was stationed at Harrogate, Mrs. More, a beautiful and amusing friend of his family, persuaded him to dress up as a woman and to let her introduce him as such to all her friends. He spent a whole day disguised and was not suspected.

deeply religious sense. His father the Earl of Buchan, a strict Presbyterian, 'a zealously religious man, strong in his anti-Roman convictions' had successfully passed on these convictions to his son, who surprised his superior officers by preaching sermons to his men when his
fellow ensigns were out riding or drinking. He had much in common
with Gordon and the two young men were very fond of each other.
But the barrister felt obliged to tell his client that he did not think much
of his chances.

Arrayed against Kenyon and Erskine were seven distinguished counsel led by the Attorney-General. The judge was to be the Lord Chief
Justice.[1]

The date of the trial was fixed for 5 February and it seemed that at
last it really would take place. The cases for both the prosecution and
the defence were finally prepared, the witnesses had been briefed, the
jurors notified.

The day when it dawned was bitterly cold. At nine o'clock it began
to rain. But in spite of the weather the crowd in front of Westminster
Hall was enormous. Within less than a minute of the doors being
opened the courtroom was full. The spectators were packed as closely
'as the bale goods in a ship' and at least one of them 'soon took himself
off rather than suffer death by suffocation'.

'The noble prisoner', as the newspapers called him, was a remarkable
figure. He stood there, tall and thin, in his black velvet suit and snow-
white stock, as apparently unconcerned by the curious staring eyes as
by his own predicament. His red hair was longer and more lank than
ever, his death-like convict's pallor emphasized by the sombre black-
ness of his clothes. He carried a Bible in one hand, his steel-rimmed
spectacles in the other. But he seemed, a journalist thought, to be in
good spirits and his dark blue eyes were bright and almost gay.

Between them he and his counsel challenged no less than nineteen of
the jurors; one of them Arthur Shakespear being challenged by Lord
George, to the delighted amusement of the court, as 'prejudiced by
interest' on account of his trade. He was a ropemaker.

The indictment in accordance with contemporary custom was extremely long and involved. Briefly it contended

that George Gordon, commonly called Lord George Gordon not having the
fear of God before his eyes but being seduced by the instigation of the devil

[1] 'Somehow or other', Walpole plaintively commented, 'the Constitution will
be brought in guilty for Lord Mansfield is the judge.'

on the second day of June unlawfully, maliciously and traitorously did compass imagine and intend to raise and levy war against our Lord the King. And
on the second day of June with a great multitude of persons, armed and
arrayed in a warlike manner (that is to say) with colours flying and with
clubs, bludgeons and staves and other warlike weapons did ordain, prepare
and levy publick war against the King. And between that day and the tenth
day of the same month did compass, imagine and intend to raise and levy
war, insurrection and rebellion against our said Lord the King.

To be guilty of such a charge could lead a man not merely to the
gallows but to an even more revolting and agonizing death. It was not
until 1814 that Sir Samuel Romilly brought in his 'Bill to alter the
punishment of High Treason'. Throughout the eighteenth century
'godly butchery' was still practised and a convicted traitor could be, and
sometimes was, sentenced 'to be taken from the prison and laid upon a
sledge or hurdle and drawn to the gallows or place of execution, and
then hanged by the neck until he be half dead, and then cut down; and
his entrails to be cut out of his body and burnt by the executioner; then
his head to be cut off, his body to be divided into quarters, and afterwards his head and quarters to be set up in some open places directed'.
As the son of a Duke, Lord George would be exempt from the extreme
horrors of this punishment which was, in fact, now rarely carried out
as fully as the law allowed even upon a commoner. But there were
more than a few men who, when hearing the charge, openly expressed
pleasure at the thought that death might not be considered punishment
enough.

The Attorney-General opened the case for the prosecution with a
calm and well-reasoned speech. He began by pointing out that to be
guilty of treason as specified in the indictment Lord George need not
be proved to have levied war against 'the *person* of the King'. If it could
be shown, and he intended to show, that the prisoner had levied war
against 'the *majesty* of the King' in order to 'effect by force an alteration
of the established law', that was enough, for that was high treason too.
He gave a short account of the penalties imposed upon Roman Catholics and of the provision of Sir George Savile's act; of the riots in Scotland and of the formation of the Protestant Associations. He was
reasonable, fair, dispassionate. He spoke of the prisoner's avowed un-
willingness to present the petition unless accompanied by twenty
thousand men and of his subsequent activities during the time of the
riots, dwelling particularly upon his conduct in the House of Com-

mons which was to be dealt with at length in the evidence which followed. Lord George refused, he said, to order the mob to disperse. 'It
was not safe for him to order them to stay and obstruct the proceedings
of the House in plain terms; but he did that which was equivalent; he
told them to be steady and persevere. He reminded them over and over
of the conduct of the Scotch'. On Tuesday, the Attorney-General went
on, the prisoner returned to the House wearing his blue cockade which
had now become the badge of insurrection and on Wednesday he sent
an advertisement to be inserted in Thursday's papers. 'Lord George
Gordon', the announcement ran, 'went in person to three different
places, when the tumults were subsisting, to harangue the mob and
exhort them to a peaceable and legal deportment; he stood for a considerable time among parties of foot soldiers, accompanied by one of
the London Sheriffs; but all this was without effect. *Lord George Gordon*', and here the Attorney-General broke off to look at the jury and to
emphasize each subsequent word—'*Lord George Gordon not being able to
give them any assurances that the act would be repealed.*'

It was evident, he concluded, that the prisoner supported and encouraged the mob throughout and went so far, as his witnesses would
prove, as to sign several papers ordering the mob to give protection to
certain favoured people.

When he sat down the prisoner's chance of acquittal seemed to most
spectators in the courtroom, more remote than ever. The Attorney
General's speech had been neither eloquent nor impassioned but it had
stated the facts quite clearly and the facts were damning enough in
themselves.

The first witness called by the prosecution was William Hay.
Examined by the Solicitor-General he deposed that he had attended
various meetings of the Protestant Association at Greenwood's Rooms
in Haymarket, 'The Old Crown and Rolls' in Chancery Lane, 'The
London Tavern' in Bishopsgate Street and St. Margaret's Hall, Southwark. At some of these meetings he had seen the prisoner. A few
evenings before the meeting in Coachmakers' Hall, he had been at 'The
Old Crown and Rolls' where Lord George had read out the Corona-
tion Oath and had said that in his opinion the King had broken it.
About a week later on 2 June he had been in the lobby of the House
of Commons where the great noise 'was generally occasioned by the
chiming of Lord George Gordon's name. Lord George Gordon's name
was the constant chime. The great noise appeared to me to be made by

chiming those words, Lord George Gordon.' He was an emphatic if repetitive witness.

'Did you', the Solicitor-General asked him, 'hear him say anything at that time?'

> *Hay:* 'Yes, he exhorted them "to continue steadfastly, to adhere to so good and glorious a cause as theirs was. He promised he would persevere in it himself, and he hoped, although there was very little expectation from the House of Commons, that they would meet with redress".'

Solicitor-General: 'Do you recollect anything else in particular?'

> *Hay:* 'That is the substance of everything I heard his Lordship say. I have repeated all the words that I thoroughly remember.'

> *One of the Jury:* 'Are you thoroughly satisfied that you have repeated the words of Lord George Gordon?'

> *Hay:* 'I am.'

Hay's evidence concluded with some revealing remarks concerning the conduct of the men at the burning of the foreign chapels on the Monday night. The men with blue cockades, he said, did not actually do the damage but stood by encouraging those who did.

He looked around him with a 'self-satisfied confident' air and his evidence was undoubtedly damaging. But before the Solicitor-General had sat down, Kenyon was on his feet. His cross-examination skilful and spirited, showed with what determination the defence were prepared to fight the case. It was an extremely effective object lesson in the difficult art of discrediting and ridiculing, without offence to the jury, an apparently assured and unbreakable witness.

He began politely: 'Pray what are you?'

Hay: 'By trade a printer.'

'Do you print on your own account or are you servant to any person?'

'I print on my own account.'

'I believe you had misfortunes in the world?. You were a bankrupt'?

'Yes.'

'When did you first resort to these meetings of the Protestant Association as they called themselves?'

'I said on the evening of the 10th of December.'

'Was that the first time?'

'Yes.'

'And you went from time to time to all the meetings that were held afterwards?'

'Yes, to the publick meetings.'

'You were at several places where Lord George did not attend?'

'Yes.'

'You have mentioned one place where Lord George was, at Greenwood's Rooms; now I desire you to recollect, and say, whether you saw him at Greenwood's Rooms?'

'I think I saw my Lord once there, and I was there once when he was not. I was there twice.'

'I caution you to be upon your guard.'

'I will. It is a very serious matter. I think Lord George was once at Greenwood's Rooms.'

'You cannot speak with certainty.'

'Unless I look at some notes I cannot tell. I have some notes here.'

'Did you make them at the time?'

'Yes, I made them that evening.'

'You may refresh your memory with them.'

'On the 21st of January Lord George Gordon was not, I find, present at Greenwood's.'

'Then you was mistaken in that part of your evidence?'

'I was mistaken.'

It was a minor triumph but there was a long pause before Kenyon asked his next question.

'How came you, from time to time, to make notes of what passed at these several meetings?'

'I shall be very free in telling you that I had an idea then, that this would be the consequence of these meetings. I went almost purposely to make notes of them.'

'How soon had you this foresight of what would happen? In the month of December you foresaw what would happen?'

'I did not. I said no such thing. I foresaw it on the 20th of February.'

'Then the 20th of February was the first time you began to draw your conclusions?'

'It was.'

'Then how came your notes and memorandums to have a date prior to that? You have notes so early as the 21st of January.'

Hay (*confusedly*): 'Without those notes, I could not come to that conclusion in my own mind about the consequences. I took notes on the 10th of December.'

'I must again return to the question I asked before. How came you first to take notes?'

'I wished to learn what those gentlemen would be at. I put down then what occurred, and then entered it down after I came home.'

'That is your constant course in all occurrences of life?'

'Yes.'

'Can you tell us any one occurrence of your life, when you have committed to writing everything that passed?'

'I do not know any one meeting of that kind when I have not put down as much as my memory would help me to.'

'How many meetings of this kind have you resorted to?'

'I never resorted to any others of this kind.'

'You said you never attended any meetings respecting this kind of business where you did not commit to writing what passed. Now I want to know: what other meeting beside the Protestant Association have you attended?'

'I have attended a great many meetings, but I cannot pretend to recite them.'

'Have you upon your oath, before God and your Country, put down everything that passed at those meetings?'

At this point Erskine noticed 'the sweat ran down his face'. The witness was confused and irritated and had for some minutes been shooting quick glances of appeal at the Solicitor-General and the Judge. It was due to Kenyon's skill that he was unsure where this questioning was leading to and how much he should admit.

Hay: 'I do not comprehend the nature of your question.'

'Have you set down any transactions at any other meetings, except those of the Protestant Association?'

'I have many times undoubtedly.'

'Tell me when and where.'

'The first notes I made in my life were in the General Assembly of the Church of Scotland, the very first church I ever was in in my life.'

'How long ago is that?'

'Twenty years ago.'

'Did you do that because you had a foresight of any ill consequences that would ensue from those meetings?'

'I wished to know what was going on there, or to oblige a friend to inform him what was doing.'

'You were not only at meetings of the Protestant Association that were advertised but happened casually to be at the chapel in Duke Street, at Mr. Langdale's, at a house burning in Lincoln's Inn, at a house burning in Great Queen Street and at Newgate?'

Kenyon spoke slowly, emphasizing the unlikely casualness of this sightseeing.

Hay: 'The first you mention was the burning the Roman Catholic chapel. I was coming home.'

'Coming home from where?'

'From Westminster.'

'From the lobby I suppose?'

Hay (with slight truculence): 'Very likely so.'

'At the time when you was in St. George's Fields had you a blue cockade in your hat?'

Hay (startled): 'I never had in my life.'

'You say you was in the lobby of the House of Commons.'

'I was.'

'Did you go into the lobby with persons who had blue cockades in their hats?'

'They were all there long before me.'

'The lobby is not a very large room. Were there a good many people of the same description as yourself, that were there merely from curiosity?'

'I saw none such. They did not come from curiosity.'

'Then you was the single individual, that stood distinguished from all the rest that was there?'

'There were more than I there. There was that man M'Millan and an apprentice of mine. I took them on purpose with me.'

'That they might be of what use?'

'I wanted to enquire after some particular friends. I was afraid they might be hurt. I was afraid of myself.'

'Being afraid of yourself, you went in the crowd in the lobby?'

'I was willing to see what they were about.'

'Which of your friends did you conceive to be in danger?'

'I cannot charge my memory with any particular friend.'

'You said Lord George Gordon desired they would meet at ten in the morning and put on their best clothes, or as you choose to put it "to be arrayed in their best clothes", which was the word as far as you can recollect?'

'I think it was "be sure to be *in* your best clothes" or "be dressed in your best clothes".'

'He gave orders they should be in four what—?'

'Divisions.'

'Columns you called them.'

'I said columns or divisions.'

'In St. George's Fields you were a considerable distance from Lord George. How near were you to the persons who carried the two flags?'

'I saw one of the flags carried by a constable on my left hand. I was in the road. I did not go into the fields.'

'The persons who carried the flags were I suppose surrounded by the rest of the multitude?'

'No they were not surrounded.'

'By what good luck did you happen to see the flag in Fleet Street? Where is your house?'

'Next St. Dunstan's Church. I was upon the leads upon purpose to see them.'

'One of the persons you saw with a flag in Fleet Street, you saw afterwards?'

'Yes, at the Fleet Prison. And at Westminster.'

'Can you describe his dress?'

'I cannot charge my memory. It was a dress not worth minding. A very common dress.'

'Had he his own hair or a wig?'

'If I recollect he had black hair. Shortish hair, I think.'

'Was there something remarkable about his hair?'

'No, I do not remember anything remarkable. He was a coarse-looking man. He appeared to me like a brewer's servant in his best clothes.'

Kenyon quickly took up this description knowing that it was a brewer's servant who had taken an active part in the attack on the Bank.

'How do you know a brewer's servant when he is in his best clothes from another man?'

'It is out of my power to describe it better than I do. He appeared to me to be such.'

'I ask you, by what mark do you distinguish a brewer's servant from another man?'

'There is something in a brewer's servant, different from other men.'

'There may be for what I know. But tell me how you distinguish a brewer's servant from another man?'

'Be so good as to state the question again.'

'If there can be any doubt what the question means in any one of this audience you shall have it repeated. I asked you by what mark you were able to distinguish a man to be a brewer's servant.'

'I think a brewer's servant's breeches, clothes, and stockings have something very distinguishing.'

'Tell me what in his breeches, and the cut of his coat and stockings it was by which you distinguish him?'

'I cannot swear to any particular mark.'

'Then you had no reason upon earth to use that word which came so flippant over your tongue that he was a brewer's servant?'

'I cannot answer that question if you put it to me a hundred times.'

'You said that one of the persons who carried one of the flags in St. George's Fields was a constable?'

'Yes.'

'How do you know he was a constable?'

'The man was very remarkable. His name is Payne. He is a City Constable.'

'Are you a Roman Catholic?'

'I am of the Church of England.'

'Did you inform the Secretaries of State or any civil magistrate of your apprehensions in February of what would happen?'

'Yes, I did communicate my fears then.'

'To whom?'

'A gentleman. I would rather not mention the gentleman's name.'

'But you must do.'

'I wrote my sentiments of these matters to a very particular friend.'

'You are asked who that particular friend is.'

'Mr. Butler of Lincoln's Inn.'

'Mr. Butler is a gentleman I have likewise the honour of knowing. Mr. Butler is I understand a Roman Catholic?'

'I never asked him the question.'

'If he is your particular friend, have you any doubt about it?'

'I have heard he is a Roman Catholic.'

'Have you the least doubt of his being a Roman Catholic?'

'I have heard he is. I will not answer the question.'

When Hay got down from the box he looked, so Erskine said afterwards, like a frightened rabbit. His former brash and rather quarrelsome manner had alienated the sympathy of the jury and Erskine was able confidently to refer to him in his speech the following morning as a 'dark Popish spy, the wretched abandoned Hay'. His evidence had certainly done a great deal more harm than good to the prosecution's case, but as the Attorney-General rose to call his next witness, he knew that his case had only just begun and that there was plenty of time yet to bring back the jury on to his side.

William Metcalf who now came into the box was as calm as Hay was agitated, as apparently disinterested as Hay was malicious. He had gone, he said, merely out of curiosity to Coachmakers' Hall and had heard the prisoner make a somewhat impassioned speech to his audience in which he had declared that 'he would not present the petition of a lukewarm people' and that he himself 'wished so well to the cause that he would go to the gallows for it'. Having established that Lord George's language at that last meeting of the Protestant Association had been, to say the least of it, indiscreet—a fact which the next witness corroborated—the prosecution turned to his behaviour in the House of Commons.

The Attorney-General hoped to show that his actions and speeches in the lobby of the House on the Friday were the cause of the acts of violence committed during the following week. The principal witness to the prisoner's outrageous behaviour on this occasion was the chaplain to the House, the Reverend Thomas Bowen, who had seen the prisoner several times during the day, had heard what he said to his supporters and had more than once tried to persuade him to get them to go home. Bowen told the Court of Gordon's having repeatedly come out of the House on to the gallery, to tell the crowd in the lobby below what was being said in the debating chamber. He told of his conversation with the prisoner in the dining-room of the House and of his enthusiastic introduction to the crowd of Sir Michael le Fleming who had spoken in support of the petitioners. 'He patted or stroked his shoulder', Bowen said, 'and expressed a kind of joy in his countenance which I hardly know how to describe; it seemed to me extravagant, and if I may use the expression, childish.' And, most damaging of all, he told of Gordon's reference to the success of the Scotch and of his refusal to suggest that the petitioners should go home, even after they themselves had asked him if they should. Bowen was not sure, he admitted, whether the prisoner had said, 'the Scotch had no redress till they pulled down the Mass houses', or 'When the Scotch pulled down the Mass houses they had redress.' But whichever it was the implication was the same.

After Bowen several witnesses were called to give evidence of the horrors of the riots themselves and great pains were taken by the examining counsel to associate the rioters with the Protestant petitioners. Much was made of the wearing of blue cockades. Justice William Hyde, in giving his evidence said that the gang of men who had attacked Lord Sandwich were all wearing blue cockades and shouting 'No Popery!' One of these men, 'a resolute, impudent fellow had a stick with a large head, with a leather apron or something twisted round the top of it. He said if they did not murder him, then he would himself before he had done with him.'

Lord Porchester was then called and said that Lord George was wearing a blue cockade when he came to the House on the Tuesday.

In fact the Attorney-General implied, through the evidence of his last witness, that the prisoner so much considered himself at the head of the rioters that he signed papers which gave protection to property. Richard Pond, who held a house on lease and who had a Roman Catholic as his sub-tenant, got Lord George to sign a paper which said: 'All true friends to Protestants I hope will be particular and do no injury to the property of any true Protestant as I am well assured the proprietor of this house is a staunch and worthy friend to the cause— G. Gordon.'

With Pond's evidence the prosecution closed their case, well aware that they had succeeded in repairing the damage done by Hay's collapse and in making the prisoner's chances of acquittal look slender indeed.

It was now well on into the afternoon and the candles in the courtroom were already lit when Erskine rose to examine the first defence witness, the Reverend Erasmus Middleton, who had been a member of the committee of the Protestant Association since February 1779. He was a reasonable, likeable witness and his stolid contented face and mild manner came as a surprise to those who had been told about the lean and hungry, fanatical looks of the leaders of the Protestant Association. He spoke in respectful and admiring terms of the prisoner and his 'good moral character'. 'His Lordship appeared', he said, 'always the most calm and dispassionate of us.' He had warned the petitioners not to take sticks in their hands for fear of appearing aggressive. His idea, Middleton insisted, was that they should march quietly to the House and show its members how formidable they were, not as a military force but as a moral one. For it was easy enough, Lord George had explained, to get signatures to a petition but signatures alone were not enough. The petition would be no more effective than any other if those who had signed it did not come to back it up with their presence. But they must do so quietly and peaceably. 'If they smite you on one cheek,' he had advised them, 'turn the other also.'

Middleton's portrait of a reasonable, moderate Lord George Gordon was backed up by the evidence of Thomas Evans who, having been warned that a number of roughs and criminals were mixing with the petitioner, had advised Gordon that there would be a riot if more than thirty or forty people accompanied him to the House. He asked Lord George if he intended to take all the petitioners with him.

'By no means', replied Gordon and went on to say that 'he intended to go to the House alone, and sometime after he had been there, the petition was to follow him to the lobby of the House of Commons and there to wait till he came out to receive it.'

'May I tell the people so?' Evans had asked him.

'Yes,' Lord George had told him, 'with all my heart.'

Another witness, John Turner, was even more helpful. According to him, Lord George had told the petitioners in St. George's Fields that 'if anything had weight with their petition it would be their quiet and peaceable behaviour and that nothing else would have weight with it.' The prisoner had gone on to say that 'he was informed since he came into the Fields that a number of persons had come abroad that day, on purpose to raise a riot or a tumult. Do not be led away by such persons.'

Having shown that the prisoner had wished and enjoined the petitioners to behave peaceably, it was the next task of the defence to prove that the prosecution's attempt to associate the petitioners with the rioters was unjustified and false. Alexander Johnston's evidence went a long way towards doing so. He had been in Westminster Palace Yard on the Friday evening, he said. He had wandered there with some friends of his who had had dinner with him in the Strand. 'There were', he found, 'about twenty boys, not one of them above ten to eighteen years of age, I suppose, and four or five men stopping the carriages. I then went over to the coach. I took hold of a man by the breast that was next to the coach door. I asked him who gave him authority to stop that carriage. He said he had got authority. I asked him, "from whom?" He said it was no matter from whom, he had got authority. Then I told him I had got authority to take him. I took him by the breast. Several about him got hold of me and held me by my hair, and I was a week after that before I could straighten my neck. I gave him in charge to one of the gentlemen that were along with me, and as soon as I did that the rest ran away, and left the carriage to itself.'

'Were the sort of people you saw making that riot', Erskine asked him, 'quite a different sort of people from the Protestant Association?'

Johnston: 'They were a set of boys, quite a set of pickpockets.'

'Did they appear like those of the Protestant Association you had seen in the morning?'

'No; not in the least appearance like them. No such thing.'

Alexander Frazer who followed Mr. Johnston in the witness box, gave evidence to the effect that even in the morning several gangs of rowdies were to be seen amongst the petitioners, looking out for trouble and hoping to find it.

'I saw', he said, 'several bodies of people collected together on the bridge: it was a very hot day. I went close to them and asked them, "Do you belong to the Association?" as they had all blue cockades.'

Kenyon: 'Did they appear to you to be of the body of petitioners?'

'No they did not, and many of them were in liquor.'

'That was before the petitioners arrived there?'

'This was about eleven o'clock.'

'When you asked them if they were of the Association, what answer did they make?'

'One with a great stick, who seemed to be in liquor, held up his stick and said, "No, damn it, *this* is all our Association".'

Erskine and Kenyon were successfully guiding their witnesses to tell a convincing story of a well-meaning honest man whose innocent intentions had been exploited by gangs of ruffians. Having built up this picture of innocence by means of unknown but apparently reputable witnesses, they called a man whose corroboration of their various eye-witness reports would be unassailable. The man they chose for this was Sir Philip Jennings Clerke, the charming and popular Member of Parliament who had been with Lord George on that frantic ride from Westminster to Alderman Bull's house in the City. Kenyon began by asking him if he had taken notice of the persons whom he had seen in St. George's Fields.

'I took very particular notice of them', he replied.

Kenyon: 'What kind of class of people did they appear to be?'

'The better sort of tradesmen; they were all well-dressed, decent sort of people. All that I conversed with told me that their desire was that there should be a stop put to publick preaching and publick teaching; they were all exceeding quiet and orderly and very civil, and they had no particular reason to be so to me, because I never put a blue cockade into my hat.'

But the people he saw later on in the evening 'were a lower kind of people, more a mob of blackguards'.

He was honest to admit how frightened he had been when he had been in the coach with Lord George who, he said, had done all he could to get the mob to disperse. 'It was impossible', he told the court, 'for any man to take more pains than Lord George Gordon did to prevail upon the people to disperse. . . . When the mob took the horses off, Lord George said, "For God's sake go peaceably home and about your business. Whilst you assemble in this tumultuous way your petition will never be complied with, the House will never consent to it" .'

Again there was presented this picture of innocence, this idea of an earnest man desperately trying to control wild and ungovernable forces. The picture was completed by the appearance in the witness box of Mrs. Yond, Lord George's faithful old servant, whose simple domesticity and appealing loyalty did much to help her master's case. Her evidence, Erskine knew, would be worthless, but the very fact of her presence, and her determined, emphatic loyalty, would gain much sympathy. Her master had arrived home, she said, on Friday at a quarter to eleven 'and did not go out again. My Lord was at home Saturday, Sunday and Monday.'

Erskine: 'You saw him at home those days?'

'I did.'

'You saw him upon every one of them?'

'Yes.'

'Are you sure of it?'

'I am sure of it.'

Court: 'Do you mean that his Lordship did not go out or only that he was at home some part of those days?'

'He was at home some part of those days.'

Erskine looked at Lord Mansfield. 'We are ready', he said deliberately, 'if the Court thinks it material to go into evidence to shew where
his Lordship was *every hour and every minute* of those days.'[1]

It sounded almost like a threat and Erskine had intended that it should
for it was already past midnight and the Court had been sitting con-
tinuously for sixteen hours. Lord Mansfield did not think it material.

Erskine, glancing at the members of the jury, was more than grateful
for this decision. Those faces that he could see in the candlelight were
obviously tired. Now that the cross-examinations were over they
would soon become bored and impatient. Already, a journalist afterwards noted, there was to be heard the sound of shuffling feet, the
infectious noise of coughing. It was in this atmosphere of growing
restiveness that Erskine rose to address them.

His speech, fluent, intelligent, literate, emotional, was one of the
greatest of his career.

He admitted from the outset to sharing his client's distrust of Roman
Catholics. 'I will not call up from the graves of martyrs', he cried with
a passion which, although extravagant, was known to be sincere, 'all
the precious blood that has been spilt in this land to save its established
government and its reformed religion from the secret villainy and the
open force of papists.' It was an appeal more to their emotions and their
patriotism than to their sense of justice; and having once reminded
them of the horrors of Popery he turned, before he had irritated
the less susceptible to that approach, to the particular points at issue.

He had, he believed, successfully established in evidence Lord
George's reasonable behaviour in St. George's Fields and his lack of
direct responsibility for the acts of outrage subsequently committed.
What was less easily defensible was his conduct in the lobby of the
House of Commons, particularly his alleged constant appeal to his
supporters to 'remember the Scotch'. 'But', Erskine said, 'it was the
constitutional unanimity and firmness of the great body of the people
of Scotland whose example Lord George Gordon recommended and
not the riots and burning'. And before his hearers could consider the
likelihood of this he went on to say, 'Mr. Bowen is the only man—*I
beseech you gentlemen of the jury to attend to this circumstance*—Mr. Bowen
is the only man who has attempted, directly or indirectly, to say that
Lord George Gordon uttered a syllable to the multitude in the lobby

[1] Lord George himself wrote an account of his movements during the riots,
which is now in the British Museum (Add. MSS. 42129).

concerning the destruction of the mass houses in Scotland'. Not even
the 'wretched abandoned Hay' had done that.

And, Erskine insisted, apart from this uncorroborated reference to
the mass houses, everything else Lord George had said had been perfectly peaceable, he merely requiring his supporters to be 'temperate
and firm'.

Regarding the signing of notes of indemnity, which the prosecution
had considered so damning, he told the jury that Mr. Fisher 'confessed
to the Privy Council that he himself had granted similar protections to
various people, yet was dismissed as having done nothing but his duty',
and recalled the evidence of a witness who had said that Lord George
was so harassed when he signed one note thrust at him that he did not
even read it. When after the week-end the banditti had begun to riot
in the name of Protestantism, he had published an advertisement in the
newspapers 'revealing the authors of these riots; and as the Protestant
cause had been made the pretext of them, enjoining all those who
wished well of it to behave like good citizens'.

The fact that so many citizens were not behaving well was surely no
fault of Lord George's. He had not incited them to riot, he had not
encouraged them when they did riot, rather had he done his utmost to
get them to disperse. The most serious crime of which he might be
thought guilty was lack of foresight but 'gentlemen', Erskine reminded
them, 'we are not trying whether he might or ought to have foreseen
mischief, but whether he wickedly or traitorously preconceived and
designed it'.

He wound up his speech on the same emotional, dramatic note on
which he had begun it.

Since Lord George stands clear of every hostile act or purpose against the
Legislature of his country, or the properties of his fellow subjects—since the
whole tenor of his conduct repels the belief of the traitorous purpose charged
by the indictment—my task is finished. I shall make no address to your
passions; I will not remind you of the long and rigorous imprisonment he has
suffered; I will not speak to you of his great youth, of his illustrious birth, and
of his uniformly animated and generous zeal in Parliament for the constitution of his country. Such topics might be useful in the balance of a doubtful
case; yet even then I should have trusted to the honest hearts of Englishmen
to have felt them without excitation. At present the plain and rigid rules of
Justice are sufficient to entitle me to your verdict; and may God Almighty
who is the sacred author of them, fill your mind with the deepest impression

of them, and with virtue to follow those impressions! You will then restore my innocent client to liberty, and me, to that peace of mind which, since the protection of that innocence in any part depended upon me, I have never known.

He sat down conscious of his success. It was a performance of great virtuosity and power, and if it was calculated to appeal to the emotions rather than to the intellect it was none the less impressive for that.

The closing speech for the prosecution which followed it was neither so long, nor so passionate. But it was coldly effective. The Attorney-General restricted himself to the facts. He referred to the Reverend Erasmus Middleton's evidence as to the prisoner's docile behaviour in St. George's Fields and frankly declined to believe it. He referred to the illegality of petitioning Parliament in the manner described by his witnesses and he referred, and this he evidently felt was the strongest point in his case, to Lord George's wild behaviour in the lobby of the House.

When he had finished, the acquittal which had appeared so necessary at the end of Erskine's speech a short time before now seemed once more in doubt.

The summing up did not restore the prisoner's confidence. During the course of it, in fact, he felt obliged to complain of its bias. And Lord George was not alone in thinking that Lord Mansfield considered him guilty and all but implied it in his speech.

It was an imputation which the old lawyer would have been anxious to avoid, and on other occasions would have taken care to avoid it. But it was by now nearly four o'clock in the morning. His kind and clever old face was lined and white with exhaustion. And in fact only once or twice did his words vaguely imply a formed opinion. It was afterwards considered a reasonably impartial speech.

He began it with a short dissertation on the meaning of high treason and said, 'without any doubt I tell you, the joint opinion of us all is that if this multitude assembled with intent, by acts of force and violence, to compel the legislature to repeal a law, it is High Treason'. He then stated the law on the legality of petitions and denied that the Bill of Rights, as had been suggested, was meant to interfere with an Act of Charles II which limited the number of people who could present a petition. On this point he said, again categorically, that 'we are all of the opinion that attending a petition to the House of Commons by more than ten persons is criminal and illegal'.

He then went carefully and skilfully through the evidence given by the various witnesses and dismissed the jury with the usual admonition that 'if the scale should hang doubtful, and you are not fully satisfied that he is guilty, you ought to lean on the favourable side and acquit him.'

At a quarter to five the jury gratefully retired and within half an hour they had returned. Erskine was certain that they had brought back with them a verdict of guilty and had already regretfully told his client so. As the jurors sat down in their places one of them caught his eye, smiled encouragingly and nodded his head. Erskine was so surprised that he fainted.

The Clerk of the Court spoke.

'Lord George Gordon, hold up your hand', he said. 'Gentlemen of the Jury. Look upon the Prisoner. How say you? Is he guilty of the indictment wherewith he stands charged or not guilty?'

'Not Guilty.'

'You say he is Not Guilty and so you say all.'

12

GORDON AND LIBERTY!

H E left the courtroom looking exhausted, 'his eyes closed, like a corpse walking'. Mrs. Yond and McQueen were waiting for him outside and they took him back with them to Welbeck Street and put him to bed.

As the sun came up and the news spread about the town, services were held in Presbyterian chapels and prayers of thanskgiving said for his acquittal. In Scotland that evening church bells rang and bonfires were lit.

Even those who disliked the man were thankful that he had been found not guilty. Hannah More who could 'less forgive an affectation of enthusiasm in him, because he is a man of loose morals', was 'glad he is acquitted, for it disappoints the party and uncanonizes the martyr'. And Doctor Johnson also was relieved because a precedent had not been created for hanging a man for 'constructive treason'.

The King and his Ministers were unconcerned by their failure to obtain a conviction. Lord George was, they felt certain, a 'broken man' anyway. As a troublemaker the riots had finished him, just as certainly as they had killed Wilkesism and changed Wilkes from the 'devil' which the King had once called him to the 'exhausted volcano', which he now considered himself to be. No one would trust Lord George any more. He would never get into Parliament again. He was a beaten failure.

They seemed at first to be right. The past nine months would have left their mark on a far more placid and balanced temperament. The excitement of the weeks before the riots, his almost hysterical frenzy during the riots themselves, his subsequent lonely imprisonment with his self-condemnation and sense of guilt, had changed him undoubtedly and had changed him, his critics believed, for the better. Although his sanity was still questionable he had, they believed, sobered down, become quieter, more reasonable, less touchy. The terrible memory of the countless lives lost in his name had drained the passion, the bitterness and the ambition out of him.

He appeared to be content to retire from public life and to devote his time and energy to his voluminous, plethoric correspondence. Every day from his study McQueen took out letters of enormous length addressed to America, to France, to Holland and in fact to any country where he had a friend or an acquaintance or knew of a man concerned in a struggle for liberty. The advice he gave was usually unsolicited, frequently unwanted and apparently often unanswered. But he was undeterred; the communications poured from his pen and he remained for the rest of his life as tireless a correspondent as Calvin.

He also seemed to be more sincerely religious. Formerly his religious beliefs had been bound up inescapably with his political convictions. Protestantism, as he so often insisted, was synonymous with Liberty, Popery with arbitrary power. The motives behind his leadership of the Protestant Association had appeared more material than spiritual. To him 'No Popery!' had been a political catch-phrase as much as a religious cry. But now religion was an end in itself and no longer a weapon with which the Pope and the enemies of freedom could be fought.[1]

He rarely went out without a Bible in his pocket and he had whole chapters of the Old Testament by heart. He now never wore his gay plaid trousers but was generally to be seen in unrelieved black. He looked more than ever like a Puritan preacher with his lank hair falling down below his shoulders; his pale face thinner than ever; his curiously deep eyes glinting darkly behind the small oval lenses of his spectacles. No longer did people gossip about his whores and mistresses, instead they told each other that his experiences had driven him a little mad.

Wraxall thought that he detected this touch of insanity in his eyes. 'He had the appearance', he said, describing him at this time, 'as well as the deportment of a man of quality. There was, however, something in his cast of countenance and mode of expression that indicated cunning, or a perverted understanding or both.' Nevertheless his conversation was, as always, 'agreeable . . . his manners gentle'.

But in spite of his still gentle manners and calmer disposition he had not lost the capacity to irritate.

[1] It was at this time that he began to study the beliefs of the Quakers which in his present mood made an understandable impression upon him. Their pacifism, their insistence that Christian behaviour is more important than Christian dogma, their concern for the poor and the unprotected were all essential to his own *credenda*. But although meetings were held in his house he never joined their sect.

On Sundays he went to chapel at the Lock Hospital near his house. This hospital was supported by a charity managed by Methodists and although the Governors were mainly Anglican, the chapel services were held in the strictest Methodist manner. When he came to worship there, he was received 'with the respect shown to an Apostle' and the reverential congregation 'always made a lane for him to pass'. This so annoyed the Duke of Richmond and Lord Rockingham that they resigned from the Board of Governors and the Earl of Hillsborough would have done so too, had he not been persuaded that without his controlling hand, the other Governors would have admitted Lord George to the Board.

The fawning flattery of the Methodists at the Lock Hospital was as delicious to Lord George as the flattery of the Protestant Association. He had never been able to resist adulation. He was now, after his days of humiliation, more susceptible to it than ever. His vanity rekindled his ambition. He began to consider once more a return to public life.

In the summer of 1781 Alderman Hayley, one of the Members of Parliament for the City of London, died. Lord George was nominated a candidate for the vacant seat and he accepted the nomination. He had returned to the scene.

But the entrance was ill-timed. The country was still at war and the war was in a critical stage. The City merchants were alarmed by the immense superiority of the combined enemy fleets over British ships not only in the Mediterranean and in American waters, but also nearer at home in the English Channel where Admiral Darby 'dared not stir out of Torbay'.

At a time of such apprehension, Lord George's opponents were able to play on the fear which his name still inspired. The Government joined in their efforts to decry the 'vile incendiary of their City' and to increase the prejudice against a Scottish candidate.

A meeting of his supporters at the St. Paul's Head Tavern in Cateaton Street was broken up by a number of his opponents who had come in apparently as friends and then overturned the tables, thrown the candles to the floor and broken the windows. The next morning the energetically spread reports of more 'Gordon riots' made Lord George's chances of election so remote that he withdrew his name from the candidature.

He never again attempted to get back into Parliament, although his proved talents as an election speaker were available to any Whig candidate who cared to avail himself of them. Like Wilkes, he was a great deal more effective when addressing a crowd on an election platform than when speaking in the House of Commons.

But his services were not much in demand. His name was more of a liability than his 'mob oratory' an asset, and his words and his principles appealed most strongly to those who had no vote. Fox, however, a fellow member of the Whig Club at 'The Shakespeare', accepted his offer of assistance when he was a candidate for Westminster and Lord George mounted the hustings with appealing energy and enthusiasm on his behalf. But the Opposition was still, for him, only one degree better than the Ministry. While it was true, he agreed, that in the words of the Parliamentary motion, the Ministry had 'lost the confidence of the people,' the Opposition, it must be admitted, 'had certainly not found it'. Both Government and Opposition were, for him, representatives of the aristocracy, without a thought for the real interests of the people. And as such he despised them equally. All Members of Parliament whatever they professed to be, whichever party they said they belonged to, and whichever of the complicated family connections and involved factions they supported, were professional or social climbers, businessmen out for contracts or gentlemen anxious to do the right thing, oblige a patron, a family or a friend, and cut a figure in the world. Few, if any of them, were in Parliament for the benefit of their electors. If there had been a Labour Party Lord George would no doubt have joined it to the consternation of its whips.

Fox was returned with a satisfying majority but Lord George was not asked to support a candidate again. And when he went to Scotland to attend the election of a new Member for Aberdeen he spoke for Mr. Skene, the Whig candidate, without his permission and in terms which implied that as the electors had to find a Member they might as well have Skene, as, although they might think him unremarkable, he was at least better than Mr. Fergusson the other candidate supported by his brother the Duke of Gordon and the Tories.

His reception in Scotland was, as on every previous visit, exhilarating. He was cheered on his way to Aberdeen Town Hall and when he left it. The news of Skene's election was greeted with shouts of 'Gordon and Liberty!' The students of King's College wrote to congratulate him upon his arrival in Aberdeen and hoped to 'accompany his Lordship in their uniform' when he thought it 'proper to leave town'. The proposed public valediction was, however, prohibited by the College authorities.

But although a hero in Aberdeen he had by now become once more a nuisance in London.

He had been in angry correspondence with Pitt, now Prime Minister in a new Tory Government, on the subject of a proposed tax on linens, cottons and Scotch gauze which, he said, would lead to riots amongst 'the working people'; one of his letters on the dispute having peremptorily ended: 'Lord George hopes to hear again from Mr. Pitt before he goes out this night'. He had protested to the House of Lords against a decision to restore the estates forfeited in the '45 rebellion to their original owners. To the fury of his family, and their friends among the Highland chiefs, he had said that it 'became the legislator to relieve the immediate wants of the *people* rather than to confer emoluments upon men who had abandoned their own country' and had 'never distinguished themselves in the cause of freedom'. He had opposed at various times the taxes on windows, candles, stamps, postages, Scotch distilleries and shops. Indeed in his attack on the Shop Tax his opposition had gone further than the writing of virulent letters. He had called meetings and distributed handbills. He had even gone out one morning from Welbeck Street and starting at the Oxford Street end of Bond Street he had worked his way along to the City calling at every shop he passed and inducing the owners to shut them up and put out long poles covered in black crape with the inscription, 'This Shop to be Let. Enquire of Billy Pitt'. Public opinion was aroused to such as extent that the Government felt obliged to withdraw the obnoxious Bill and Lord George had got much of the credit.

Towards the end of 1784 he joined issue with Pitt on a much more serious and dangerous topic. For some time Protestant volunteers, most of them discharged soldiers and sailors idle since the end of the American war, had been applying for permission to go to the help of the Dutch in their war against the Catholic Austrian Empire. As President of the Protestant Association which he still was, Lord George put himself at the head of this movement and called upon the Dutch Ambassador, to make him an extraordinary proposition. He suggested that the Association led by himself and accompanied by the Ambassador, should march to St. James's to prove to the Court how steadfast was the support of the Association for the Dutch cause. The proposal was rejected with horror. But Lord George, fired by his own enthusiasm, was undeterred. His subsequent behaviour was so bizarre, so outrageously Quixotic, that even his supporters could no longer deny that on occasions now he showed symptoms of that mental aberration of which his critics had for so long complained.

On the morning of 10 November he dressed himself up in a Dutch naval uniform with a large leather belt over his shoulder. Through the belt he tucked an immense Highland broadsword that had 'opposed with success the usurpations of the See of Rome'. So caparisoned he went to St. James's and persuaded the officer in charge of the Guard to put up the Dutch flag and then waited outside the Palace for the arrival of the Ambassador. As His Excellency approached, Lord George drew his rusty sword and saluted the embarrassed diplomat with great fervour, declaring he would 'protect to the utmost of his power the Dutch and their interests'.

The next day in fulfilment of this promise he sent Pitt a letter:

Sir, several hundred seamen have addressed me today. Many of them lately arrived from India came in coaches; acting lieutenants, mates, midshipmen of the Royal Navy are among them. The following is a copy of their address:

'To Rt. Hon. Lord George Gordon, President of the Protestant Association. May it please your Lordship, we the seamen whose names are underwritten are able, willing and ready to serve the United Protestant States of Holland against the King of the Romans and their Popish enemies. And your petitioners will ever pray for Lord George Gordon. Signed Edward Robinson and 34 other seamen at The Kettle Drum, Radcliffe Highway. November 17 1784.'

He followed up this letter with another one in which he told Pitt that a Captain Rawlinson had offered his frigate *The Prince William*, 'to cruise in support of all the United States of Holland' and that there were many soldiers including several artillerymen and more than a thousand seamen who were of the same sentiments.

Pitt replied the next day. 'I have hitherto', he told Lord George with irritation,

returned no answer to the letters I received because I did not think it my duty to enter into a correspondence with your Lordship on the subject, but having been informed that many seamen have been induced to quit their occupation in the expectation of being employed to serve against the Emperor, I think it my duty to remind you that whatever steps you have taken have been without the smallest degree of authority or countenance from his Majesty's Ministers and that it is for your Lordship to consider what consequences may be expected from them.

The Government was by this time seriously alarmed. On the 19th 'a vast crowd of sailors' went to the Queen's House to demand employment. A vague promise was given them by Lord Sydney and they went away; but later they formed themselves into 'numerous bodies' and marched threateningly about the town. A rumour was circulated among them by a disgruntled ship's company, discharged that morning at Wapping, that Lord George had taken advantage of their loyalty and in some unspecified way betrayed them. It was accordingly suggested that they should pull his house down. Given a satisfying outlet for their resentment they agreed and marched towards Welbeck Street. Lord George, warned by a friend of their approach, was apparently quite unmoved and 'sat down to breakfast with the greatest composure'.

The mob soon arrived outside his house and a leader went up to the front door and rattled on it with a stick. Lord George went and opened it himself and walked out to face them with a calm which seemed close to indifference.

Faced with such composed, disdainful unconcern, the sailors stood still and a 'profound silence succeeded' as Lord George began to address them. He was in his best form. He knew just how to talk to these men. He had been a sailor himself, he told them, and had always been a 'friend of the people'. Before he had finished the air resounded with shouts of 'Gordon and Liberty!' It was a remarkable, a masterly performance. 'When he had concluded his harangue one of them asked him if they might go and "pull down Mr. Pitt's house" .' He made a 'low bow and withdrew'. Fortunately the suggestion was not adopted and they went away quite quietly.

The man was becoming more than an ordinary nuisance, the Government decided after this last episode, he was beginning to be dangerous again. It was suggested he might be certified a lunatic, but between his wild spasms of extravagant derangement there were, it had to be admitted, long periods of sense and rational behaviour. His conversation was nearly always intelligent and polite, his manner gracious. If he had no close friends he had no personal enemies and many reasonable supporters. You could hate his views and despise his behaviour, but you could not dislike the man himself.

But then, after some months of relative quiet, he played into the Government's hands and at the end of 1786 they were able to arrest him on two charges.

The first arose from a personal attack on the Queen of France.

He had visited Paris again four years before and had hated it. The contrast between the lofty 'palaces and wretched hovels', between the 'unfeeling Noble and haughty Prelate' and the peasant 'trudging in the mire', had appalled him. He had met Marie Antoinette but his imagination was not 'enraptured' by what he referred to with cynical derision as 'Burke's celestial vision'.

When Count Cagliostro, therefore, was banished from France after a scandalous case in which the Queen had been involved,[1] Lord George had a particular reason, apart from his natural interest in the curious man himself, for befriending him when he came to London.

For weeks the two men saw each other almost every day and spent hours in absorbing conversation. In spite of his reputation as a charlatan, magician and saltimbanco whose secret cures for all manner of ailments had made him famous throughout France and Italy, Cagliostro was at the same time a serious student of social problems and had done much to help the poor in Paris. Most Englishmen dismissed him as a posturing, if admittedly brilliant, quack and certainly he took

[1] The remarkable Case of the Diamond Necklace, as it came to be called, had far-reaching effects. Goethe said that it 'laid the foundation of the state in ruins'; Mirabeau that it was the 'prelude of the revolution'.

It began innocently enough. Knowing Marie Antoinette's passion for diamonds the Court jewellers Mm. Böhmer et Bassange had for some time been making a collection of them for a magnificent necklace which they hoped to sell to her. When they had made a fine collection and worked them into a beautifully fashioned necklace, they sent the masterpiece to the Queen, who was enchanted by it but as the price was well over a million livres felt compelled to decline it.

A woman who called herself the Countess Jeanne de la Motte de Valois and who was the lover of the immensely rich Prince Cardinal de Rohan, conceived a plan to cheat the jewellers.

De Rohan had recently been declared *persona non grata* by the Viennese Court to which he had been sent as Ambassador by the Court of Versailles. He had offended the grim Marie Thérèse by his conscious and flamboyant charm and she had told Marie Antoinette, her daughter, not to receive him when he got back to Paris. The Prince naturally told his lover Jeanne of the Queen's refusal to see him but she assured him that all he had to do to regain her favour was to guarantee payment of the necklace which she so badly wanted.

Immediately a contract was drawn up which Jeanne took to the jewellers stamped '*Approuvé. Marie Antoinette de France*'. The next day the necklace was delivered at Jeanne's house where, she said, a royal messenger would come to pick it up. And that was the last which was seen of it. Jeanne and her husband, the bogus Count, disappeared.

Prince de Rohan called in Cagliostro for his advice and both of them were arrested. They were subsequently acquitted but Cagliostro was ordered out of the country.

no trouble to show them that he was anything other than a mounte-
bank. He claimed to have been present at the time of the creation of
the world and at all the main events which had subsequently taken
place. Jesus Christ and he had been on the most intimate terms.

'Do you remember that evening at Jerusalem', he once asked his
servant, 'when they crucified Christ?'

'You forget, sir', the servant humbly replied, 'that I have only been
in your service for fifteen hundred years'. When asked his name by
ladies in polite society he would reply in tones of vaguely menacing
but irresistible lugubriousness, 'I am he who is.' It was an attitude of
bantering contempt which held a natural appeal for Lord George
Gordon.

In August 1786 Cagliostro received notification from M. Barthelemy, who in the absence of Count d'Adhemar represented the Court
of Versailles in London, that he had had instructions from Paris to tell
him that he was now at liberty to return to France. Cagliostro accompanied by Lord George called on Barthelemy to learn what lay behind
this offer. Barthelemy asked to see Cagliostro alone but Lord George
would not leave the room, so the acting Ambassador read out in his
company the letter he had received from France. Cagliostro asked
for a copy of it and was refused one.

Two days later the following advertisement appeared in the *Public
Advertiser*:

> Count de Cagliostro has declared he will hold no intercourse with any
> messengers from France except in the presence of Lord George Gordon. The
> gang of French spies in London are trying the most industrious arts to trap
> the Count. . . . The friendship and benevolence of Count de Cagliostro in
> advising the poor Prince Louis de Rohan to be upon his guard against de
> Valois and the intrigues of the Queen's faction (who still seek the destruction
> of the noble prince) has brought upon the Count the hateful revenge and
> perfidious cruelties of a tyrannical government.

The announcement went on to list the merits of the Count and the
cruelties of Marie Antoinette, criticizing in the strongest possible terms
the French Ambassador and M. Barthelemy.

It was brought to the attention of the Attorney-General who reported to Pitt that its author could, in his opinion, be successfully
charged with libel.

Before bringing the charge, however, the Government waited until the Attorney-General was ready to proceed on an alternative charge, also for libel. This was thought to be contained in a pamphlet written by Lord George, supposedly a petition from the prisoners of Newgate begging his Lordship to 'interfere and secure their liberty and prevent their being sent to Botany Bay'.

'We have reason to cry aloud from our dungeons and prison ships', the pamphlet declared, 'in defence of our lives and liberties that the just punishment ordained by God for our trespasses of thievery is profanely altered . . . and that the true record of the Almighty is falsified and erased by the Lawyers and Judges (who sit with their backs to the words of the living God and the fear of men before their faces) till the streets of our city have run down with a stream of blood.'

The pamphlet was considered to represent a libel on the 'Judges and Administration of the Laws of England' and he was accordingly indicted for publishing it and for publishing the 'libel on the Queen of France and the French Ambassador' in his announcement in the *Public Advertiser.*

Immediately he asked Erskine once more to defend him, but by this time his cousin had accepted a general retaining fee from the Crown and was unable to accept the brief. Lloyd Kenyon was also unavailable. Unwilling to entrust his defence to less skilful hands he decided to undertake it himself. It was a decision of extreme stupidity. Few cases can ever have been so ill managed, few prisoners so ill defended.

He began by attempting to serve a subpoena upon Mrs. Fitzherbert, the Prince of Wales's 'papistical wife' with whom he had had a conversation in Paris two years before. What he hoped to prove by this conversation is not clear, and as he was turned out of her house by her servants and threatened with a whipping by her brothers, he was unable to get her into the witness box. There is no reason to suppose however, that Mrs. Fitzherbert's evidence would have been any more relevant than the rest of the extraneous, inapposite information with which he bored the Court.

On his first appearance he exasperated the Judge by quibbling over some obscure and involved legal terminology which he protested was 'unintelligible and unnecessary'; and on his second appearance he refused to accept the indictment drawn up against 'George Gordon, Esquire'. 'Can the process', he asked the Court in innocent amazement, 'be intended for the Right Honourable Lord George Gordon?' And not bothering to wait for an answer he walked from the court-room.

When the indictment was correctly worded and there were no fur-ther technicalities with which he could quarrel, he came back to Court for the third time, on 6 June 1787, apparently at last prepared to stand trial.

He started his case with an enormously long and muddled speech which included a by no means brief summary of English Criminal Law from the time of Athelstan. He had been persuaded, he said, to investigate these laws when a servant of his had been sent out to buy a fowl costing three shillings. The servant had said that it cost four shillings and sixpence and had therefore been guilty of stealing one and sixpence which was a capital offence. His butler had wanted him to hand the man over to the authorities but he would not do it. 'I looked into the law of God', he said, 'and found it required no man's blood to be taken away; and there are many other countries besides this where no man's blood is shed for the trespass of thievery. Having considered this and the number of persons whose blood is shed in this country and that it did not deter others from thievery . . . I chose to communicate my sentiments to the Judges before I did it to the public or the prisoners themselves'. He went to Lord Mansfield but 'could gain no admittance'. Then he went to Justice Gould who had 'tears in his eyes' when he was talking about it and recommended him to put his sentiments upon paper. Afterwards he went to the Recorder who told him he wished 'the legislature would take up the business'. But when he went to Sheriff Le Mesurier for permission to speak to the condemned convicts, his reception was less friendly. He told the Sheriff that his 'heart was full of it, and the heart of every man ought to be full of it, to see the lives of fellow creatures taken away, contrary to the laws of God. But he said: "Pooh! Pooh! I shall not attend to it at all".'

At this point Mr. Justice Ashurst felt obliged to interrupt the flow of talk and to explain that it was all very well but that he could not see where it was getting the Court. Lord George breathlessly apologized and went on as before.

But his arguments were worse than useless. The jury looked at him in amazement. Only cranks like John Howard were interested in penal reform. No honest citizen, no gentleman, certainly no aristocrat, con-cerned himself with capital punishment. Did he not realize what would happen to the property of honest folk if thieves were not hanged? The country would be reduced to anarchy. The fellow was patently mad.

The case for the prosecution, the jurors were pleased to note, was quite clear. Lord George frequently came to Newgate, Mr. Pitt, a turnkey deposed, to see the prisoners.

'He used to come in', Mr. Pitt reported, 'and say: "Don't you think it cruel that so much blood should be spilt? Don't you think it hard so many should suffer?" I said I could not help it nor he neither, I believed. He said, "No man ought to suffer death without he spilt blood." '

When his pamphlet was published, Lord George had employed a man and a woman, as well as his butler, to distribute copies about the prison to both prisoners and jailors. A copy was sent to Mr. Akerman who was in court to testify to the fact. Lord George's cross-examination of the Keeper showed how completely he was failing to answer the prosecution's case by merely insisting, which was not doubted, that the pamphlet was not distributed for personal reasons.

Gordon: 'Had I the smallest connection with those prisoners that they have asked you about?'

Akerman: 'Not that I know of.'

'Had I any connection in sending the petitions to any particular prisoners? Or did I direct them to you, to the turnkeys or Mr. Villete, the Ordinary?'

'I got one of them. I read it and decided that they should not deliver any.'

'Did you understand that I had the smallest connection with the prisoners?'

'I never heard that you had. I heard that you had been at the debtors' side, and had seen a debtor in the Lodge, but not to go into the Prison.'

'How long was that before this time?'

'A great while before.'

Faced with so inept and prevaricating a defence, quite out of sympathy with the Prisoner's obvious sincerity and his extraordinary attitude to capital punishment and the penal code, the Jury had no difficulty in returning an immediate verdict of guilty.

Before passing sentence the Judge had to consider the libel published in the *Public Advertiser*. The trial on this charge was postponed for a week and took place on 13 June.

The Attorney-General opened his case with a colourful catalogue of the virtues of the Queen of France, describing her as the 'most high, mighty and puissant Marie Antoinette, a great and illustrious princess, eminently distinguished and renowned for her wisdom, prudence, justice, grace, clemency, charity . . .' He would have gone on had not the Prisoner at this point interrupted him and in a loud stage whisper said, behind his hand with a broad and disarming smile, 'Everybody knows she is a very *convenient* lady'.

The outrageous comment set the tone for his defence. It was not, in fact, a defence at all. He repeated with extravagant but good-humoured vehemence the libels which he had previously committed to print, and more. 'The French Ambassador', he said, 'is a low man of no family; but being plausible, cunning and clever he has pushed himself forward to the notice of men in authority; in short what Jenkinson was in Britain, d'Adhemar is in France.'

A gust of laughter greeted this reference to the unpopular Charles Jenkinson, who was secretary-at-war under Lord North and was believed to have had enormous influence at Court as one of the King's most trusted and obedient freinds. Encouraged by the apparent appreciation of his audience, Lord George then turned with vigour upon the Queen of France. It was impossible, he said, to libel the woman. Her character was well known in every street in Paris. But he was interrupted in the middle of the next sentence and the further scurrilous remarks which were obviously on the tip of his tongue remained unsaid. The Judge felt 'compelled to interfere and the Attorney-General told him he was a disgrace to the name of Briton'.

'One is sorry', Mr. Justice Ashurst observed when the Jury had brought in their inevitable verdict, 'that you, descended of an illustrious line of ancestors, should have so much dishonoured your family . . . that you should prefer the mean ambition of being popular among thieves and pickpockets and to stand as the champion of mischief, anarchy and confusion . . . that you should insult her most Christian Majesty.'

He worked himself up to such a pitch of indignation that he decided not to pass sentence that evening. He adjourned the Court until the following day when he said, looking hard at the Prisoner, the punishment would be decided.

The next day, however, when the Court reassembled Lord George did not appear. He had been released without bail and had taken advantage of the oversight to make his escape. His house was empty; his servants gone. For seven months he was not seen in London and no one knew where he was.

At the end of January the following year Mr. McManus, a Bow Street runner, brought out of a house in Birmingham, in a poor, largely Jewish quarter known as the Froggery, a curious figure. He wore a straggling black beard which was in strange contrast with his rust-coloured hair, and a dirty gaberdine coat which hung on his thin body like a cloak. On his head was a large wide-brimmed black hat such as those worn by Polish merchants. He was treated by the people of the filthy house in Dudley Street where he had been found, and of the whole district, with a respect which verged on veneration.[1] He gave his name to McManus as Israel bar Abraham George Gordon.

He declined to accompany the policeman back to London as it was the Sabbath. The Justice to whom the matter was referred insisted, however, and a Jewish friend gave him a box of Kosher food for the journey.

On the night his trial had ended Lord George had fled to Amsterdam but the burgomaster, on hearing of the reception he had been given by a group of revolutionaries, had told him he regretted the necessity for his departure and had arranged for him to be taken back to Harwich, where he disembarked with a group of Dutch soldiers whose orders were merely to see him back on to English soil but not to hand him over to the authorities, who indeed, although his return to England was announced in the papers, made no apparent efforts to arrest him. He had consequently been able to go on to Birmingham to the house of a Jewish woman, who made a living as a street hawker of capers and anchovies, where he could go into hiding with people of his own religion.

Just when he had been accepted into the Jewish faith is obscure. He had, it was known, been interested in it for some time. One day while having luncheon at Count Cagliostro's house in Knightsbridge, Sophie Van la Roche had noticed that while the others ate an extremely good meal of roast veal, codling, lamb, and pork Lord George only had watercress sprinkled with salt; and once, while on holiday in East Anglia, when he had seen over a doorway in Ipswich a quotation from

[1] A letter from a Birmingham clergyman quoted in *The London Chronicle* said that his Jewish landlady gave 'a most flattering character of this unaccountable man, saying he is endowed with the most engaging manners and possessed of the greatest learning of any one living'.

the *Haggadah* which read: 'Let all who are hungry enter and eat', he had gone inside and had afterwards often said how greatly impressed he had been by the simple kindness and generosity of the Jews he had met there.

But apart from liking the Jews as a people and admiring their loyalty, their artistic gifts and their deep historical sense, he deeply respected their stern God who was, after all, not so very different a figure from the God of Wesley and Calvin. For years he had had doubts as to the basic truths of Christianity[1] but no doubts at all about the magnificence, the rightness and the importance of the Old Testament, which for years had never left his pocket and which had inspired so many of those long speeches in the past and was to inspire so many turgid letters in the future. It represented more to him now than a way of life, it pointed out the only way a man could live at peace with his conscience and his God. For the Jewish view of humanity, the Jewish sense of justice and the Jewish hope for the world were all very much his own.

It was said at the time that his conversion was an elaborate and cynical device to give publicity to his financial schemes for the outlawing of war. For as a pacifist he had long been endeavouring to persuade Jewish financiers to withhold their support from any bellicose enterprise and thus make it difficult for any country to go to war. It was also said that the frustrations and disappointments of his life had made him bitter and that bitter men 'love to associate with victims of persecution'. It was even said that he expected to lead back the Israelites to their fathers' land, preferring to be a leader of Jews than a humble disciple of Christ. It was, of course, frequently suggested that he had now gone completely mad and this was the latest symptom of that madness. It was impossible to believe that he was sincere in his conversion. But sincere he undoubtedly was and proved himself to be.

[1] In May 1786 he had quarrelled with the Archbishop of Canterbury for refusing to appear before an Ecclesiastical court in connection with a dispute concerning the estate of a friend of his who had been a dissenting minister and had died intestate. In his opinion it was a matter for a civil magistrate. The Archbishop of Canterbury fearful of the consequences of an unfortunate precedent and jealous of Church revenues asked if he might call on Lord George at Welbeck Street. Lord George said he would be pleased to see him but his mind was made up. The Archbishop of Canterbury excommunicated him from the Church of England in a ceremony at the church of St. Mary La Bonne. Lord George's only comment was that to expel him from a society to which he never belonged was 'an absurdity worthy of an archbishop'.

For having become a Jew he remained one with all the fervour of a convert.[1] In Birmingham he was circumcised and 'preserved with great care', so Wraxall said, 'the sanguinary proofs of his having undergone the amputation'. He had spent much of his time while he was in hiding in learning the Hebrew language and each morning was seen with his phylacteries on his forehead and forearm. He was an essentially religious man, 'constitutionally religious' Watson called him, and in Jewry he had found his spiritual home. 'Wise men change their opinions often', he was fond of saying, 'fools never.' But this was one opinion he did not afterwards change. He remained a Jew, devout and strict, for the rest of his life.

When McManus got his strange, 'very grotesque' but elaborately polite charge back to London he was brought to the Court of King's Bench to hear his sentence.

'He was wrapped up in a greatcoat', the *Public Advertiser* reported, 'his hair lank as usual, his beard about three inches long, extending under his chin and throat from ear to ear and differing from the colour of his hair'.

For the 'prison libel' he was sentenced to three years' imprisonment, for the 'French libel' to a fine of £500 and a further two years' imprisonment at the end of the first three. He was required to find £10,000 as security for his good behaviour for fourteen years and two sureties of £2,500 each.

Although the large sum he was obliged to find was well beyond his means, he heard the severe sentence without emotion and was committed to Newgate.

After a few days of terrible discomfort in the Common Felons' Ward, where the appalling stench hung like a fog in the dark stagnant air and the prisoners fought each other and the rats for the scraps of food thrown at them by the gaolers, he was able to buy his way into a more salubrious part of the prison in which he had a room to himself and was able to live in decency and eventually in great comfort.

---

[1] He had become one with some difficulty. David Tevele Schiff, the rabbi of the fashionable synagogue in Duke's Place, St. James's, had refused to accept him, probably, Israel Solomons thinks, upon the advice of the lay heads of the community, as being too dangerous and suspect a convert; and he had eventually to seek instruction from Aaron Barnett, the Reader of the congregation at the Hambro synagogue, an unorthodox community. The Jews, of course, are not proselytizers and view converts with some suspicion.

A man of regular habits he rose each morning punctually at eight and read the newspapers over breakfast. He then dealt with his still enormous correspondence,[1] reading and writing letters until twelve o'clock when he received his numerous visitors. The large cell was often so crowded in the early afternoons that there was no room to sit down even on the floor. His visitors were not only men and women who shared his views and sympathies and wished to discuss them with him. He would see anyone who wanted to see him. On one occasion he spoke to 'a young lady from Oxford Street' who said, after much hesitation, that although she was pregnant, she had conceived virgin-ally. She had been very miserable, she added, until the Archangel Gabriel had appeared to her in a vision and told her the end of the world was at hand, commanding her to convey the news to Lord George Gordon.

Having no rent and few other expenses to pay, he was able to afford some simple hospitality for his guests and rarely less than eight sat down at table when dinner was served at two o'clock. Although the food was unexceptional it was adequate and well cooked. One day there was fish, the next meat; always there was soup and a good pudding. His guests had beer or wine, but he himself never had more than a single glass of porter.

After dinner he lit his pipe and started a discussion on social problems, religion or more often politics. He spoke little himself, occasionally making an astute comment, a sensible observation or opening up

[1] Letters from his cell went all round the world and particularly to Holland and America and after 1789 to France. On 23 July 1789 he wrote to the National Assembly explaining why he was in prison and requesting that 'your most honourable Assembly in your wisdom and sympathy will apply to the Court of London to relieve your petitioner from the above mentioned sentence and imprisonment'. He did not receive a reply until the end of February the following year when Grégoire, a devout Catholic although a revolutionary, told him he was 'sincerely grieved' but as he was a foreigner 'it would be improper to deliberate upon the subject'.
He wrote numerous letters to Gouverneur Morris, one of the founders of the American Republic and to Benjamin Franklin and Henry Laurens warning them that John Adams the American Envoy in London was a principal actor in what he called the 'Liberticide plot to subvert the republican Government by raising up an Emperor and Senate like that of Rome, dependent on France, upon the ruins of the betrayed Commonwealth under the auspices of the Washington Convention'.
He wrote also many letters to the House of Commons, particularly about the slave trade, denouncing the Members for only '*talking* about *regulating* the slave trade instead of *abolishing* it as the National Assembly had done'.

some new line of thought. He seemed always more anxious that the conversation should be entertaining and instructive and enjóyed by his guests than that he should play a large part in it. How strange, one of them once thought, that this quiet, unassuming, contented, intelligent man with his long Jewish beard and sad kind eyes should have been not so long ago the wild reckless 'mad Scotchman', the 'Whoring Puritan', at once the bore, the despair and the laughing-stock of the House of Commons.

The quiet pleasant conversation lasted until six o'clock, when his guests and his two little maids, one Gentile and one Jew, had to leave the prison and go home. When he was left alone he had some tea, a plateful of salad, lit his long-stemmed pipe once more and spent an hour or two in quiet contemplation and prayer before going to bed.

The next morning at eight o'clock the two maids came back again and another day began.

Sometimes, to break the monotonous pattern of the days, there would be a party at which the company would, by any standards, be remarkable and by contemporary standards fantastic. Dukes would meet Italian barbers, ladies of fashion would dance with Jewish shop-keepers, soldiers would drink with Members of Parliament, Polish noblemen with American merchants, rabbis with infidels. There were no observances of protocol, no rules of precedence. Everyone who believed in democracy was welcome. Everyone, that is, except un-orthodox Jews who trimmed their beards or who uncovered their heads. For Lord George retained unimpaired his convert's impatience with laxity and his insistence upon the strict observance of the ordained laws.[1]

The party would begin with a concert in which Lord George him-self entertained his guests on the several instruments which he could play with an expertise which was more than talent. He still had, how-ever, that distressing fondness for the bagpipes which had endeared

[1] He once refused to see a poor Jew, Angel Lyon, because his beard was too short. He explained his reasons in a letter of familiar verbosity.

'ANGEL LYON, my answer is that I will not admit thee. I have given a general order to the turnkeys of the prison to let in no Jews without beards, and I can see no reason to make thee an exception as thy transgression is voluntary. . . . Tarry, therefore, in Fenchurch Street until thy beard is grown and then return to thy sincere friend and servant,

Israel bar Abraham G. Gordon.'

him to the Scots in his electioneering days, so that occasionally the entertainments provided for his guests were perforce not wholly pleasurable.

The concert would be followed by dancing. Quite often the Duke of York would lend his band, and sometimes he would come himself with his servants and aides-de-camp, who felt quite out of place in so curious an assembly. Particularly so as Lord George seemed not in the least impressed by their master's presence. Once when His Royal Highness was there his host greeted him with a few polite words and then went off to talk to his maids who seemed embarrassed and over-awed by the royal entourage and noticing a turkey roasting at the fire he 'very obligingly turned it'.

The parties ended with a few traditional Scottish tunes and finally, after 1789, with the stirring, triumphant *Marseillaise*.

On the days when he had no visitors, 'which was but seldom' he would go into the other wards of the prison and give concerts to the prisoners on his violin or play with them the ball games which they had invented for themselves. He spent hours talking with them, making occasional wry jokes, comforting the old and the unhappy, arguing with the gaolers for some alleviation of their lot, giving them what money he could afford. He sought out French and German and Italian prisoners and had long conversations with them in their own languages all of which he had taught himself. The prisoners loved him and he deserved their love.

Every Saturday, with the help of ten Polish Jews, a public service was held in his cell when the walls were hung with Jewish signs like a synagogue. A wall plaque listed the ten commandments and the *mezuzah* was fastened to the door post. The room was always full an hour before the service began.

And so life for him went on, placid, regular, unchanging until the first sentence had expired.

At the end of January 1793 he was taken to the Court of King's Bench. He refused, faithful to his Jewish custom, to take off his hat in court and it was snatched from his head by an official. Whereupon without comment he bound his head in a turban with an enormous multi-coloured handkerchief. He produced as sureties for his good behaviour, in the sum of £2,500 each, two dirty and obviously penni-less Polish Jews. Their guarantees were naturally refused and when two Englishmen got up to guarantee him instead, their capacity to pay if necessary was also questioned..They admitted the improbability of being able to meet the sum required.

'As it is a mere fiction', Lord George remarked, 'which the Court themselves chose to adopt by supposing me worth £10,000, the same fiction ought in justice to be held good in proportion to the sureties. Unless the Court really intended imprisonment for life when they demanded such excessive and unprecedented bail'.

He seemed disinclined to accept help from those who could have afforded the £2,500 if called upon to find it and was in consequence returned to prison.[1]

He left the Court looking, for all his spirit and gay turban, like an old man. He was only just forty-one but those who had not seen him for many years were shocked to notice that he looked as if he might be sixty. His pallor was remarkable, his face deeply lined, his body as thin as a stick. His beard was still black but his hair, longer, straighter and even more outlandish than before, was beginning to turn grey. He walked with a slight limp and the gaberdine hung like a tent on his sharply bent and stooping shoulders.

He must, his doctor advised him, guard against gaol fever, that virulent form of typhoid which killed hundreds of Newgate prisoners every year. And the doctor's caution was justified.

In October when he thought that he had escaped the usual summer epidemic, Lord George contracted the dreaded disease. The doctor stayed by his bedside for three days and nights as he grew weaker and weaker. Scores of prisoners waited outside his door for news of him. Friends regardless of infection, stood whispering in the room and praying for his recovery. Polly Levi, his little Jewish maid, soothed his burning chest with cold hands dipped in water. On the morning of

---

[1] Whether his family offered to stand bail for him is not known. Watson, unashamedly bitter about his hero's family, said that 'most of his relations gamble more in one evening than would have secured his liberty' and made no effort to help him. They had been bought off, he suggested, by the Government's having heaped upon them 'honours and places of profit'. This is unlikely..The Duke of Gordon was an amiable, good-looking, contented if dim-witted fellow with an income of over £20,000 a year and Lord George appears to have remained on good terms both with him, and his other brother Lord William, until his death. His sister Lady Susan the wife of Colonel Woodford, was a frequent visitor in Newgate. They all could well have afforded to stand him bail and probably offered to do so. But he, in his stubborn pride, refused them. He had during his first year in prison refused to make a public recantation of his opinions, as the Duke had wished him to do in exchange for his freedom, saying that to 'sue for pardon was a confession of guilt'.

1 November he became delirious and lay panting and sweating on his bed, his brow twitching convulsively, murmuring scraps of long forgotten speeches, the names of his brothers and favourite sister and of women he had loved.

In the afternoon he lay quiet for an hour, his brow at last relaxed, breathing slowly. And then he began to murmur again and the people in the room stopped whispering and listened to the tired, weak, dying voice struggling brokenly to repeat the words of the *Ça Ira*, the cry of freedom.

BIBLIOGRAPHY

The Aberdeen Journal
Adams's Weekly Courant
AIKIN, John
    Annals of the Reign of George III (1816)
ALBEMARLE, Earl of
    Memoirs of the Marquess of Rockingham (1852)
The American Catholic Quarterly
ANGELO, Henry
    Reminiscences of Henry Angelo, with Memoirs of his Late Father and Friends (1830)
The Annual Register
ANSON, Sir William (Editor)
    Autobiography and Political Correspondence of the Third Duke of Grafton (1898)
ASQUITH, H. H.
    Studies and Sketches (1924)

BARRETT, Mrs. Charlotte Francis (Editor)
    The Diary and Letters of Mme. D'Arblay (1842)
BEAVAN, Arthur H.
    James and Horace Smith. A Family Narrative (1899)
BENHAM, Daniel
    Memoirs of James Hutton (1856)
BENTLEY, R. (Editor)
    The Diaries and Correspondence of James Harris, 1st Earl of Malmesbury (1844)
BESANT, Sir Walter
    London in the Eighteenth Century (1902)
BLACK, Clementina (Editor)
    The Cumberland Letters, 1771–1784 (1912)
BLEACKLEY, Horace
    Life of John Wilkes (1917)
BLUNT, Reginald
    Mrs. Montagu, Her Letters and Friendships (1923)

BOSWELL, James
    Life of Johnson (various editions)
BRASBRIDGE, Joseph
    The Fruits of Experience (1824)
BULLOCH, J. M.
    Territorial Soldiering in the North-east of Scotland During 1759–1814 (1914)
    The Gay Gordons (1908)
    The Bibliography of the Gordons (1924)
BURTON, Edwin H.
    The Life and Times of Bishop Challoner, 1691–1781 (1909)
BUTTERFIELD, Herbert
    George III, Lord North and the People, 1779–1780 (1949)

CAMPBELL, Lord
    The Lives of the Chief Justices of England (1849)
CASTLE, E. Egerton (Editor)
    The Jerningham Letters, 1780–1843 (1896)
CASTRO, J. Paul de
    The Gordon Riots (1926)
COLERIDGE, Ernest Hartley
    The Life of Thomas Coutts (1920)
COLSON, Percy
    Their Ruling Passions (1949)
    The Strange History of Lord George Gordon (1937)
CRABBE, The Rev. George
    The Life and Poetical Works of the Rev. George Crabbe (1853)
CROSTHWAITE, J. Fisher
    A Brief Memoir of Major-General Sir John George Woodford (1881)
CURNOCK, Nehemiah (Editor)
    The Journal of the Rev. John Wesley (1909–1916)

Dictionary of National Biography
Dolman's Magazine
DONNE, W. Bodham (Editor)
    The correspondence of King George III with Lord North, 1768–1783 (1867)
DOUGLAS, Sylvester
    Reports of Cases in the Court of King's Bench in the 19th, 20th and 21st years of George III (4th Ed., 1813)
The Downside Review
The Dublin Review

The English Historical Review

Fergusson, Lt. Col. Alex
    The Hon. Henry Erskine (1882)
Fitzmaurice, Lord
    Life of William Earl of Shelburne (1912)
Fitzwilliam, Earl, and Bourke, Lt. Gen. Sir Richard
    The Correspondence of the Rt. Hon. Edmund Burke (1844)
Fortescue, The Hon. Sir John (Editor)
    The Correspondence of King George III (1927)
Franklin, Benjamin
    Memoirs of the Life and Writings of Benjamin Franklin (Edition of 1833)
Fraser-Mackintosh, Charles
    Letters of Two Centuries (1890)

The Gazeteer and New Daily Advertiser
The General Advertiser and Morning Intelligencer
The General and New Daily Advertiser
The General Evening Post
The Gentleman's Magazine
George, M. Dorothy
    London Life in the Eighteenth Century (1925)
Gilchrist, Alexander
    Life of William Blake (1880)
Gordon, Lord George
    Innocence Vindicated and the Intrigues of Popery (1783)
    The Memorial which Lord George Gordon has written in the Prison of Newgate
    (1789)
    A Letter from Lord George Gordon in Newgate to Baron de Alvensleben,
    Minister from Hanover (1792)
    A Letter from the Rt. Hon. Lord George Gordon to E. Lindo, Esq., and the
    Portuguese and N. Salomon, Esq. and the German Jews (1783)
    A Letter from G. Gordon to W. Smith, Esq., M.P. (1792)
    Prisoners' Petition to the Rt. Hon. Lord George Gordon to preserve their lives
    and liberties and to prevent their banishment to Botany Bay (1786)
    Narrative of My Proceedings (1780) Add MSS. 42129
Griffiths, Arthur
    Chronicles of Newgate (1884)

Hanway, Jones
    The Citizen's Monitor (1780)
Hawkins, Laetitia
    Memoirs, Anecdotes, Facts and Opinions (1824)

HAYWARD, A. (Editor)
Autobiography, Letters and Literary Remains of Mrs. Piozzi (1861)
HAZLITT, W. (Editor)
Memoirs of Thomas Holcroft (1816)
HILL, Constance
The House in St. Martin's Street (1907)
HILL, G. Birkbeck (Editor)
Doctor Johnson's Letters (1892)
History of the Rt. Hon. Lord George Gordon to which is added several of his speeche
in Parliament (1780)
HOLLIDAY, John
Life of William late Earl of Mansfield (1797)
HUISH, Robert
The Public and Private Life of George III (1821)

ILCHESTER, The Countess of, and Lady STAVORDALE (Editors)
The Life and Letters of Lady Sarah Lennox (1901)

JACKMAN, R. W. *The Letters of Samuel Johnson* (1952)
JESSE, J. H.
George Selwyn and His Contemporaries (Edn. of 1901)
Memoirs of the Life and Reign of George III (Edn. of 1901)
JUNIUS
A serious letter to the Public on the late Transaction between Lord North and the
Duke of Grafton (1778)

KEARSLEY, G.
Fanaticism and Treason (1781)
KENYON, George T.
The Life of Lloyd 1st Lord Kenyon (1873)
KETTON-CREMER, R. W.
Horace Walpole (1940)

LANSDOWNE, The Marquis of
Mrs. Thrale's Letters (1934)
LECKY, W. E. H.
A History of England in the 18th century (1892)
LEITH, W. F. (Editor)
Memoirs of Scotch Catholics during the 17th and 18th Centuries (1909)
LEWIS, W. S. (Editor)
Horace Walpole's Correspondence (Yale Edition, 1937–1948)

LLANOVER, Lady (Editor)
The Autobiography and Correspondence of Mary Granville (1861–1862)
The London Chronicle
The London Courant and Westminster Chronicle
The London Evening Post
The London Gazette

MACKENZIE, Henry (Editor)
The Works of John Home with an account of his life (1822)
MAHON, Lord
History of England (1854)
MARKHAM, Sir Clements
Markham Memorials (1913)
MAYO, Lawrence Shaw
Jeffery Amherst (1916)
The Morning Chronicle and London Advertiser
The Morning Post and Daily Advertiser

NAMIER, Sir Lewis
The Structure of Politics at the Accession of George III (Edition of 1957)
The National Review
Narrative of the Proceedings of Lord George Gordon and the persons assembled under the denomination of the Protestant Association (1780)
NICHOLS, John
Literary Anecdotes of the 18th Century (1812)
NORTON, J. E. (Editor)
Letters of Edward Gibbon (1956)
Notes and Queries

Old Bailey Sessions Papers

PAUL, Sir James Balfour (Editor)
The Scots Peerage (1904)
PEMBERTON, Noel W. B.
Lord North (1938)
PHILLIPS, Hugh
The Thames about 1750 (1951)
PHILO-VERITAS
A letter to the Lord Archbishop of Canterbury occasioned by the Excommunication of Lord George Gordon (1786)
POSTGATE, Raymond
That Devil Wilkes (1930)

Proceedings at Large on the trial of George Gordon Esq. commonly called Lord George Gordon for High Treason (compiled from the shorthand writing of Mr. William Blanchard), (1781)

PRYOR, F. R. (Editor)
Memoirs of Samuel Hoare by his daughter Sarah and his widow Hannah (1911)
The Public Advertiser

PUBLIC RECORD OFFICE
Records of the State Paper Office—State Papers Domestic George III. Papers relating to the Lord George Gordon Riots 1780, vols. 20 and 21.
Records of the War Office—Miscellanea. Select unnumbered papers (W.O.40).
Records of the Commissioners of Works and Public Buildings—Miscellanea (Works 6).

RADZINOWICZ, Leon
A History of English Criminal Law (1948)
RAIMBACH, M. J. S. (Editor)
Memoirs and Recollections of Abraham Raimbach (1843)
REYNOLDS, Frederick
The Life and Times of Frederick Reynolds, written by Himself (1826)
RIDGWAY, James (Editor)
Speeches of Hon. Thomas Erskine (1810)
ROBERTS, William (Editor)
Memoirs of the Life and Correspondence of Mrs. Hannah More (1834)
ROCHE, Sophie, Von La
Sophie in London (1933)
ROMILLY, Sir Samuel
Memoirs of the Life of Sir Samuel Romilly, written by Himself (1841)
The St. James's Chronicle

SCHOLES, Percy A.
The Great Dr. Burney (1948)
SHARPE, Reginald Robinson
London and the Kingdom (1894)
SNOWDEN, W. Crawford
London Two Hundred Years Ago (1948)
SOLOMONS, Israel
Lord George Gordon's Conversion to Judaism (1913)
SOMERVILLE, Thomas
My Own Life and Times, 1741–1814 (1861)
SPENSER, Alfred (Editor)
Memoirs of William Hickey, Vol. II, 1775–1782 (1919)

STANHOPE, Earl
Life of the Rt. Hon. William Pitt (1861)
STEUART, A. Francis (Editor)
The Last Journals of Horace Walpole (1910)
SYDNEY, W. C.
England and the English in the Eighteenth Century (1892)

The Temple Bar Magazine
TINKER, C. B. (Editor)
Letters of James Boswell (1924)
TOYNBEE, Mrs. Paget (Editor)
The Letters of Horace Walpole (1903-1905)
Transactions of the Jewish Historical Society of England
Trial of George Gordon Esq., commonly called Lord George Gordon for High
Treason (taken in shorthand by Joseph Gurney) (1781)
Trial of the Hon. George Gordon for High Treason (taken in shorthand by W.
Vincent) (1781)
Trial of Lord George Gordon for High Treason (Edinburgh, 1781)
TURBERVILLE, A. S. (Editor)
Johnson's England (1933)
TWINING, Thomas
Recollections of a Country Clergyman of the 18th Century (1882)
TWISS, Horace
Life of Lord Chancellor Eldon (1844)

VILLETTE, J.
The Annals of Newgate (1776)
VINCENT, William (Thomas Holcroft)
A Plain and Succinct Narrative of the Late Riots and Disturbances (1780)

WALPOLE, Horace
Journal of the Reign of George III, 1771-1783 (1859)
WARD, George Atkinson (Editor)
The Journals and Letters of the late Samuel Curwen (1842)
WATSON, Robert
The Life of Lord George Gordon with a philosophical review of his political
conduct (1795)
WEMYSS, Millicent Erskine
A Notable Woman and other Sketches (1893)
WENDEBORN, F. A.
A view of England towards the close of the 18th century (1791)
The Westminster Magazine

WHITFIELD, G.
  Memoirs of the life of the Rev. Peard Dickinson (1803)
Whole Proceedings on the trials of two informations against Lord George Gordon.
  One for a libel on the Queen of France and the French Ambassador; the other
  for a libel on the Judges and the Administrators of the Laws in England
  (Taken in shorthand by Joseph Gurney) (1787)
WILKES, John
  Diary (Add. MSS. 30866 BM)
WILKINS, W. H.
  Mrs. Fitzherbert and George IV (1905)
WORTLEY, Mrs. E. Stuart (Editor)
  A Prime Minister and his Son (1925)
WRAXALL, Sir Nathaniel William
  Historical Memoirs of My Own Time (1815)
WRIGHT, Thomas (Editor)
  The Correspondence of William Cowper (1904)

INDEX

Adams, Samuel, 85
Addington, Mr. Justice, 46, 47
Adelphi, 85
Admiralty, The, 36, 73
Akerman, Mr., 74–77, 83, 163
Aldeburgh, 66
Aldgate, 105
Amherst, Jeffrey, 90, 92, 111 ,112, 116, 119, 120, 126, 128
Angelo, Henry, 38n, 49, 73, 76, 82, 95, 99, 114
Apsley House, 94
Artillery Ground, Moorfields, 59, 94, 119
Ashburnham, Lord, 38, 90
Ashurst, Mr. Justice, 162, 164

Bank of England, 84, 90, 93, 97, 100, 102–104, 108, 111, 114, 116, 126
Bartholomew Lane, 97
Bathurst, Earl, 91, 94
Bavarian Embassy, 51
Beauchamp, Earl, 60, 107
Beaufort, Duchess of, 90, 107
Bethnal Green, 32
Bishopsgate, 35
Blackfriars Bridge, 86, 99, 103, 104, 112, 113, 115, 121
Blackfriars Stairs, 103, 104, 107
Bloomsbury Square, 82, 83, 90, 114, 127
Borough Clink, 98
Boston, Lord, 40, 41, 42
Boswell, James, 74, 124
Bow Street, 54, 55, 72, 73
Bowen, Rev. Thomas, 46, 143
Brasbridge, Joseph, 58, 60
Bridewell, 79, 119, 130, 131
Broad Street, 104, 105, 107
'Brown Bear, The', 72
Buckingham House, 88

Bull Alderman Frederick, 43, 44, 46, 64, 65, 70, 93
Burdon, Mr. (Magistrate), 82, 83
Burke, Edmund, 6, 7, 9, 18, 26, 38, 44n, 62, 67n, 86, 87, 121, 122n, 127
Burney, Charlotte, 57n, 62, 70, 72, 109
Burney, Dr. Charles, 35n, 110, 114, 121
Burney, Susan, 62, 67n, 70–72, 95, 108, 110, 114
Burns, Robert, 1
Bute, Lord, 27, 103, 119

Cagliostro, Count, 159, 160, 165
Cane, William, 10, 11
Canterbury, Archbishops of: (Frederick Cornwallis); 12, 77, 78n, 79; (John Moore, 166n)
Cavendish, Lord Frederick, 46
Cavendish, Lord John, 47–48
Challoner, Bishop, 17, 51
Charing Cross, 35, 99, 107
Cheapside, 35, 70, 96, 97, 102, 116
Clerke, Sir Philip Jennings, 46n, 48, 69, 146
Coachmakers' Hall, 31, 33
Coleman Street, 102n
Conway, General, 45, 68, 107
Cornhill, 35, 97
Coutts, Mr. (Banker), 114, 118, 124
Crabbe, Rev. George, 66, 74, 76
Cripplegate Ward, 117n
Cumberland, George, 119, 122
Cumberland, Rev. Richard, 123
Customs House, 116

Dalrymple, Sir John, 17, 18, 23, 28
Denbigh, Lord, 41, 42
Dennis, Edward, 130, 131
Dirty Lane, 33
'Dog & Duck', Lambeth, 34

Donovan, Mr., 104, 105
Dowgate Wharf, 104
Downing Street, 108
Dung Wharf, 115
Dunning, John, 18

East India Company, offices of, 116
Edinburgh, 21, 22
Effingham, Earl of, 86, 104
Erskine, Thomas, 133, 134, 139–150, 161
Esdaile, Sir James, 57

Fagniani, Maria, 94n
Farringdon Ward Without, 120
Fielding, Sir John, 50, 54n, 55, 65, 72
Fisher, James, 23, 29, 30, 129
Fleet Bridge, 116
Fleet Ditch, 103
Fleet Market, 86, 101
Fleet Prison, 80, 98, 99, 100, 103, 107, 113, 130
Fleet Street, 35, 70, 106, 116
Fox, Charles James, 7, 30, 87, 121, 155
Franklin, Dr. Benjamin, 85, 86, 125n, 132, 168
Fraser, General Simon, 6, 109
Frederick's Place, 97, 98

Geary, Admiral, 123n
George III, 27, 28, 89–92
Glasgow, 21
'Globe Tavern', Fleet Street, 106
Gordon, Duchess of, (Lady Catherine), 1
Gordon, Lord George, boyhood of, 2–3; as midshipman, 4, 14; visits West Indies, 5; stays in Paris, 12; invited to Edinburgh, 23; starts march to House of Commons, 34; at House of Commons, 43; attempts to stop riots, 102; in Tower of London, 128; first trial, 135–151; second trial, 161–164; flees to Amsterdam, 165; brought back to Harwich, 165; goes to Birmingham, 165–167; committed to Newgate, 167
Gordon, Lord William, 2n
Great Queen St., 48, 49, 107
Greenwich Hospital, 116
Grimaldi, 94–95
Guildhall, 38, 92, 93

Hay, Bishop George, 17, 21, 22, 28
Haymarket, 107, 108, 132
Hertford, Lord, 107, 123
Hickey, William, 10, 11, 13, 113
Hillsborough, Lord, 38, 41, 42, 53, 112, 119, 133, 154
Hoare, Mrs. Samuel, 104, 105
Holborn, 100–102, 107, 114
Holroyd, Colonel, 45, 102
Huntingdon, Lady, 78, 80
Hyde, Mr. Justice, 66, 69–72, 144
Hyde Park, 93, 94, 113, 119

Inns of Court, 93, 106
Islington, 71

Jackson, James, 70, 72
Jenkinson, Charles, 164
Jersey, Lord, 69, 109n, 118, 128
Johnson, Dr., 34, 88

Kennett, Alderman, 58–61, 90, 93, 129
Kenyon, Lord Lloyd, 133, 134, 137–143, 161
King's Bench Prison, 98, 99, 107, 113, 119, 130, 170

Lambeth Butts, 126
Lambeth Palace, 78
Lambeth Road, 34
Langdale's Distillery, 100, 101, 113, 114, 127
Laurens, Citizen, 132, 168
Le Fleming, Sir Michael, 46n, 143
Leicester Fields, 62, 70, 71, 108
Leith Wynd, 21
Lichfield, Bishop of, (Richard Hurd), 38
Lincoln, Bishop of (Thomas Thurlow), 38, 106
Lincoln's Inn Fields, 48, 49, 79, 106
Lock Hospital, 154
Lowther, Sir James, 46n, 47

Maberley, Mr., 49, 50, 63, 79
Macpherson, Sir John, 108, 109
Malo, Mr., 56–59, 61, 127
Mann, Sir Horace, 122, 125

Mansfield, Lord, 27, 37, 38n, 41, 43, 63, 77–82, 91, 94, 121, 122, 127, 134n, 150, 162

Mansion House, 70, 90, 97, 98

Marie Antoinette, 159n, 160, 164

Maskall, Henry John, 84n

Mason, William, 121, 125

Mawley, Sir Joseph, 46n

Melancholy Walk, 33

Middleton, Rev. Erasmus, 29, 30, 144, 145

Montagu, Mrs., 94n, 123, 132

Moorfields, 56, 57, 59–61, 68, 102, 103, 129, 131

Navy Pay Office, 116

New Gaol, 98

Newgate, 56, 72–74, 79, 80, 82, 83, 86, 88, 111, 113, 114, 118, 167

Newgate St., 73, 95

New Palace Yard, 36

New Prison, Clerkenwell, 79, 107, 111n

North, Lord, 7, 9, 16, 17, 22, 30, 38, 42, 44, 89, 108, 109, 128, 164

Northampton Chapel, Clerkenwell, 79, 80

Northumberland, Duke of, 37, 55

Old Bailey, 73, 88, 130

Old Crown and Rolls Tavern, Chancery Lane, 29

Old Jewry, 97, 98

Paddington, 32

Palace Yard, 38, 39, 46, 47, 48

Parliament St., 36, 39, 69

Percy, Lord Algernon, 22, 102

Petre, Lord, 18, 25, 26n, 29

Piccadilly, 94, 107

Pitt, William, 118, 156, 157

Polhill, Mr., 46n

Poultry, 70, 97, 102

Poultry, Compter, 98, 119

Rainforth, Sampson, 49, 50, 63, 65, 79

Ranelagh, 108, 109

Reynolds, Frederic, 36, 46, 48, 76, 86, 91

Reynolds, Sir Joshua, 63

Richmond, Duke of, 39–41, 53, 121, 154

Rockingham, Lord, 54n, 107, 117, 121, 154

Roget, Rev. John, 39, 68

Romilly, Samuel, 20, 39, 68, 94, 125, 135

Ropemaker's Alley, 59, 60, 65

Royal Exchange, 93, 99, 118

St. George's Fields, Southwark, 31, 33, 99, 113

St. George's Spa, Southwark, 34

St. Giles's, 56, 81, 119

St. James's Palace, 27, 119n

St. James's Park, 113, 119n

St. John, Lord Jack, 38, 108, 109

St. Margaret's Hall, Southwark, 33

St. Margaret's Street, Southwark, 46

St. Martin's Street, 62, 70

St. Paul's Cathedral, 118

St. Paul's Churchyard, 103, 118

St. Paul's, Covent Garden, 117n

St. Sepulchre's, Holborn, 117

Sandwich, Lord, 13, 40, 67, 144

Sardinian Ambassador, Chapel of, 48, 63

Savile, Sir George, 18, 38, 47, 48, 62, 63, 71, 135

Savoy, 50

Selwyn, George, 6, 10, 94, 106, 122

Shelburne, Lord, 37, 42, 43, 54, 55, 121

Sheldon, William, 18

'Ship, The', Southwark, 98n

Shrewsbury, Earl of, 18

Shoreditch, 81

'Simon The Tanner', Southwark, 98n

Snowhill, 114

Somerset House Barracks, 50

South Sea House, 116

Southwark, 20, 33, 98, 130

Spencer, Countess, 69, 118

Spitalfields, 32, 53, 57, 63, 81, 118

Stormont, Lord, 37, 59, 89–91, 119–121

Strand, 35, 72, 107

Stuart, Colonel, 103, 111, 119, 124, 128

Surrey Bridewell, 98

Taplin, Thomas, 96

Tavistock St, 110

Temple, The, 106

Thrale, Mrs Henry, 34, 88, 100n

Thrale's Distillery, 100n
Threadneedle St, 97, 102
Tollemache, Mr, 46n
Topham, Captain, 46, 47, 91
Tothill Fields, Bridewell, 119
Tower of London, 59, 93, 94, 112, 128, 132
Townshend, Lord, 41, 114
Trentham, Lord, 38
Turner, Charles, 38, 96
Twining, Thomas, 108, 121
Twistleton, Colonel, 103, 119

Walpole, Horace, 9, 27, 38, 46, 51, 56, 86, 90, 95, 96, 107, 109, 114, 121, 122, 125, 126, 130, 133, 134
Wapping, 105, 106
Warwick Street, Charing Cross, 51, 107
Watson, Dr. Robert, 3
Welbeck Street, 22, 25, 29, 30, 47, 128, 158

Wesley, John, 20, 28, 132
Westminster, 36, 66
Westminster Bridge, 36, 112
Westminster Hill, 134
Weymouth, Lord, 32
Whitechapel, 29, 130
Whitehall, 30, 36, 69, 70, 96, 129
Wilkes, John, 8, 18, 36, 87n, 92, 93, 128
Willoughby de Broke, Lord, 38
Wilmot, Mr., 84, 90
Wood, St. Compter, 119
Woodford, Colonel John, 82, 83, 171
Woolwich, 124
Wraxall, Sir Nathaniel, 91n, 96, 100, 101, 103, 107, 118, 125, 131, 153, 167
Wright, Sampson, 41–43, 46, 50

York, Archbishop of (William Markham), 38, 77, 83, 84, 90, 91, 123, 126